THE MINI ROUGH GUIDE TO

COPENHAGEN

There are more than one hundred and fifty
Rough Guide travel, phrasebook, and
music titles, covering destinations from
Amsterdam to Zimbabwe, languages from
Czech to Vietnamese, and musics from
World to Opera and Jazz

Forthcoming titles include

Devon & Cornwall • Ibiza • Iceland
Malta • Tenerife • Vancouver

Rough Guides on the Internet

www.roughguides.com

Rough Guide Credits

Text editor: Gavin Thomas
Series editor: Mark Ellingham
Production: Julia Bovis, Robert Evers, Rob McKinlay
Cartography: Ed Wright

Publishing Information

This first edition published February 2001
by Rough Guides Ltd,
62–70 Shorts Gardens, London WC2H 9AH

Distributed by the Penguin Group:

Penguin Books Ltd, 27 Wrights Lane, London W8 5TZ
Penguin Putnam, Inc. 375 Hudson Street, New York, NY 10014, USA
Penguin Books Australia Ltd, 487 Maroondah Highway,
PO Box 257, Ringwood, Victoria 3134, Australia
Penguin Books Canada Ltd, 10 Alcorn Avenue,
Toronto, Ontario, Canada M4V 1E4
Penguin Books (NZ) Ltd,
182–190 Wairau Road, Auckland 10, New Zealand

Typeset in Bembo and Helvetica to an original design by Henry Iles.
Printed in Spain by Graphy Cems.

ISBN 1-85828-668-9

The publishers and authors have done their best to ensure
the accuracy and currency of all the information in
The Rough Guide to Copenhagen; however, they
can accept no responsibility for any loss, injury or
inconvenience sustained by any traveller as a result of
information or advice contained in the guide.

THE MINI ROUGH GUIDE TO

COPENHAGEN

by Lone Mouritson
and Andrew Spooner

ROUGH
GUIDES

We set out to do something different when the first Rough Guide was published in 1982. Mark Ellingham, just out of university, was travelling in Greece. He brought along the popular guides of the day, but found they were all lacking in some way. They were either strong on ruins and museums but went on for pages without mentioning a beach or taverna. Or they were so conscious of the need to save money that they lost sight of Greece's cultural and historical significance. Also, none of the books told him anything about Greece's contemporary life – its politics, its culture, its people, and how they lived.

So with no job in prospect, Mark decided to write his own guidebook, one which aimed to provide practical information that was second to none, detailing the best beaches and the hottest clubs and restaurants, while also giving hard-hitting accounts of every sight, both famous and obscure, and providing up-to-the-minute information on contemporary culture. It was a guide that encouraged independent travellers to find the best of Greece, and was a great success, getting shortlisted for the Thomas Cook travel guide award, and encouraging Mark, along with three friends, to expand the series.

The Rough Guide list grew rapidly and the letters flooded in, indicating a much broader readership than had been anticipated, but one which uniformly appreciated the Rough Guide mix of practical detail and humour, irreverence and enthusiasm. Things haven't changed. The same four friends who began the series are still the caretakers of the Rough Guide mission today: to provide the most reliable, up-to-date and entertaining information to independent-minded travellers of all ages, on all budgets.

We now publish more than 150 titles and have offices in London and New York. The travel guides are written and researched by a dedicated team of more than 100 authors, based in Britain, Europe, the USA and Australia. We have also created a unique series of phrasebooks to accompany the travel series, along with an acclaimed series of music guides, and a best-selling pocket guide to the Internet and World Wide Web. We also publish comprehensive travel information on our Web site: www.roughguides.com

Help us update

We've gone to a lot of trouble to ensure that this Rough Guide is as up to date and accurate as possible. However, things do change, and any suggestions, comments and corrections are much appreciated, and we'll send a copy of the next edition (or any other Rough Guide if you prefer) for the best letters.

Please mark letters
"Rough Guide Mini Copenhagen Update" and send to:
Rough Guides, 62–70 Shorts Gardens, London WC2H 9AH, or
Rough Guides, 4th Floor, 345 Hudson St, New York, NY 10014.

Or send email to: mail@roughguides.co.uk
Online updates about this book can be found on
Rough Guides' Web site (see opposite).

The authors

Lone Mouritsen was born in Brazil to itinerant Danish parents, and has since travelled the globe incessantly, though always returning between times to the family home in Copenhagen for rest and relaxation, while a longer stint in the city as a student at Copenhagen University gave her the chance to fully appreciate the city's unique ambience. She began writing for Rough Guides in 1998, and has previously contributed to guides to West Africa and Europe.

Andrew Spooner disappeared with a notorious UK punk band to Norway in 1986 and liked it so much he ended up spending the next seven years there, playing and touring with various bad but well-intentioned musicians. In 1993 he returned to London, where he ended up studying for a master's degree in cultural studies and humanities. He has previously contributed to the Rough Guides to Scandinavia and Europe, and also appears regularly in the *Guardian*.

Acknowledgements

A big thank you to all the many, many people who made this book possible (and apologies to anyone we've forgotten): Andrea Vaugn Jensen, Britt Lightbody from the Danish Tourist Board in London, Christina Bilde, Dorthe Lindgren, Greg Pilley, Henrik Thierlein of Wonderful Copenhagen, Jakob Levinsen, John and Karen, Kajak Ole, Lars Ringgård and Betina Lemtorp, Mikkel Toksvaerd, Nicolaj Steen Moller, Steen Petersen from City Safari, Tina Schneider, Petronella Perret, Steve and Marie Allen, and Gavin Thomas for editorial wisdom and input.

The editor would also like to thank Kate Berens for making this book happen; Ed Wright for consummate cartography; Robert Evers for patiently shouldering the twin burdens of proofreading and typesetting; and Rob McKinlay for additional production.

CONTENTS

MAP LIST

Introduction

openhagen (København) is Scandinavia's most vibrant and affordable capital, and one of Europe's most user-friendly cities. Small and welcoming, it's a place where people rather than cars set the pace, as evidenced by the multitude of pavement cafés and the number of thoroughfares that have been given over to pedestrians and bicycles. Amenable and relaxed, it also offers a range of entertainment which belies its relatively modest size: at night there are plenty of cosy bars and an intimate club and live-music network that could hardly be bettered, while in summer, especially, there's a varied range of entertainment as the city's population takes to the streets. This is not to mention a beckoning range of cultural attractions, including major national museums, a selection of magical art galleries, a healthy assortment of performing arts events and one of Europe's most interesting film scenes.

Physically, much of Copenhagen dates from the seventeenth and eighteenth centuries, a cultured ensemble of handsome renaissance palaces, parks and merchant houses laid out around the waterways and canals that give the city, in places, a pronounced Dutch flavour. Successive Danish monarchs left their mark on the place, in particular Christian IV, creator of many of the city's most striking landmarks – including Rosenborg Slot and the districts of

Nyboder and Christianshavn – and Frederik III, who graced the city with the palaces of Amalienborg and the grandiose Marmorkirke church, along with the elegant royal quarter of Frederikstad in which they are located. These landmarks remain the highest points in a refreshingly low and undeveloped skyline which continues to measure things on an emphatically human scale.

Historically, Copenhagen owes its existence to its position on the narrow Øresund strait separating Denmark from Sweden and commanding the entrance to the Baltic – one of the great trading routes of medieval Europe and now the site of the region's grandest engineering project, the massive Øresund Bridge. It's this location, poised on the dividing line between Europe and Scandinavia, that continues to give Copenhagen its distinctive character. Compared to the relatively staid capitals further north, Copenhagen has a decidedly European flavour, from the innocent hedonism of the famous Tivoli gardens to the sleazy goings-on around Vesterbro's red-light district. It's no surprise that the city's most famous export is a beer, Carlsberg, and the freedom with which it flows in the city's thousands of bars is in stark contrast to the puritanical licensing laws found elsewhere in Scandinavia – a fact attested to by the thousands of thirsty Swedes who descend on the city each year. Yet Copenhagen is also a flagship example of the Scandinavian commitment to liberal social values, as exemplified by its laid-back attitudes to everything from gay marriages to toplessness and pornography, and is also home to the unique "Free City" of Christiania, whose drop-out community is one of Europe's most intriguing social experiments.

For all its twentieth-century success, however, the new millennium finds Copenhagen facing an important set of changes and challenges. On the one hand, the magnificent new Øresund Bridge, opened in 2000 to link the city with Malmö and southern Sweden, has given Copenhagen the infrastructure to become the western Baltic's leading urban centre, and there are many who would like to see the city develop into a suitably internationalist and forward-looking metropolis. On the other hand, there are many Copenhageners who regard the bridge, at best, as an irrelevance or, at worst, as a symbol of all those foreign influences that threaten to undermine traditional Danish values. Above all, these influences are typified by Copenhagen's burgeoning immigrant community, and simmering racial tensions – and the resulting rising power of the right wing – pose increasing challenges to the city's tolerant image. At the same time, Denmark's landmark decision in a referendum of October 2000 to opt out of the single European currency also suggests a national desire to remain isolated from the continental mainstream, with the possible result that Copenhagen will be relegated to a position of provincial irrelevance. For all that, it's worth remembering that the city's occasional smugness and resistance to change is the result of its citizens' pride in their capital and determination to protect its unique character, and as a visitor you'll be made to feel welcome wherever you go, especially since absolutely everybody speaks English.

Copenhagen, as any Dane will tell you, is no introduction to Denmark – indeed a greater contrast with the sleepy provincialism of the rest of the country would be hard to find. Thanks to the rapid transport links which connect the capital with its surrounding countryside, however, you can enjoy all the pleasures of rural Zealand without ever being much more than an hour away from the bright lights of the capital. Amongst the many attractions which ring the city are the great castles of **Kronborg** (the "Elsinore Castle" of Shakespeare's *Hamlet*) and **Frederiksborg**, while the ancient Danish capital and ecclesiastical centre of **Roskilde**, with its magnificent cathedral and museum of Viking ships, offers another enticing day-trip.

When to visit

Copenhagen is on exactly the same latitude as Edinburgh and Moscow, and **winters**, as you'd expect, are wet, windy and cold, with temperatures regularly falling below zero, though if you're prepared to brave the weather there's the chance to go skating on the frozen city lakes before retreating for a comforting glass of hot *gløgg*. The city is at its prettiest in **spring**, when the trees come into leaf and people emerge from their layers of winter clothing. **Summer** weather can be variable: rain is a common occurrence, though when the sun appears the locals turns out in force, occupying every last corner of every park and pavement café, while the long summer evenings see the city at its liveliest.

	°C		RAINFALL
	AVERAGE DAILY		AVERAGE MONTHLY
	MAX	MIN	IN
Jan	2	-2	1.9
Feb	2	-3	1.5
March	5	-1	1.3
April	10	3	1.5
May	16	8	1.7
June	19	11	1.9
July	22	14	2.8
Aug	21	14	2.6
Sept	18	11	2.4
Oct	12	7	2.3
Nov	7	3	1.9
Dec	4	1	1.9

THE GUIDE

THE GUIDE

1

Introducing the city

Copenhagen is one of Europe's most manageable capitals: it takes just thirty minutes to walk across the compact centre, and the wealth of green spaces and pedestrianized areas makes exploring the city a relaxed and thoroughly civilized experience. The historic core of the city is the small district of **Slotsholmen**, originally the site of the twelfth-century castle from which Copenhagen derived its earliest wealth and now home to the city's highest concentration of historic buildings, foremost among them the huge royal and governmental complex of Christiansborg. Facing Slotsholmen over the Slotsholmen Kanal is the medieval maze of **Indre By**, the bustling heart of the modern city, traversed by Strøget, the world's longest pedestrianized street, and packed with an abundance of swish cafés, shops and bars, and an eclectic clutch of museums and churches. On the opposite side of Slotsholmen from Indre By, the island of **Christianshavn** – popularly known as "Little Amsterdam" on account of its Dutch-style canals and gabled houses – was built on reclaimed land in the seventeenth century. It's now one of the inner city's most relaxed and bohemian areas, and is also home to the "free city" of Christiania, Copenhagen's famous alternative-lifestyle community.

Northeast of Indre By, the fairy-tale palace of **Rosenborg**, one of several royal residences in the city, sits at the heart of the inner city's greenest area, with the immaculate lawns of Kongens Have and the lush green-houses of the Botanisk Have close by. Abutting Kongens Have are the wide, aristocratic streets of **Frederikstad**, Frederik V's royal quarter, dominated by the huge dome of the Marmorkirke church and centred on the royal palaces of Amalienborg, while just to the north are the green ramparts of **Kastellet**, Europe's oldest working military fort. Back across Indre By to the south is the city's transport and entertainment hub, grouped around the famous **Tivoli** pleasure gardens, close to both the city's main transport terminus, Central Station, and its main square, Rådhuspladsen.

Ringing the centre are a series of distinctive and contrasting inner-city areas: to the west, down-at-heel, multicultural **Vesterbro**, home to the city's red-light district, next to the genteel, villa-lined streets of **Frederiksberg**, where you'll also find another royal palace, Frederiksberg Slot, and the city's zoo. To the north is the formerly working-class but increasingly gentrified district of **Nørrebro**, centred on the trendy bars and restaurants of Skt Hans Torv and Blågårdsgade. East of Nørrebro, snooty **Østerbro** is home to Copenhagen's old money, as well as the national football stadium Parken and the city centre's largest open space, Fælled Park.

All Danish telephone numbers have eight digits – there are no separate area codes. To call Copenhagen from abroad, dial the international access code, followed by the Danish country code (45) and the subscriber's number.

ARRIVAL

However you arrive in Copenhagen you'll find yourself within easy reach of the city centre. Kastrup **airport** is just a few kilometres south on the island of Amager, while almost all **trains** and **buses** deposit you right in the centre at the city's main transport hub, Central Station.

By air

Modern Kastrup **airport**, 8km from the city, is the air hub of Scandinavia and your most likely point of arrival. Getting into the city from here couldn't be easier: a rail line, one of the fastest airport-to-city links in Europe, runs directly to Central Station every ten to twenty minutes (daily 5am–midnight, Sat from 5.30am, Sun from 6.30am; 18kr), taking just twelve minutes. Half these trains continue to the town of Helsingør (45min; 50kr), calling en route at Nørreport (16min; 18kr) and Østerport (18min; 18kr) stations. There's also a slower, but equally expensive, city bus (#250S; 18kr) from the airport to Rådhuspladsen. A taxi to the centre will cost about 125kr – there's a rank outside the arrivals hall.

There's a not particularly helpful **information desk** (daily 8am–7pm) just by arrivals where you can pick up a copy of the English-language *Copenhagen This Week* and free maps of the city. There's also a **currency exchange booth** (daily 6.30am–10pm) and a **hotel booking service** (daily 6am–11pm; 50kr per reservation).

By train and bus

Almost all coaches and trains to Copenhagen arrive at **Central Station** (in Danish, Hovedbanegården or København H), the city's main transport hub, from where there are excellent connections to virtually every part of the city via bus or local train. The station is also home to an array of shops, exchange booths (daily 7am–9pm), a bicycle rental service (see pp.14–16), places to eat and, downstairs,

ARRIVAL

COPENHAGEN AND MALMÖ

For centuries, the Swedish city of **Malmö** (in Danish, Malmø), 20km distant from Copenhagen across the Øresund, and the surrounding province of Skåne were part of a Danish empire with its capital in Copenhagen. With the Swedish capture of Skåne in the seventeenth century, however, Malmö was reduced from the second city of a major northern European power to a neglected outpost of a greater Sweden in which power rested firmly with distant Stockholm. The sense of rejection persists – Malmö's residents derisively call people from Stockholm *null åttas*, "zero-eights", after the telephone code for Stockholm.

In July 2000, Malmö's historical ties with the Danish capital were renewed with the opening of the **Øresund Bridge** – Scandinavia's biggest-ever engineering project. The "bridge" (actually a road and rail link made up of a four-kilometre tunnel, a four-kilometre artificial island and an eight-kilometre cable bridge) has brought the two cities within a thirty-minute train ride of one another, effectively transforming Malmö into a satellite-cum-suburb of Copenhagen, placing the Danish capital at the heart of a new region, the so-called **Øresund**, which now looks set to dominate the western Baltic for the foreseeable future.

Trains run roughly every 15–20min from Copenhagen's Central Station to Malmö (65kr each way), via Kastrup airport, with fast onward connections from Malmö to Stockholm, Gothenburg and Oslo (reservations always required). A single journey across the bridge by car costs 230kr. The Copenhagen Card (see p.10) is not valid for the crossing but can be used to get reductions at some museums in Malmö. For more information, contact the tourist office at Malmö Central Station (℡46 40/30 01 50, Ⓦ *www.tourismmalmoe.com*).

a left-luggage office (Mon–Fri 10am–5pm, Sat 10am–1pm; 20kr per item per day). Also downstairs, the seasonal InterRail Centre (July to mid-Sept daily 7am–1am) offers an array of facilities including showers and microwave ovens, although you can only use it if you hold an InterRail or Eurail pass. The national train company, DSB, has a travel agency and **information centre** just inside the main entrance off Vesterbrogade (daily 6.30am–11pm; ⊤70 13 14 15, ⓦ *www.dsb.dk*).

Euroline **coaches** (⊤99 34 44 88) from around Europe pull up just outside Central Station on Reventlowsgade. Long-distance buses from Århus stop at Valby, a couple of stations west of Central Station on several S Tog lines; buses from Aalborg stop at Ryparken Station on S-Tog line H.

By boat

The port of Copenhagen has long been in decline, and the opening of the Øresund bridge (see opposite) connecting Copenhagen with Sweden may have dealt it a death blow. **Ferries** currently connect with Oslo in Norway (2 daily; 16hr), Malmö in Sweden (23 daily; 45min–1hr 30min), Swinoujscie in Poland (5 weekly; 10hr), and the Danish island of Bornholm (1 daily; 7hr). All except the Swinoujscie ferry – which docks near the Little Mermaid (see p.75) – arrive at points very close to Nyhavn, a few minutes' walk from the city centre; bus #550S and the transport hub of Kongens Nytorv (see p.46) provide transport links to the rest of the city.

INFORMATION

Copenhagen boasts two excellent free information resources: **Use It**, centrally located at the back of the Huset complex at Rådhusstræde 13 in the heart of Indre By (map

COPENHAGEN ON THE WEB

There are several excellent Copenhagen-related Web sites that are worth checking out before your visit – all have numerous links to other useful sites.

www.aok.dk The most comprehensive English-language site about Copenhagen, with up-to-date listings and reviews of nearly every restaurant, bar, café and shop in town.

www.billetnet.dk Billetnet (see p.188) Web site listing all events that they sell tickets for, allowing you to purchase with a credit card online. It's exclusively in Danish, but easy to use, even so.

www.ht.dk The city transport company site – unfortunately, only in Danish – with a useful and easy-to-use route planner. Enter any starting and finishing address and you'll be given the appropriate bus or train routes.

www.woco.dk Wonderful Copenhagen tourist office site, with regularly updated listings in English.

3, F6; mid-June to mid-Sept daily 9am–7pm; mid-Sept to mid-June Mon–Fri 10am–4pm; ⓣ 33 15 65 18), and the **Wonderful Copenhagen** tourist office just outside Central Station at Bernstorffsgade 1 (map 3, D8; personal callers only May Mon–Fri 9am–5pm, Sat 9am–2pm, Sun 9am–1pm; June to mid-Sept daily 9am–6pm; mid-Sept to April Mon–Fri 9am–5pm, Sat 9am–noon; ⓦ*www.woco.dk*).

If you want to book accommodation before you arrive, Wonderful Copenhagen runs a telephone booking line (Mon–Sat 10am–4pm ⓣ 33 25 38 44).

Both offices can provide details of accommodation (budget accommodation only at Use It; all price ranges at Wonderful Copenhagen), eating, drinking and entertainment venues. Use It also holds mail and stores luggage, and in summer issues *Playtime*, a small but extremely useful free English-language newspaper packed with listings. The Wonderful Copenhagen office provides countrywide information and distributes the free quarterly *Copenhagen This Week* – an up-to-date news and listings magazine – as well as an excellent, free fold-out map which shows all city bus routes, attractions and most hotels.

The **maps** at the back of this book and those handed out by the tourist offices should be sufficient for most purposes. If you need something more detailed, the Kraks Citykort is the definitive map of Copenhagen; you can buy it either in book form (130kr; covering a large part of Zealand), or fold-out form (80kr; covering the city centre and suburbs only). Both are available at major bookstores (see p.213).

CITY TRANSPORT

The best way to explore Copenhagen is either to walk or cycle: the inner city is compact, much of the central area pedestrianized and the entire city has a comprehensive network of excellent cycle paths – you'll often find it just as quick to walk or cycle as to wait for a bus. For travelling further afield, there's an integrated network of buses and S-Tog and local trains.

Tickets

All city transport operates on an integrated – and complicated – **zonal system**. There are dozens of zones (pick up a free leaflet from any S-Tog station); you may find it easiest at first simply to state your destination and you'll be sold the

THE COPENHAGEN CARD

The **Copenhagen Card** (155kr for 1 day; 255kr for 2; 320kr for 3) allows unlimited travel on the entire metropolitan system (which includes the towns of Helsingør, Roskilde and Hillerød) and also gives entry to virtually every museum in the Copenhagen area. The cards are quite pricey, however, and unless you're planning to cram a lot of museums into a very short space of time it's difficult to make them pay – the one exception might be if you use the three-day card to visit several of the outlying attractions. Note too that on Wednesdays entrance to nearly every museum in the city is free. The card also gives twenty- to fifty-percent discounts on some car rental and ferry rides, and on certain museum entry prices in southern Sweden. It's available from the tourist office, travel agents, hotels and most train stations in the metropolitan region – get it stamped when you use it for the first time and sign the back.

appropriate ticket. The city centre and immediately surrounding area, as you'd expect, are in zones 1 and 2. **Fares** are based on a combination of zones and time: the cheapest ticket costs 12kr and is valid for one hour's travel within any two zones, with unlimited transfers between buses and trains. Another option is the **klippekort** ticket, containing ten stamps which you cancel individually according to the length of your journey and the value of the *klippekort*. The cheapest *klippekort* cost 80kr, with each stamp being valid for an hour's travel within any two zones; each stamp in a 110kr *klippekort* is valid for ninety minutes' travel within any three zones – good value if you plan to travel outside the city centre – and is also valid to and from the airport; seven-zone and over *klippekort* stamps are valid for two hours. Unlimited transfers are allowed within the time period of the ticket, and two or more people can use the same *klippekort* simultaneously, provided you clip the required number of stamps per person. There's also an excellent-value **24-hour ticket** (70kr) which is valid on all transport in all zones as far afield as Helsingør and Roskilde, as well as night buses. All types of ticket can be bought on board buses, at train stations or in the city's many newsagents. They should be stamped when boarding the bus or in the machines on station platforms. Except on buses, it's rare to be asked to show your ticket, but if you don't have one you face an instant fine of 250kr.

Trains

The **S-Tog** train service (see colour map 7 at the back of the book) is a metropolitan network covering Copenhagen and the surrounding areas. It is laid out in a huge U shape, with almost all services passing through Central Station (in Danish, Hovedbanegården or København H); each line runs about every ten to fifteen minutes between 5am and 12.30am. The network is rather confusing, so study the map thoroughly before boarding your train. There are both slow and fast trains – check carefully or you could whizz straight past your destination. The network can be a bit erratic, running some odd routes and being occasionally plagued by inexplicable delays, but it's still the fastest way to reach outlying points. Stations are marked by red hexagonal signs with a yellow "S" inside them.

There is also a local network of **Danish State Railway** (DSB) trains which connect to Helsingør and Roskilde, calling at Østerport and Nørreport stations and some suburban destinations; remember that the S-Tog and DSB stations have different entrances at Nørreport station. The same tickets are valid on both networks, though note that Eurail passes and InterRail are valid only on DSB trains.

CITY TRANSPORT

UNDERGROUND AND OVERDUE

The idiosyncrasies of Copenhagen's S-Tog and bus routes mean that getting quickly to the centre from the outskirts can be a frustrating experience. The city's transit system will be getting a much-needed boost in 2002 or 2003, however, when its first **underground train line** finally opens, with stations conveniently located in Christianshavn, at Kongens Nytorv and on Strøget. The evidence of this work is obvious all over the city centre, disrupting views and traffic in high-visibility areas such as Christianshavn and Nørreport. By 2003 the plan is to run a light railway or underground train every couple of minutes during rush hour, linking central Copenhagen not just to its own suburbs but also with the new Øresund bridge to Sweden and with Kastrup Airport. The project is currently plagued by delays, however, and it looks like it will miss its proposed opening date by months, if not years.

Buses

The city's **bus** network is much more comprehensive than the S-Tog system and can be a more convenient way to get around once you get the hang of finding the stops – marked by yellow placards on signposts – and as long as you avoid the rush hour. The excellent free city map produced by the Wonderful Copenhagen office (see p.8) includes a list of all bus routes. The city's main bus stand is adjacent to Rådhuspladsen, a block from both Central Station and the Tivoli Gardens. Other useful buses leave from Central Station's Vesterport side entrance, the Tivoli side entrance and the bridge at the end of the tracks (including the #550S, which goes straight to the ferry docks every ten minutes). Buses with an "S" suffix only make limited stops,

USEFUL BUS ROUTES

#5 Bellahøj, Assistens Kirkegård, Nørrebrogade (near Skt Hans Torv and Blågårdsgade), Nørreport Station, Gammel Torv and Nytorv, Rådhuspladsen.

#6 Experimentarium, Østerbro (near Parken Stadium), Kastellet, Marmorkirken, Nyhavn, Slotsholmen, Ny Carlsberg Glyptotek, Tivoli, Central Station, Vesterbro, Frederiksberg Slot and the City Zoo.

#8 Holmen, Christiania, Christianshavns Torv, Slotsholmen, Ny Carlsberg Glyptotek, Tivoli, Central Station, Åboulevard Ågade, Bellahøj.

#16 Grundtvigs Kirke, Assistens Kirkegård, Nørrebrogade (near Skt Hans Torv and Blågårdsgade), Rådhuspladsen, Tivoli, Central Station, Istedgade, Carlsberg Brewery, Valby.

#28 City Zoo, Frederiksberg Slot, Vesterbro, Central Station, Tivoli, Ny Carlsberg Glyptotek, National Museum, Slotsholmen, Christianshavns Torv, Amager.

offering a faster service – check they make the stop you require before you get on. All buses have a small electronic board above the driver's seat displaying both the zone you're currently in and the correct time – so there's no excuse for not having a valid ticket. There's a skeletal **night bus** service, though fares are almost double daytime rates. Night bus numbers always end with "N"; stops are well marked by yellow signs on major routes into and out of the city.

Taxis

Taxis are plentiful, and with several people sharing can be good value for cross-city journeys. Within Copenhagen there's a basic **fare** of 22kr, plus a charge of 10–13kr per kilometre depending on day and time. There's a handy taxi rank

THE "HARBOUR BUS"

A cheap way of taking a trip on the water in Copenhagen is to ride the small ferry, the so-called "Harbour Bus", which runs from Nodre Toldbod (near the Little Mermaid) to Holmen, Nyhavn, Knippelsbro and the Black Diamond. Services leave daily every twenty minutes from about 6.30am to 7pm (unless the harbour area is frozen) and cost 24kr. Tickets are valid for one hour and are transferable to the rest of the transport network; bikes cost an extra 12kr.

outside Central Station, or hail any cab in the street that's showing a green "Fri" (free) sign on top. Alternatively, phone Københavns Taxa (℡35 35 35 35), Hovedstadens Taxi (℡38 77 77 77), or Amager/Øbro Taxi (℡32 51 51 51). If you're in a big group, you can phone for a minibus on ℡35 39 35 35. Note that when booking a taxi it's standard practice for the customer to pay for the journey the taxi makes to pick them up.

Bicycles

If the weather's good, the best way to see Copenhagen is to go native and ride a **bicycle**. Cycling is also excellent for exploring the immediate countryside – bikes can be taken on S-Togs for 10kr through any number of zones; you can also buy a special bicycle *klippekort*, valid for ten journeys and costing 90kr. The excellent, city-wide cycle lanes make cycling very safe, though remember that lights are a legal requirement at night (you'll be stopped and fined if the police catch you without) and helmets are recommended at all times.

There are a number of excellent cycle **rental outlets** in central Copenhagen: Københavns Cyklebørs, Gothersgade

GUIDED TOURS

Copenhagen Excursions (℡ 32 54 06 06) Bus tours (with multi-lingual headphone commentary) departing from the Palace Hotel on Rådhuspladsen. Tours include a "City and Harbour" tour, by coach and boat (daily June–Sept 1.30pm & 3pm; 175kr; 2hr 30min), the "City Tour", which passes all the major sites (daily May–Sept 9.30am, 1pm & 3pm; 130kr; 1hr 30min), the "Grand Tour", which also includes the suburbs (daily 11am, April–Sept also at 1.30pm; 170kr; 2hr 30min); other tours cover the rest of Zealand, taking in places such as Helsingør and Roskilde.

City Safari (℡ 33 23 94 90, ⓦ *www.citysafari.dk*) Two-hour guided bike tours starting by an old World War II bunker at the end of Rewentlowsgade beside Central Station and visiting various well-known and less well-known city attractions. Tours run twice daily in summer (daily June–Aug 10am & 1pm; 150kr including bike hire) and during the rest of the year according to demand – book in advance at all times.

Copenhagen Adventure Tours (℡ 40 50 40 06, ⓦ *www.kajakole .dk*) Original and challenging tours using well-designed, safe and easy-to-handle kayaks. Based on Gammelstrand, Indre By (look carefully for the canalside sign), these trips give a unique view of the city and on a warm summer's day make an almost perfect trip. Standard ninety-minute tours (mid-April to mid-Aug; 165kr) take in the central city canals and Christianshavn; longer trips include the Little Mermaid and Holmen. The price includes a free drink in a canalside floating bar.

DFDS Fifty-minute canal tours (daily April–Oct; 50kr; ℡ 33 42 33 20) taking in various city sights including the Little Mermaid, Nyhavn and Holmen island. Boats depart from Gammel Strand or Nyhavn every 30mins from 10am until about an hour before sunset and have English-speaking guides – bring a raincoat and warm clothing if the weather is bad, as the boats are quite exposed.

Continued overleaf

GUIDED TOURS

GUIDED TOURS (continued)

Wonderful Copenhagen Tourist Office English-language guided walking tours (May–Sept Mon–Sat at 10.30am; 50kr; ☎ 32 84 74 35) taking in most of the city-centre highlights. Tours start at the Wonderful Copenhagen office on Bernstorffsgade and last two hours.

157, Indre By (Mon–Fri 8.30am–5.30pm, Sat 10am–1.30pm; ☎ 33 14 07 17; 40kr/day, 185kr/week, 200kr deposit); Dan Wheel, Colbjørnsensgade 3, Vesterbro (Mon–Fri 9am–11am & 4pm–5.30pm, Sat & Sun 9am–2pm; ☎ 31 87 14 23; 35kr/day, 165kr/week, 200kr deposit); Københavns Cykelcenter, Reventlowsgade 11, along the side of Central Station (Mon–Fri 8am–6pm, Sat 9am–1pm, July & Aug also Sun 10am–1pm; 50kr/day, 225kr/week, 300kr deposit). The city also provides 2500 **free bikes**, easily recognized by the advertisements painted onto their solid back wheels, which are scattered about the city in racks at S-Tog stations and other busy locations; a 20kr refundable deposit unlocks one. Unfortunately, many of the bikes are in a bad state of repair, though you should be able to find a decent one if you look carefully. When you've finished with it leave the bike in a rack (you get your coin back automatically as you re-lock the bike), or just leave it on the pavement, in which case someone will happily return it for you and pocket the deposit. Don't secure one with your own lock and remember not to take one outside the inner-city limits or you risk a fine. It is also possible to rent a **scooter** – those under 50cc can use cycle lanes – from Peugeot, Frederiksborgvej 59, Nørrebro (☎ 38 33 40 04; 250kr/day, 1000kr deposit) – you'll need to be over 18 and hold an international driver's or motorcycle licence.

CITY TRANSPORT

Slotsholmen

The district of **Slotsholmen** is the historical and geographical heart of Copenhagen. It was here, in 1167, that Bishop Absalon founded the castle that became the nucleus of the future city, and it's been the seat of Danish rule ever since. Here you'll find the highest density of historic sites in Copenhagen, foremost among them the buildings of the massive **Christiansborg** complex, comprising all the surviving portions of the various palaces, castles and other royal and governmental edifices which have occupied this site since 1167. At the heart of the complex is the severe grey **Christiansborg Slot**, now home to the Danish parliament. Behind Christiansborg Slot, Christiansborg's **Outer Courtyard** is all that remains of the original Baroque palace built by Christian VI in the early eighteenth century, while on the **northern side of Christiansborg** is the recently restored Slotskirke (Palace Chapel) of 1826, and Thorvaldsens Museum, a captivating museum devoted to the work of Denmark's most famous sculptor. **South of Christiansborg**, the Royal Arsenal Museum, containing the world's largest collection of historical guns and cannons, leads to the Royal Library and its sleek modern extension, the so-called Black Diamond.

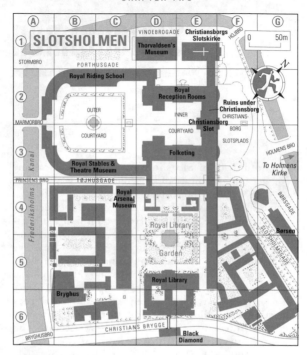

SLOTSHOLMEN: CHRISTIANSBORG SLOT

CHRISTIANSBORG SLOT

Map p.18, E2–E3. Bus #1, #2, #6, #8, #10, #37, #550S or #650S.
The history of Christiansborg (see the box opposite for a full account) is inseparably linked to that of Copenhagen. The centrepiece of the present-day complex is **Christiansborg Slot** – a heavy, granite-faced neo-Baroque building topped by an enormous green, copper spire – which was constructed between 1907 and 1928 using the

CHRISTIANSBORG THROUGH THE AGES

There has been a castle of some sort on the site of today's Christiansborg since 1167, when Bishop Absalon of Roskilde was granted the small village of Havn (on the site of modern Indre By) by his foster brother King Valdemar the Great. Absalon set about constructing a castle to protect herring traders in the village from Wendish pirates, and the castle subsequently ensured Danish domination of Øresund and a large part of the Baltic, until in 1369 a strong Hanseatic fleet finally succeeded in occupying the town and set about methodically dismantling the castle to ensure that it would never be rebuilt.

A new castle, known as **Københavns Slot**, was built by the church to replace Absalon's castle. Completed in 1417, it was promptly confiscated by the Danish king, Erik of Pomerania, who made it the seat of Danish rule and residence of the royal family. Over the years, the Slot was extended and modernized innumerable times. Christian IV completely refurbished it and added a spire to the infamous Blue Tower (in which, after his death, his unfortunate daughter Leonora Christina was wrongly imprisoned for treason for 22 years). Over the years, foreign visitors and dignitaries became increasingly amused by the Slot's mish-mash of architectural styles, until, to avoid further ridicule, the newly crowned Christian VI decided in 1730 to have the castle demolished and a much grander palace, inspired by the Rococo palaces of France's Louis XIV, erected in its place. Architects from all over Europe were called in to furnish **Christiansborg**, as it became known, with some of the finest art and decoration of the period. Christian VI died long before the palace was completed in 1766, and only 28 years later, in 1794, it burnt down in all its splendour. The Outer Courtyard and its two low, Baroque wings (which now house the Royal Stables, the Riding School and the small Court Theatre) are all that remain of this original palace.

Continued overleaf

CHRISTIANSBORG THROUGH THE AGES (continued)

The building of a **second Christiansborg** was delayed by the country's dire position following the war with England and the bombardment of Copenhagen in 1807. The palace square and its ruins were used as emergency housing for homeless Copenhageners, and when construction finally began, the walls of the ruins were incorporated into the new palace to save money. By 1828, a new Romanesque-style palace had arisen, but its lifetime was short: in 1884 it, too, burnt to the ground. The chapel – the present Christiansborgs Slotskirke – is all that remains from this second Christiansborg.

Today's Christiansborg Slot, the **third Christiansborg**, took 32 years to complete, since the three parties it was to house – the royal family, the parliament and the high court – couldn't agree on a suitable style. In the end, the royal family decided to stay at Amalienborg (see p.69), where they have been ever since. Christiansborg now houses the parliament, the Royal Reception Rooms and Library, the High Court, and the prime minister's office.

remains of the previous palace, which had been destroyed in a fire in 1884. It now houses the Folketing (Danish Parliament), the High Court, the prime minister's office and other ministries, and the Royal Reception Rooms.

The main entrance to Christiansborg Slot, is on the square of **Christiansborg Slotsplads**, adorned with an equestrian statue of Frederik VII – a favourite spot for demonstrations against king or parliament. Head left around the outside of the building from here to reach the Folketing; head right to reach Christiansborg Slotskirke and Thorvaldsen's Museum. The entrance to the Ruins under

Christiansborg is inside the main entrance, beyond which is Christiansborg Slot's Inner Courtyard and the entrance to the Royal Reception Rooms.

The Folketing

Map p.18, D3–E3. Free access to the spectators' gallery during sittings of parliament. Guided tours on Sun at 10am, 11am, 1pm, 2pm, 3pm & 4pm; free (call ⓣ 33 37 55 00 or visit Ⓦ *www.folketing.dk* for info on English-language tours).

The **Folketing** is located in Christiansborg Slot's south wing — walk left around the outside of the building from Christiansborg Slotsplads to reach the entrance. You can visit the main parliamentary chamber, the **Folketingssal**, at any time during the surprisingly informal parliamentary sittings (usually after 1pm on Tues & Weds, and after 10am Thurs & Fri; no sessions June & July) and see Danish democracy at work, but you'll get a much better impression of the Folketing by taking one of the tours. Well-informed guides lead you up the magnificent staircase to the seemingly endless **Vandrehal** (Hall of Wandering), where the original Danish constitution from 1849 is exhibited in a silver chest, along with other important historical documents. You're also introduced to the Folketing and its somewhat complicated seating arrangement (left wing politicians sometimes sit to the right of the podium, depending on their length of service), and the surprisingly engaging collection of paintings of prominent politicians.

The Royal Reception Rooms

Map p.18, D2–E2. Guided tours in English: May–Sept daily at 11am & 3pm, June–Aug also at 1pm; Oct–April Tues, Thurs, Sat & Sun at 11am and 3pm; 40kr.

The **Royal Reception Rooms** are located in the palace's

north wing – go through the main entrance into the courtyard and they're on your right. The rooms are used mainly
by the royal family as a place in which to wow important
visitors, though given the Danish royals' easygoing attitude,
the formality and stateliness of these meticulously kept
chambers can come as a surprise. The Throne Room has
walls covered in delicate and richly decorated silk from
Lyon, while the Alexander Hall is encircled by
Thorvaldsen's magnificent frieze depicting Alexander's
arrival into Babylon. In the Great Hall, Bjørn Nørgaard's
tapestries (a fiftieth birthday present to the present queen)
depict the history of Denmark in an unusually modern and
colourful way that somehow seems to fit the otherwise classical room.

Ruins under Christiansborg

Map p.18, E2. May–Sept daily 9:30am–3:30pm; Oct–April Tues,
Thurs, Sat & Sun 9:30am–3:30pm; 20kr.

In 1907, during the digging of the extraordinarily deep
foundations necessary for Christiansborg's soaring new
spire, the foundations from previous castles – Absalon's castle and Københavns Slot (see box on p.19) – were discovered. Prior to this, nobody had known what Absalon's castle had looked like – or indeed whether it was only a myth
– so massive efforts went into excavating the ruins.

The entrance is actually inside Christiansborg's main
entrance, from where a staircase leads down to the ruins.
These comprise two massive rooms, connected by archways,
that follow the circumference of Absalon's castle. Signs indi-
cate which bits of the stone and brick wall are from
Absalon's castle and which from Københavns Slot, and
though there's not actually much to see, it's all surprisingly
absorbing, the mood enhanced by the semi-darkness and the
lack of external noise. Also on display in a room adjacent to

the ruins are the astonishingly intricate pieces of carved granite and sandstone discovered during excavations – it's thought they formed part of Absalon's chapel and were dumped here by the Hanseatic fleet while the castle was being dismantled in 1369. In the same room are sketches and paintings of the various castles and palaces that have existed on the site since Absalon's time – most interesting are the drawings illustrating the confused development of Københavns Slot, with it's mishmash of building styles.

THE OUTER COURTYARD

Walk through Christiansborg Slot's main entrance and inner courtyard to reach the so-called **Outer Courtyard**, all that survives from the original Christiansborg, which burnt down in 1794. The courtyard is flanked by two long, low wings that curve around to meet at the **Marmorbro** (Marble Bridge), once the main entrance to Christiansborg, from where there's a stunning view of the palace complex.

The courtyard's north wing is home to the magnificent Baroque **Royal Riding School**, an exquisite, light-filled indoor riding arena flanked by delicate arches and a balcony running into a royal box at the far end – it's considered Denmark's most important piece of eighteenth-century architecture and gives a clear indication of how highly equestrian skills were valued. The arena is open most days until 4pm – if you're lucky you may see the queen's horses being exercised here or on the Outer Courtyard itself in the morning.

The Royal Stables and Coach Museum

Map p.18, B3–C3. May–Sept Fri–Sun 2–4pm; Oct–April Sat & Sun 2–4pm; 10kr.

In the south wing of the Outer Courtyard is all that

remains of the **Royal Stables**, which once occupied both wings of the Outer Courtyard and housed the royal family's retinue of 200 horses (there are now just twenty). Even if you're not interested in horses, the stables, part of the original Baroque Christiansborg, are worth seeing for their lavish interiors, with pillars, vaulted ceilings, and walls and cribs of Tuscan marble – apparently not even the king's own chambers were this extravagantly decorated.

The stables also include the **Coach Museum**, the royal family's formidable collection of coaches and carriages (some of them still in use) which ranges from Dowager Queen Juliane Marie's state coach from 1778 – the collection's oldest and most elaborately decorated carriage – to Frederik IX's Bentley T, left here since his death in 1972.

The Theatre Museum

Map p.18, B3–C3. Wed 2–4pm, Sat & Sun noon–4pm; 20kr.

Upstairs from the Royal Stables, the **Theatre Museum** (Teatermuseet) occupies the former eighteenth-century Court Theatre, a small Italian-style auditorium created by Frederik V out of an old tack room above the stables (the original Christiansborg lacked a theatre, thanks to the pietistic Christian VI, who prohibited theatre performances throughout Denmark). The auditorium remained in use until the fire authorities closed it down in 1881, after a disastrous theatre fire in Vienna that same year.

The building was reopened as the Theatre Museum in 1922, displaying original costumes, set-models, and the old dressing rooms and royal boxes from the Court Theatre. Each room follows a theme from Danish theatrical history, and though most are not particularly captivating, the auditorium itself, with its deep stage and beautifully decorated oriental ceiling (painted for a royal masquerade in 1857), evokes a real sense of theatrical excitement. The theatre is best experienced during a live performance – consult the tourist office or Ⓦ *www .kulturnaut.dk* for information about the plays which are occasionally staged here.

AROUND CHRISTIANSBORGS SLOTSPLADS

Head back through the main entrance onto Christiansborg Slotsplads and walk left around the outside of the building to reach **Christiansborgs Slotskirke** (Palace Chapel; Sun noon–4pm and daily noon–4pm during Easter and from July 16 to the third week of Oct; free), all that remains of the second Christiansborg, which burnt down in 1884. Consecrated in 1826, the chapel – designed by C.F. Hansen, one of the most important Danish Golden-Age architects – is a beautiful example of the simple Neoclassical architecture typical of the period. Ironically, having escaped the fire of 1884, the chapel went up in flames in 1992, when a flare landed on its roof during Copenhagen's Lent carnival and the inside was burnt out. It has since been returned to its original state, with Thorvaldsen's magnificent angel frieze encircling the dome and Bissen's four angel reliefs hanging from the walls beneath. Regular services are no longer held here, and the chapel is today mainly used by the Royal Danish Music Conservatory for organ lessons. Concerts are sometimes held here (check with the tourist office).

Thorvaldsen's Museum

Map p.18, D1. Tues–Sun 10am–5pm; July & Aug guided tours in English Sun 3pm; 20kr, free on Wed; Ⓦ *www.thorvaldsens.dk*.
Right next door to Christiansborgs Slotskirke is **Thorvaldsen's Museum**, converted from Christiansborg's old Coach House in 1839. The unusual museum building,

with its simple but strikingly coloured Neoclassical architecture, houses an enormous collection of works and memorabilia (and the body) of Denmark's most famous sculptor. Despite negligible schooling, **Bertel Thorvaldsen** (1770–1844) drew his way into the Danish Academy of Fine Arts before moving on to Rome, where he perfected the heroic, classical figures for which he became famous. Nowadays he's not widely known outside Denmark, although in his day he enjoyed international renown and won commissions all over Europe. The labels of the great, hulking statues here read like a roll-call of the famous and infamous: Vulcan, Adonis, John Russell, Gutenberg, Pius VII and Maximilian, while the Christ Hall contains the huge casts of the statues of Christ and Apostles which decorate Vor Frue Kirke (see p.35). The bright, multicoloured walls enhance the white statues and reliefs, while a magnificent frieze by Jørgen Sonne on the building's ochre facade depicts the triumphant reception accorded to the sculptor when he returned to live in Denmark after 41 years in Rome.

Thorvaldsen was something of a wit too. Asked by the Swedish artist J.T. Sergel how he managed to make such beautiful figures, he held up the scraper with which he was working and replied, "With this".

Holmens Kirke and Børsen

Map p.18, G3–G5.

Just over the far side of Holmens Bro from Christiansborg Slotsplads is **Holmens Kirke** (May–Sept Mon–Fri 9am–2pm, Sat 9am–noon; Oct–April Mon–Sat 9am–noon), looking almost lost between two busy main roads. Originally built as an anchor forge for the naval dockyard in 1562, Christian IV converted it into a church for naval personnel from Bremerholmen (the naval yard) and Slotsholmen in 1619. The long chapel along the canal, added in the early eighteenth century, is dedicated to Denmark's seafaring heroes and has two fine models of ships hanging from its ceiling.

Back on Slotsholmen, just south of Christiansborg Slotsplads, is the long, low seventeenth-century **Børsen** (Stock Exchange), with its distinctive green copper roof and spire formed out of four entwined dragons' tails. Created by Christian IV, Børsen was originally built as a stock exchange – stock as in goods rather than money – before money traders and bankers began moving in during the eighteenth century. It's now owned by the Chamber of Commerce and not open to the public.

SOUTH OF CHRISTIANSBORG

Most of the buildings in the area **south of Christiansborg** are connected to Christian IV (1577–1648) and the period when Slotsholmen was home of the Danish Royal Navy. The buildings here are mostly much older than those of Christiansborg, with a predominance of solid-looking red-brick constructions capped by massive tiled roofs.

Royal Arsenal Museum

Map p.18, C4. Tues–Sun noon–4pm; 20kr.

Walking from Christiansborg Slotsplads past the main entrance to the Folketing brings you to the **Royal Arsenal Museum** (Tøjhusmuseet), housed in the old Tøjhus. Completed in 1604, the Tøjhus (Arms House) was originally an armoury created to supply Christian IV's large navy with cannons, guns, ammunition and gunpowder, while the adjacent Proviantgården (Victuallers' Building) provided clothes, food and drink. Eighty years later, the royal naval base moved to Nyholm on Christianshavn and the Tøjhus and Proviantgården fell into disuse (the latter now houses parliamentary offices and isn't open to the public).

The museum's collection of military paraphernalia is a treasure trove for arms buffs. Downstairs, the **Cannon Hall** contains more than 500 historic guns, mortars, artillery and tanks – the oldest guns, from the fifteenth century, are to the left of the entrance; it's reputedly the world's finest collection of eighteenth- and nineteenth-century armaments. The atmospheric hall itself is equally impressive – at 163 metres it's the longest arched room in Europe. Upstairs, in the **Armoury Hall**, an endless collection of firearms is displayed in order of technological advance. The glorification of weaponry can be a bit overwhelming to the innocent pacifist (most of the visitors seem to be wide-eyed young army cadets), though the well-informed custodians will do their best to help you appreciate the military significance of the items on display.

The Royal Library and Black Diamond

Map p.18, D5–E6. Mon–Sat 10am–7pm; free; Ⓦ*www.kb.dk*. Bus #8.
The basin in which ships used to dock while being provisioned at the Tøjhus and Proviantgården was filled in during the 1860s and is now the site of the tranquil **Royal Library Garden** – the mooring rings in its northern walls are the only reminder of its past incarnation. The gardens are an excellent venue for a picnic, with a fishpond and assorted statues, including one of a lovesick Søren Kirkegaard looking over to where his fiancée, Regine Olsen, used to live. At the far end of the gardens is the old entrance to the **Royal Library** (Det Kongelige Bibliotek), a Venetian-inspired building of 1906 with large, curved windows and slim pillars. (You can't actually get in this entrance now – walk around the library to the waterfront to reach the new entrance.)

Reflected in the waters of the Inderhavn is the elegantly tilted black-glass library extension known as the **Black Diamond** (Sorte Diamant), jutting out into the harbour and connected to the original library building by a walkway above the road. The extension has doubled the library's capacity and added a concert hall, exhibition and conference rooms, a café and an expensive restaurant (the only one on Slotsholmen). The library contains manuscripts by Hans Christian Andersen, Karen Blixen and Søren Kierkegaard, though to see them you'll have to convince those at reception that you're a bona fide scholar – a student card should suffice. Exhibitions and concerts are open to the general public (prices vary according to what's on). The Black Diamond also houses the fascinating **National Photo Museum**, with more than 25,000 Danish and foreign photos from 1839 to the present – selected photos are displayed in the museum's changing exhibitions (free).

The ground floor of the Black Diamond has free-to-use PCs with Internet access, a café with a selection of foreign newspapers and a peaceful waterfront view.

Bryghus

Map p.18, B5–B6.

Turn right out of the Black Diamond and walk down Christians Brygge to reach the historic Bryghus (brewery) and Langebro (long bridge). Constructed by Christian IV in the early seventeenth century, the **Bryghus** is a classic building of its time: a monumental red-brick structure with a massive roof, built to house the king's brewery and to provide rations to the navy, as well as to defend what was then the most outlying point of the island of Slotsholmen. Beer was brewed here only until 1767, when the building partially burnt down, since when it has served as a storage facility for the navy and later for the Arsenal Museum. It's not currently open to the public.

Indre By

Compared to the monumental edifices of Christiansborg across the Slotsholmen canal, the district of **Indre By** presents Copenhagen on a more human scale. The heart of both medieval and modern cities, Indre By occupies the site of the Copenhagen area's original settlement, the small and marshy fishing village of Havn, whose fortunes were transformed by the arrival of Bishop Absalon in 1167. Whilst Absalon and his successors raised their castles on the island of Slotsholmen, the settlement of Havn on the mainland opposite prospered through tax and trade, acquiring the name of København ("Merchant's Harbour") and becoming capital of Denmark in 1445.

Within its fortifications – which survive as a ring of parks, lakes and green areas surrounding Indre By – Copenhagen grew rapidly. Although it was ravaged by a series of major fires, as well as being bombarded first by the Swedish, then the British, the medieval town's tangle of tiny streets, squares and ancient churches survived, and is still very much in evidence, in sharp contrast both to the state buildings of Slotsholmen and to the relatively modern areas outside the old fortifications, where permanent settlement only started after 1851.

Nowadays, Indre By (literally, "inner city") is the hub of the city's day-to-day activity and very much the public face of Copenhagen, with lively streets perfectly suited to idle ambling amongst crowds of locals, tourists and street entertainers. Two main pedestrianized thoroughfares cross the area: the first is **Strøget**, the collective name given to the series of streets (Frederiksberggade, Nygade, Vimmelskaftet, Amagertorv and Østergade) which run across Indre By from Rådhuspladsen in the west to Kongens Nytorv in the east. The second, **Købmagergade**, leaves Strøget at Højbro Plads, heading north towards Nørreport Station via Kultorvet square. These two main drags form the backbone of the city's shopping district, lined by high-street shops that are all rather mainstream and expensive, though the side streets conceal an intriguing array of second-hand and antique shops, as well as many popular and unusual inner-city bars, cafés and restaurants.

The area covered by this chapter is shown in detail
on colour map 3.

RÅDHUSPLADSEN TO HØJBRO PLADS

Central Copenhagen's principal square, **Rådhuspladsen** (map 3, D7–E7), was nothing more than a simple hay market until the old city ramparts became obsolete in 1851 and it was decided to build a new city hall here, on what was then the city's largest available central space. Today Rådhuspladsen is the main meeting point for the city's buses, and although it's one of central Copenhagen's least scenic squares, it makes a convenient place from which to start exploring Indre By, and a useful point from which to orientate yourself in the city as a whole, with Indre By on one side, and the Tivoli Gardens and the district of Vesterbro on the other.

**The new travel centre on Rådhuspladsen – a black,
shed-like building – can help you with information about
city transport, tickets, timetables and routes.**

The square's main feature is the monumental, red-brick
Rådhus (City Hall; Mon–Fri 10am–3pm, free; guided tours
Mon Fri 3pm, Sat 10am & 11am, 30kr), designed by
Martin Nyrop and completed in 1905. You're free to wander around during working hours, though given the building's massive size, and the ease with which you can get lost
here, it's worth joining a guided tour. Beyond the impressive
entrance, the spacious and elegant main hall has retained
most of its original features, such as the Italianate wall decorations and the sculpted oak banisters heading up from the
ground floor. Upstairs, the reception hall and balcony overlooking the square are used for civic celebrations. Look out
too for a row of painted portraits of the city's past mayors: as
with the portrait gallery at the Folketing, it's interesting to
see how politicians' appearances reflect the times they live in
– note the picture of left-wing Villo Sigurdson portrayed
with a poster of the Clash in the background.

At 106m, the city hall **tower** (tours June–Sept Mon–Fri
10am, noon & 2pm, Sat noon; Oct–May Mon–Sat noon;
20kr) is Denmark's highest. There are about 300 steps up to
the balcony, and a further fifty through a narrow passageway
to the spire, passing the bells used as Danish Radio's hourly
chime. From the top there's a good view of the city and
down the length of Strøget all the way to Kongens Nytorv.

In a side room close to the entrance, what looks like a
mass of inscrutable dials is in fact the astronomical time-
piece of **Jens Olsen's World Clock** (Mon–Fri
10am–4pm, Sat 10–1pm; 10kr; ⓦ *www.copenhagencity.dk*).
Set going in 1955, the clock features a 570,000-year calen-
dar plotting eclipses of the moon and sun, solar time, local

time and various planetary orbits – all with incredible accuracy. It's fascinating to watch, too, as hundreds of ticking dials track the movements of the planets of the solar system.

Also on Rådhuspladsen is **Ripley's Believe It Or Not!** (Mon–Thurs & Sun 10am–6pm, Fri & Sat 10am–8pm; 66kr; ⓦ *www.ripleys.dk*), a collection of oddities based on the cartoons of American Robert L. Ripley – a life-sized model of the world's tallest man and a bicycle made from matchsticks are just two of hundreds of exhibits.

East to Larsbjørnstræde

Map 3, D6–E7.

Head east from Rådhuspladsen down Frederiksberggade, the first of the series of streets collectively known as **Strøget**, which runs across Indre By from Rådhuspladsen in the west to Kongens Nytorv in the east. Walk down here for five minutes then head left along Kattesundet to reach **Larsbjørnstræde**, one of the liveliest streets in the city. Despite being nicknamed *Pisserenden*, "the urinal" (in its dilapidated past it was a favourite spot for people to relieve themselves in), the street has shed its smelly past and now overflows with trendy shops selling secondhand clothes and books, chic organic cafés and a buzzing nightlife. **Studiestræde** and **Skt Peders Stræde**, which run across Larsbjørnstræde at right angles, are similarly lively.

The Latin Quarter

Map 3, D5–E5.

Walking up Larsbjørnstræde then right along Skt Peder Stræde brings you to Copenhagen's **University**, at the centre of the so-called **Latin Quarter** – Latin once being the *lingua franca* here. The university, founded in 1475 to train Catholic priests, is the oldest in Scandinavia, though today most of its departments have moved out of the city centre, and the impressive neo-Gothic main building from 1836 is used mainly for administration. Statues of the university's most distinguished graduates – including Nobel Prize-winner Niels Bohr, who discovered the structure of the atom – stand in front of the building.

Across from the university on the other side of Nørregade is **Skt Petri Kirke** (St Peter's Church; Tues–Sat 11am–3pm), one of the city's characteristic red-brick churches. In 1585 the church was donated by King Frederik II to the German Lutheran congregation, and sermons are still held only in German. The core of the present church dates back to the mid-fifteenth century, though it's been enlarged a number of times since, and was refurbished following the Great Fire of 1723. Be sure to stroll through the atmospheric side chapel from 1691 – resting place of many prominent Danish government ministers.

Immediately south of the university is Copenhagen's cathedral, **Vor Frue Kirke** (Our Lady's; Mon–Fri 8am–5pm, Sat noon–5pm). Built on the site of a twelfth-century church, the present Neoclassical edifice dates only from 1829, when it was erected to a design by the prolific C.F. Hansen amidst the devastation caused by the British bombardment of 1807. Inside the church, a weighty figure of Christ behind the altar and the solemn statues of the apostles – some crafted by Bertel Thorvaldsen, others by his pupils – merit a visit. Organ concerts are held here through July and August.

Gammeltorv and Nytorv

Map 3, E6.

Head south from Vor Frue Kirke down Nørregade to get back to Strøget, here flanked by the busy squares of **Gammeltorv** and **Nytorv** ("old" and "new" squares), two

RÅDHUSPLADSEN TO HØJBRO PLADS

ancient spaces which mark the site of the earliest market-place in Havn when it was still a fishing village. The city's **Domhus** (Law Courts), on Nytorv, is marked by a suitably forbidding row of Neoclassical columns built by the ubiquitous C.F. Hansen, town planner and architect, whose simple, Neoclassical designs were a distinctive feature of Copenhagen's Golden Age.

Busy Gammeltorv's most striking feature is the **Caritas Fountain**, by Statius Otto, dating from 1608. Ten years older than the similarly risqué – but much more famous – Mannikenpis in Brussels, the fountain's water flows from Caritas's breasts and from the little boy at her feet taking a leak (the three holes were sealed with lead during the puritanical nineteenth century). The fountain supposedly symbolizes Christian IV's compassion for his people: the well on top of which it stands was the city's first external water supply, linked by lead piping to a source six kilometres north of the city. There's a small fruit-and-veg market in front of the fountain, along with stalls selling handmade jewellery and bric-a-brac.

It's also worth detouring south from Nytorv to visit **Kompagnistræde**, one of Europe's best hunting grounds for antiques. The range of outlets here, both up- and downmarket, yields all sorts of treasures if you look hard enough, from Persian carpets and oak furniture to silver candlestick holders, ancient plates, delicate crystal glassware and collectable old children's toys.

Gråbrødretorv

Map 3, F5.

Continue east down Strøget, then left just before reaching Helligåndskirken down cobbled Valkendorfsgade and through Kringlegangen – a pedestrian passageway that goes straight through no. 17 – to reach **Gråbrødretorv**, a

charming cobbled square filled with good cafés and restaurants and often crowded with buskers. The square dates
back to 1238, when Franciscan monks started the city's first
monastery here – the name Gråbrødretorv ("Grey Brothers'
Square") is a reference to their grey habits. The monks left
Copenhagen shortly before the Reformation and today the
square is a gathering place for locals in the know, who
come in good weather to dine well or just sit by the fountain and enjoy a cold *høker* beer. Concerts are held on the
square during the summer.

East to Højbro Plads

Map 3, F5–G5.
Returning to Strøget and turning left brings you to
Helligåndskirken (Church of the Holy Ghost; Mon–Fri
noon–4pm), founded in 1296 as part of a Catholic
monastery of the same name, and one of the oldest churches
in the city. The monastery was dissolved during the
Reformation, but the church survived as a Lutheran parish
church until being completely gutted by the Great Fire of
1728; it has been largely rebuilt since. Entrance is through a
beautifully carved sandstone portal, dating back to 1620,
which was originally intended for the old stock exchange
(Børsen) on Slotsholmen; inside, look out for an impressive
altarpiece donated by Christian VI depicting the ascension
of Christ. Also dating from 1296, **Helligåndshuset** (entered
from the church close, left of the main church entrance), the
west wing of the original monastery, survived the fire of
1728 and is today the only completely preserved medieval
building in Copenhagen. It's now used for art shows and
other exhibitions and is worth going into for a peek at the
formidable vaulted ceiling and slender granite columns.

A few steps further along Strøget is the **Tobacco
Museum** (Tobaksmuseet; Mon–Thurs 10am–6pm, Fri

10am–7pm, Sat 10am–2pm; free), a low-key exhibition in the cellar of the old W.Ø. Larsen tobacco shop, whose two rooms contain a briefly diverting clutter of vintage pipes from as far back as the sixteenth century, along with ornate cigar holders, diamond-covered snuff boxes and every conceivable smoking accessory, plus paintings and drawings satirizing the deadly habit.

Opposite the Tobacco Museum is **Georg Jensens Silverware Shop**. Georg Jensen became famous in the early twentieth century for his Art Nouveau silverware – ranging from jewellery to cutlery – and there's a small museum in the shop dedicated to him and his designs, including some beautiful examples of his early work. Next door, connected by an inside passageway, is one of Copenhagen's oldest buildings: dating from 1616, it miraculously survived the city's many fires and now houses the **Royal Copenhagen Porcelain Shop**, selling glass and porcelain from the most famous Danish factories; you can also watch porcelain being painted. Upstairs, **Konditoriet** (see p.159) offers some of the best – and most expensive – pastries in Copenhagen.

If you want to see how Royal Copenhagen porcelain is made, tours are held daily at the factory at Frederiksberg (see p.96).

HØJBRO PLADS AND AROUND

The cobbled **Højbro Plads**, created to make space for the city fire brigade's trucks after the devastating fire of 1795, is lined with banks and other relatively dull buildings. It's traditionally been home to generations of street vendors, formerly selling flowers to wealthy locals, today flogging bric-a-brac to tourists. In the centre of the square, the

Storkespringvandet ("The Stork Fountain", though the birds which adorn it are actually herons) has repeatedly been a focal point of Danish anti-establishment culture, most memorably during the flower-power era, when hippies sat around it singing protest songs, though today you're more likely to encounter rollerbladers, street entertainers and a few local drunks.

Around Gammel Strand

Map 3, G5. Bus #1, #6 or #29.

At the southern end of Højbro Plads is **Gammel Strand** ("Old Beach"), adorned with an equestrian statue of the founder of Copenhagen, Bishop Absalon, positioned on the spot where he is presumed to have first sighted Slotsholmen, site of his future castle. The statue, by Wilhelm Bissen, dating from 1901, was criticized for its aggressive portrayal of Absalon – perched on a rearing charger, he looks more like a warrior than a man of the church – though the plinth, by Martin Nyrop, was much praised; some critics even suggested that horse and rider be removed, leaving the plinth alone to stand as more worthy memorial to the bishop.

Turning right along the canal down Gammel Strand brings you to another statue, *The Fisher Woman*, commemorating the tough ladies who used to line up along the beachfront here, selling the fish their husbands had caught (the canalside by the statue is now one of the DFDS docking points – see p.15 for more details). From here, there's a fine view across the canal to Slotsholmen, with the brightly coloured Thorvaldsen's Museum standing out next to Christiansborg and Christianborgs Slotkirke, best appreciated during spring and summer from the outside tables of the row of canalside restaurants here, including the popular *Thorvaldsens Gourmetbar & Café* and, a few doors further along, Denmark's oldest and most famous fish restaurant, *Krogs*. In summer there's a flea market here on Saturdays from 8am to 2pm.

For reviews of *Thorvaldsens* and *Krogs*
Gammel Strand, see pp.160 and 163.

Squeezed in between the canalside cafés and restaurants is the impressive **Kunstforeningen Gammel Strand** exhibition hall (Tues–Sun 11am–5pm; art gallery 30kr, photographic centre 25kr; ⓦ *www.kunstforeningen.dk*), devoted to temporary exhibitions of contemporary art. The **Photographic Centre** (ⓦ *www.photography.dk*) on the first floor displays the work of internationally renowned photographers.

NORTH ALONG KØBMAGERGADE

From Højbro Plads you can either continue east along Strøget – a route described on p.45 – or head north up Indre By's other main thoroughfare, the pedestrianized **Købmagergade**, which takes you to Kultorvet before changing its name to Frederiksborggade. With its many chic boutiques and designer shops, Købmagergade is becoming an increasingly close competitor to Strøget. On the corner of Købmagergade and Strøget, **Illums** department store, Copenhagen's answer to Harrods of London, sets the tone with its pricey merchandise and snooty service.

The Erotica and Post museums

Map 3, F4–G4. Bus #31, #42, #43 or Nørreport S-Tog.

A bit further down Købmagergade, on the same side as Illums, a dark entrance hall leads to one of the city's most original museums, the **Museum Erotica** (May–Sept

Mon–Sun 10am–11pm; Oct–April Mon–Fri & Sun 11am–8pm, Sat 10am–9pm; 65kr; ⓦ *www.museumerotica.dk*), a shrine to the erotic – and just plain pornographic – through the ages. Exhibits range from saucy Indian miniatures to a written description of Hans Christian Andersen's sex life (or lack of), plus a bank of videos showing porn movies.

On the corner of Købmagergade and Løvstræde (which also leads down to Gråbrødretorv – see p.36) is the surprisingly interesting **Post and Tele Museum** (Tues & Thurs–Sun 10am–5pm, Wed 10am–8pm; 30kr, free on Wed; ⓦ *www.ptt-museum.dk*), devoted to the history of communication by post and phone and displaying an impressive collection of items such as Christian IV's first mail coach – constructed in an odd spherical shape to minimize air resistance, allow water to run off, and prevent the coachman from taking along passengers – and postal curios through the ages.

The Post and Tele Museum's rooftop café offers scrumptious lunches, and a fine view of the city's many towers. There's also free Internet access at the first-floor B@lkony, a children's museum workshop and a playroom by the rooftop café.

Rundetårn

Map 3, E4. June–Aug Mon–Sat 10am–8pm, Sun noon–8pm; Sept–May Mon–Sat 10am–5pm, Sun noon–5pm; 15kr; ⓦ *www.rundetaarn.dk*. Bus #5 or Nørreport S-Tog.

Further along Købmagergade is one of the city's oddest structures, the **Rundetårn**, a round tower built by Christian IV as part of the **Trinitatis** complex, which combined three important facilities for seventeenth-century scholars: an astronomical observatory, a church, and a university library. The tower functioned both as observatory lookout (it's now the oldest functioning observatory in Europe) and as the Trinitatis church tower – and perhaps also as a vantage point from which Copenhagen's citizens could admire Christian's additions to the city. Inside the tower a spiral ramp winds its way to the top, from where there's a good view of the hive of medieval streets below. Legend has it that Peter the Great sped to the top on horseback in 1715, pursued by the tsarina in a six-horse carriage – a smoother technique than descending on skateboard, a short-lived fad in more recent times. Left unused for many years, the library, which is housed in the church attic, was recently restored and turned into an **art gallery** with changing artistic, cultural and historical exhibitions. So, if you're not quite up to reaching the top, the halfway point is usually a worthwhile stop.

North to Kultorvet

Map 3, D4–E4.

Turning left down Krystalgade takes you past **Regensen** on the left-hand corner, a crooked old student hostel originally founded by Frederik II in 1628 for students without means, a function it still fulfils today. Many of Denmark's most prominent philosophers lectured here, and over the years Regensen became the hub of the city's intellectual life. Further down Krystalgade on the right-hand side is Copenhagen's **Synagogue**, a classical-style basilica dating from 1833. It's the main synagogue for Denmark's Jewish community, but is only open during services.

The short stretch from Rundetårn to Kultorvet is unremarkable, as is **Kultorvet** itself, though it buzzes with life during the summer months when its numerous restau-

rants, cafés and music venues offer entertainment to satis-
fy most tastes and ages. Close to Nørreport Station, it's
also an easy place to stagger home from after a lively
night out.

Musical History Museum

Map 3, D3–E3. May–Sept Mon–Wed & Fri–Sun 1–3.30pm;
Oct–April Mon, Wed, Sat & Sun 1–3.30pm; 20kr;
Ⓦ *www.kulturnet.dk/homes/mhm*. Bus #31, #42, #43, #350S or
Nørreport S-Tog.

Just behind Kultorvet, the thoroughly entertaining
Musical History Museum has an impressive quantity of
musical instruments and sound-producing devices spanning
the globe and the last thousand years. Naturally the bulk
come from Denmark, and there are some subtle insights
into the social fabric of the nation to be gleaned from the
yellowing photos of country dances and other get-togeth-
ers hung alongside the instruments. There are recordings of
most of the instruments to listen to (helpful with some of
the odder ones, where it's a mystery even which end the
sound comes out from), two rooms where children can
play with sounds, and a resident violin-maker demonstrat-
ing the delicate art of instrument-building. Concerts using
instruments from the museum are occasionally held in the
small concert hall – check with the museum for details on
Ⓣ 33 11 27 26.

AROUND NØRREPORT

Less musical sounds are provided by the cars hurtling along
Nørre Voldgade, north of Kultorvet, which marks the position of the former ramparts and the end of the pedestrianized streets of the old city. The site of the Nørreport city
gate is now occupied by **Nørreport Station**, the city's

busiest train station, serviced by S-Tog, regional trains and – from 2001 – a metro to Christianshavn, Ørestad and Malmö. No construction was allowed in the area outside the old ramparts until 1856, which is why most developments in the area north of Nørre Voldgade up to the lakes are relatively new.

Around Israels Plads

Map 3, C4. Bus #5, #14, #16 or Nørreport S-Tog.

Shortly after the old city gates were demolished, the city's vegetable market moved from Christianshavn to what is now **Israels Plads**, just northwest of Nørreport Station. It didn't take long, however, before the surrounding area was completely built up and, as further expansion became impossible, the market moved again, this time to Valby. The fruit, vegetable and flower retailers stayed behind, however, and are still much in evidence today, trying to out-shout and out-sell one other. There's a **flea market** on the playground behind the vegetable market on Saturdays – you may find some good deals if you're lucky, though rumour has it that many of the stands are owned by mainstream city shops and that the keepers dress down for the occasion.

Just behind Israels Plads is **Ørstedsparken**, named after the famous Danish physicist, H.C. Ørsted, who discovered electro-magnetism. It's one of the few areas where the layout of the old ramparts has been preserved – the lakes here (part of the old defence system) follow the shape of the former ramparts – and there are also a number of unimpressive statues scattered around the hills, sponsored by brewing magnate Carl Jacobsen. In the summer you can get refreshments at the park café in the centre and watch the world pass by. It's also one of the city's most popular gay cruising grounds.

The Workers' Museum

Map 3, C3. Daily 10am–4pm, closed Mon Nov–June; 35kr;
Ⓦ *www.arbejdermuseet.dk*. Bus #5, #14, #16 or Nørreport S-Tog.

On the far side of Norrebrogade, halfway down
Rømersgade, is the **Workers' Museum** (Arbejdermuseet),
an engrossing guide to working-class life in Copenhagen
from the 1870s onwards. Entering the museum, you walk
down a reconstructed Copenhagen street, complete with
passing tram and a shop window hawking the consumer
durables of the day, continuing via a backyard where washing hangs drying and a printing works subsidized by the
Marshall Plan into a coffee shop, which sells cups of an old-
fashioned coffee and chicory blend. Elsewhere, mocked-up
house interiors contain family photos, newspapers and TVs
showing newsreels of the time. The four permanent displays
– each describing different periods of Danish workers' history – are backed up by some outstanding temporary exhibitions from labour movements around the world, both
factual and artistic. In the basement, an 1890s-style
lunchtime **restaurant** serves traditional Danish food from
the era – the only listed restaurant in the city. The museum
also has a lunch room where you can eat your packed
lunch, as long as you buy your drinks at the bar.

EAST TO NYHAVN

Back at Højbro Plads, head east off the square along the alley
named Lille Kirkestræde and then left to reach the grandiose
Skt Nikolaj Kirke (daily noon–5pm; 20kr, Wed free).
Although one of the oldest churches in the city, and mother
church of the Danish Reformation in 1536, it
hasn't been used for ecclesiastical purposes since 1795, when
the city's second great fire destroyed everything except the
tower (which, ironically enough, was subsequently used to

house the municipal fire brigade). The massive red-brick church wasn't rebuilt until early in the twentieth century, and now houses stimulating exhibitions of contemporary art: the main body provides a grand venue for multimedia art shows; the tower is mostly used for audio and video installations.

Heading east along the final section of Strøget – here called Østergade, and undoubtedly the most exclusive section of the entire thoroughfare – you'll pass a number of classy stores and shopping arcades, along with another international tourist pull: the **Guinness World of Records Museum** (June–Aug daily 9.30am–10pm, 69kr; Sept–May daily 10am–6pm, 65kr; Ⓦ *www.guinness.dk*) – much as you'd expect, with family-oriented exhibits on the world's tallest, fastest and smallest.

Kongens Nytorv

Map 3, H3–I3. Bus #1, #6, #9, #10, #29 or #650S.

For most Copenhageners Strøget ends, rather than begins, at **Kongens Nytorv**. This is where the shopping spree finishes and the search for a place to sit down and rest the feet starts. In summer, weary shopaholics head for the outdoor seats of the square's high-ceilinged, glass-fronted cafés; in winter, for the cosy dens selling *gløgg* and *æbleskiver* (warm mulled wine with nuts, raisins and spices served with round dough balls that are supposed to have slices of apple in them, but never do).

At the centre of Kongens Nytorv is an equestrian statue of Christian V, who completed the square by ordering the owners of land bordering it to erect houses of a certain regal standard or sell up, which is why the square is entirely surrounded by pompous-looking buildings from the seventeenth century, such as the swish *Hôtel d'Angleterre*. In more recent times it has become the tradition for newly graduated high-school students to celebrate by dancing around the king's statue in a ring – watch out for cheery, white-clad youngsters in late spring. In winter, the square is transformed into a free open-air ice-skating rink; a stall nearby hires out skates.

Turning right as you leave Strøget, you pass the **Magasin du Nord** – after Illums, the city's most exclusive department store – before reaching **Det Kongelige Teater** (Royal Theatre; guided tours every Sun Aug–May; 50kr (book in advance on ☎33 69 69 77)). Hans Christian Andersen supposedly tried his luck here as a ballet dancer while attempting to court the prima ballerina. True to his reputation, he failed miserably – whereupon he wrote yet another fairy tale with a rosy ending. The present theatre is one of the few in the world where ballet, opera and drama are performed under one roof. An extension, **Stærekassen**, was added in 1931 in Danish Art Deco style, its plain surfaces and clean decoration in sharp contrast to the Italianate "old stage", as the main building is now called. The front of the main entrance is adorned by statues depicting poet Adam Oehlenschläger and playwright Ludvig Holberg, both prominent in eighteenth-century Danish cultural life.

For details of performances at Det Kongelige Teater, see pp.199 and 205.

Next door to Det Kongelige Teater is **Charlottenborg Palace** (daily 10am–5pm, Thurs until 7pm), built by an illegitimate son of Frederik III in 1677 and now the oldest building on the square. It was handed over to the Royal Academy of Fine Arts in 1754, since when many prominent artists, such as Thorvaldsen, have lived here. It's still home to the Royal Academy, and though there are no specific public displays, it's worth dropping in just to glimpse the palace's elegant interior. The spacious, light rooms of

EAST TO NYHAVN

the **exhibition hall** (20kr) at the back, in a separate building from 1883, provide a perfect setting for eclectic exhibitions of contemporary art, architecture and decorative art.

Nyhavn

Map 3, I3–K3. Bus #1, #6, #9 or #10.

Nyhavn ("New Harbour") – created in 1671 as a canal
leading from the city's main port to Kongens Nytorv – is
mostly known for its sunny northern side, with its long row
of bars, cafés, taverns and restaurants set in brightly
coloured and picturesque gabled houses, some dating back
as far as 1681. During the past twenty years this canalside
promenade has become one of the trendiest places in the
city to live and be seen, a complete turnaround from its
seedy past as a disreputable sailors' haunt.

Frequent DFDS boats run from Nyhaven to the Little
Mermaid and Christianshavn – see p.15 for details.

On the corner of Nyhavn and Bredgade, the **Amber
Museum** (Ravhuset; Mon–Sat 10am–6pm, Fri until 7pm;
free) is located on the first floor of the Amber House, a historic building from the 1670s now devoted to producing
and selling amber artefacts. The surprisingly captivating
museum takes you through the economic and geological
history of amber, while rows of display cases equipped with
magnifying glasses show specimens of the many odd creatures found trapped in the resin from the enormous pine
forests of northern Europe twenty to fifty million years ago.
There's also an in-house craftsman showing how amber is
worked, plus the world's largest piece of Baltic amber, a
massive lump weighing 8.8 kilos.

Christianshavn

F acing Indre By and Slotsholmen across the waters of Inderhavnen, and linked to them by Knippelsbro bridge, is the island of **Christianshavn**. Nicknamed "Little Amsterdam" on account of its many small canals, cobbled streets, crooked houses and brightly painted facades, it's an easygoing area, and a pleasant place to hang out with a *høcker* beer while watching the wooden boats meander up and down the canals.

Until the seventeenth century, however, Christianshavn didn't even exist. The area now occupied by the island was under water, creating a breach in Copenhagen's defences which left the city vulnerable to attack from the sea, until Christian IV reclaimed an arc of land facing Copenhagen and built a ring of defensive fortifications on it. The reclaimed land became the island of Christianshavn and an autonomous borough was created on it to house Dutch merchants, with a Dutch architect – Johan Semp – being employed to plan the new district, explaining the many features on Christianshavn today which are more redolent of Amsterdam than of Copenhagen. The Dutch merchants never arrived, however, and the island was instead distributed between rich Danish merchants and aristocrats, who moved into the elegant dwellings along the waterfront and Wilders Kanal, and the workers, who were assigned the dark and dingy areas between.

Christianshavn's main thoroughfare, **Torvegade**, runs across the island from mainland Copenhagen in the north towards the island of Amager in the south – at right angles to the picturesque **Wilders Kanal** that flows down the centre of Christianshavn and divides the island in two. **Christianshavns Torv**, slap bang in the middle, is the district's busy central square – all buses crossing Christianshavn stop here and it's also the site of a new metro station due to open in 2001. On the northeastern corner of the island is the so-called "free city" of **Christiania**, whose improvised dwellings and community of alternative types have long been one of Christianshavn's main tourist attractions. At the far end of Christianshavn are the islands and former naval station of **Holmen**, now the site of many interesting new cultural developments and well worth exploring on a sunny afternoon.

The area covered by this chapter is shown in detail on colour map 3.

Christians Kirke and the B&W Museum

Map 3, K6–K7. Bus #2, #8, #9, #19, #28 or #350S.

The bustling square of **Christianshavns Torv** is the natural point from which to begin exploring Christianshavn. From here, walk up Torvegade towards Indre By and then down Strandgade on your left to reach **Christians Kirke** (daily: March–Nov 8am–6pm; Dec–Feb 8am–5pm), squeezed in between blocks of flats on one side and the new Unibank headquarters – four magnificent rectangles of glass and copper – on the other. The main feature of the church is its theatrical interior (not altogether surprising, given that Eigtved also designed the old royal theatre), with a three-storey arched gallery reminiscent of an old music-hall. Although still a functioning church, Christians Kirke also stages rock concerts, theatre and performances by the Royal Danish Ballet (information on ☏ 32 96 94 11).

Next door to Christians Kirke, hidden away in a back-yard warehouse, is the small and quirky **B&W Museum** (Mon–Fri and first Sun of the month 10am–1pm; free), a must if you're into diesel engines and surprisingly captivat-ing even if you're not. B&W was Denmark's oldest and most prestigious shipyard until being forced to close most of its operations in the early 1990s, and the museum's two upper floors are mainly devoted to the B&W diesel engine, with a multitude of models taking you through the various stages in the engine's evolution, and buttons you can press to see how they work. The museum staff, all former ship engineers, are more than happy to tell you all about the mechanical intricacies on display.

Along Strandgade

Map 3, K6–L3. Bus #2, #8, #9, #19, #28, #350S.
Heading north along Strandgade, across Torvegade, you'll pass the massive yellow-brick eyesore of the Danish Foreign Ministry before reaching the **Danish Architecture Centre** (Dansk Arkitektur Center; Mon–Fri 10am–5pm, Sat & Sun 11am–4pm; 30kr; ⓦ *www.gammeldok.dk*) at Gammel Dok. Housed in one of the oldest warehouses on Christianshavn, this beautifully renovated building is devot-ed to fascinating exhibitions concentrating on architectural design and urban culture. There's also a popular café from which you can watch boats pass by on the canal outside, and the bookshop stocks Denmark's largest selection of titles on architecture and design.

Continuing along Strandgade you cross over onto another small island to reach **Grønlands Handelsplads**. This is where ships from Denmark's old colonies in the North Atlantic – Greenland, Iceland and the Faroe Islands – used to dock, and where dried fish, whale oil and skins were stored or treated in the area's many enormous warehouses before being sold off to the rest of Europe. Although the magnificent warehouses were turned into offices in the early 1980s, they are still redolent of history – you can still detect a faint odour of fish. The Grønlandsk-Islandsk Pakhus warehouse is currently being transformed into a **North Atlantic Cultural Centre** (Nordatlantisk Center) featuring North Atlantic exhibitions, a café serving delicacies from the region, and diplomatic representations from the three countries – always useful to know if you need a visa for Greenland.

Royal Danish Naval Museum

Map 3, M5. Tues–Sun noon–4pm; 30kr. Bus #8.

South of Grønlands Handelsplads, in the beautifully restored Naval Hospital of 1780 on the corner of Bådsmandsstræde and Overgaden Oven Vandet, is the mildly diverting **Royal Danish Naval Museum** (Orlogsmuseet). Devoted to the history of the Danish Navy, the museum boasts an unusually large collection of ship models (some dating back to the sixteenth century), ships' equipment, pompous-looking uniforms, weapons, nautical instruments, maritime art and minutely detailed models of the many sea battles the Danish Navy has fought (they even include the smoke clouds from the cannons). You can also go aboard the *Spækhuggeren* ("Killer Whale") submarine – radio broadcasts help you to relive the moment it narrowly escaped the Germans during World War II. There's an eating area downstairs where you can consume your packed lunch in the company of a vast selection of cannons.

Vor Frelsers Kirke

Map 3, M6. Daily: April–Aug 11am–4.30pm; Sept–March 11am–3.30pm. Bus #8.

Poking skywards through the trees near the naval museum is the unmistakable blue-and-gold spire of **Vor Frelsers Kirke**. The spire, with its helter-skelter exterior staircase and large golden globe carrying a three-metre Jesus waving a flag, was added to the otherwise plain church in the mid-eighteenth century, instantly becoming one of the city sky-line's most recognizable features – it's said to have been used as a target by Nelson during the English bombardment of Copenhagen in 1807, though fortunately he only managed to hit a leg. Rumour also has it that the spire's architect, Laurids de Thurah, threw himself off the top when he dis-covered that the stairs wound to the right instead of the left, as the king had requested – although plausible, this is untrue.

To ascend the spire (20kr; note that for safety reasons the spire is closed Nov–March and on wet or windy days) you'll have to climb a total of 400 steps, 150 of them out-side, slanted and slippery (especially after rain), and gradual-ly becoming smaller and smaller. The reward for reaching the top is a great view of Copenhagen and beyond. The interior of the building, the largest Baroque church in Copenhagen, is covered in a wealth of incredible detail. Look out for the two large stucco elephants holding a gigantic organ – the animal became the symbol of the nation's highest order, the Order of the Elephant, which still exists today.

Lille Mølle

Map 3, M6. Guided tours May–Sept Tues–Sun at 1pm, 2pm, 3pm & 6pm; 40kr. Bus #2, #9, #19, #28, #31 or #37.

Between Torvegade and Bådsmandsstræde is **Lille Mølle**,

the only surviving example of the many windmills which formerly stood on the Christianshavn ramparts. Built in 1783 to a Dutch design, the windmill ground wheat for the ever-increasing numbers of Copenhageners until being converted into a private home at the beginning of the twentieth century. In 1973 it was given to the National Museum by its last owners, and today it bears witness to their lavish lifestyle, with many odd rooms furnished in a mixture of styles from quaintly Germanic to romantic British. Next door, in the miller's old domicile, is a fine new café-restaurant, *Bastionen og Løven* (see p.164), set outdoors on the edge of the ramparts.

Christiania

Map 3, N4–N5. Bus #8 (the "Christiania Express").
Stretching for almost a kilometre along either side of the moat north of Lille Mølle, the remarkable "Free City" of **Christiania** is living proof of Copenhagen's liberal social traditions (see box opposite). Christiania's population of around one thousand is swelled in summer by the curious and the sympathetic – although residents ask tourists not to camp here or point cameras at the weirder-looking inhabitants. The craft shops and restaurants are fairly cheap, and generally good, as are a couple of innovative music and performance art venues. For information on the district call in at Galopperiet (daily noon–5pm) right of the main entrance on Prinsessegade.

Guided tours of Christiania (book on ☎ 32 57 96 70; 20kr) leave from the main entrance and are a good introduction to the nooks and crannies of this rather complicated area.

Christiania spreads out on both sides of Christian IV's old moat between Christianshavn and Amager (a bridge,

THE FREE CITY

Christiania occupies an area that for centuries housed Christianhavn's army barracks, before the soldiers moved out and it was colonized by young and homeless people in the spring of 1971. Christiania was declared a "free city" by its residents later that year, with the aim of operating autonomously from Copenhagen proper and pursuing more egalitarian and environmentally friendly lifestyles. Its continued existence on some of Copenhagen's finest real estate has fuelled one of the longest-running debates in Danish (and Scandinavian) society.

One byproduct of its idealism and the freedoms assumed by its residents (and, despite recent lapses, generally tolerated by successive governments and the police) was that Christiania became a refuge for petty criminals and shady individuals from all over the city. But the problems have inevitably been overplayed by Christiania's critics, and a surprising number of Danes – of all ages and from all walks of life – do support the place, not least because Christiania has performed altruistically when established bodies have been found wanting. An example has been in the weaning of heroin addicts off their habits (once, a 24-hour cordon was thrown around the area to prevent dealers reaching the addicts inside: reputedly the screams – of deprived junkies, and of suppliers being "dealt with" – could be heard all night). And Christiania residents have stepped in to provide free shelter and food for the homeless at Christmas – the free Christmas dinner they provide is now a popular annual event, even among the not-so-homeless, as up to 2000 people descend on the Grå Hal for a traditional Danish feast. In recent years Christiania has become a more integral part of Copenhagen – the inclusion on the newest official map of Copenhagen of "Pusherstreet" (see box on p.56) illustrates its gradual acceptance into the mainstream of city life.

Dyssebroen, connects the two sides), comprising a mixture of solid old warehouses – some dating back to 1688 – and colourful and alternative new dwellings, including some unusual structures built on stilts. The **main entrance** on Prinsessegade leads straight into the heart of the "city". This is where you'll find most of Christiania's bars, restaurants and nightlife, along with the infamous **Pusherstreet**, where lines of stalls sell pre-rolled joints and an international selection of grass – wildly popular with tourists in summer. The remainder of the Free City is mainly residential, and entirely pedestrianized, dotted with the craftshops that have become an important feature of the area. The oldest structures are the bastions overlooking the Christianshavn side of the moat – Vilhelms Bastion, Carls Bastion, and

CANNABIS IN COPENHAGEN

At times, Copenhagen can appear like an Amsterdam of the north: young people searching for thrills and cheap drugs from other, less tolerant Nordic nations descend on the city, and the smell of marijuana smoke pervades the city's parks and even some bars. Christiania's **Pusherstreet** hashish market – the largest source of the drug in northern Europe – is entirely open, whilst scattered throughout the city are numerous, unsignposted outlets that sell the drug.

Though all this might seem to suggest that Copenhagen is entirely tolerant of cannabis, it's not. Police may be lenient to locals – usually a warning or an on-the-spot fine – but visitors can be expelled from the country. If you want to smoke pot, it's best to stick to the confines of Christiania, where cannabis is tolerated. Note, though, that hard drugs are *not* welcome in Christiania, and also remember that attempting to smuggle even a small quantity of cannabis into the UK or any other country is illegal and carries stiff penalties, including prison.

Frederiks Bastion; the oldest, Vilhelms Bastion, dates back to 1688 and looks all the more solid compared to the rest of Christiania's improvised dwellings.

Holmen

Map 3, M1–N3. Bus#8.

Continue north along Prinsessegade to reach the old naval station of **Holmen**, founded by Frederik III and built on five reclaimed islands. Most of the base was moved elsewhere in the early 1990s, and the islands' many listed buildings now house four art schools, with more planned – check for current developments. There's nothing particular to do, but the old listed buildings and the area as a whole are captivating; there's also a wildly popular and fun restaurant with a military theme, *Base Camp Holmen* (see p.164 and p.178), here as well.

At the northern tip of Holmen on the island of Nyholmen, **Nyholms Hovedvagt**, completed in 1745, is one of Holmen's oldest buildings, with a slightly out-of-proportion tower capped by a huge crown – the Danish flag is still raised and lowered here by the navy every sunrise and sunset. Next door is the Elephanten Dock, constructed on an old ship which was deliberately sunk to establish the foundations of the dock. There's a line of old cannons nearby, and you can walk along the top of the fortifications overlooking Inderhavnen – on a sunny day, the view from here over to mainland Copenhagen and the spires and domes of Frederikstad is incomparable.

CHRISTIANSHAVN

Rosenborg, Frederikstad and Kastellet

There's quite a contrast between the narrow, tangled streets of Indre By and the open parklands and boulevards of the more modern areas on the northeastern side of the city centre. This part of Copenhagen owes its character to two royal builders, Christian IV – creator of the fanciful palace of **Rosenborg Slot** and the more functional fortress of **Kastellet** to the north – and Frederik V, whose name is preserved in the district he created, **Frederikstad**, a sumptuous royal quarter boasting proud aristocratic monuments such as the Marmorkirken and the palaces of Amalienborg.

The area covered by this chapter is shown in detail on colour map 4.

ROSENBORG

Immediately north of Gothersgade the medieval streets of Indre By give way to the open parklands surrounding the royal palace of **Rosenborg Slot**. Opposite here is the glorious cornucopia of Copenhagen's **Botanisk Have** (Botanical Gardens), while scattered around the surrounding parklands are some good museums, including the **Geological Museum**, the **Davids Samling**, with its fine Islamic collection, and the impressive artworks of the **Royal Museum of Fine Arts** and the **Hirschsprung Collection**.

Rosenborg Slot

Map 4, F8–G8. May–Sept daily 10am–4pm; Oct daily 11am—3pm; Nov–April Tues–Sun 11am—2pm; 50kr. Bus #5, #10, #14, #16, #31, #42, #43 or Nørreport S-Tog.

Rising enchantingly from the carefully manicured lawns of Kongens Have, the Dutch-Renaissance palace of **Rosenborg Slot** looks like a setting for one of Hans Christian Andersen's more romantic tales. Surrounded by a moat and decorated with spires and towers, the playful, red-brick palace was built by Christian IV in 1607 as a summer residence, becoming over the centuries a storehouse for various royal collections which now include artworks, a small armoury and assorted curiosities, along with well preserved living quarters and the crown jewels. Note that there's no lighting in the palace and it can get pretty gloomy inside – you can borrow a torch from the ticket office for a small deposit.

You can buy a combined ticket (60kr, valid for two days) to Rosenborg Slot and the Royal Danish Collection at Amalienborg (see p.69).

ROSENBORG

The first section of the **ground floor** of the castle is a relatively sombre affair – oak-panelled rooms, royal busts and grand paintings of sea battles abound – though in later rooms the panelling gives way to stuccoed nymphs and marble, and the gloomy atmosphere is lightened by some bizarre curiosities. The highlight is a seventeenth-century armchair: hidden tentacles in the armrests would grab the wrists of anyone unlucky enough to sit in the chair, and the victim would then be doused in water before being released to the sound of a small trumpet. Look out, too, for the piece of alchemical "gold" (item 612) – the lead it was made from is kept beside it – and there's also a small armoury featuring crossbows, ornate rapiers and dozens of flintlock pistols.

Access to the two upper floors is via a spiral stone staircase. The **first floor** is a labyrinth of run-down rooms stuffed with largely uninspiring pieces of furniture or artwork. The one highlight is the **Mirror Cabinet** – all four walls are covered in mirrors – designed to indulge the king's erotic fantasies: the floor mirrors allowed him to peer up his partner's dress, before whisking her off to a connecting bedroom. The **second floor** is dominated by the **Long Hall**, its walls covered with enormous tapestries from 1690 showing Christian V's victories in the Scanian War of 1675-79. It's also home to one of the biggest collections of silver furniture in the world (from the 1700s) and three large silver lions which used to guard the king's throne.

Back outside the ground floor, a small flight of stairs leads down to the **basement**, where the **Green Cabinet** is home to a sumptuous collection of regalia and jewellery – an elaborate embroidered saddle takes centre stage. Another flight of stairs leads down through massive steel doors into the **Treasury**, where you're immediately confronted by Christian III's magnificent Sword of State, dating from 1551, beyond which are hundreds of incredibly detailed gold items and the fabulous silver Oldenborg Horn, allegedly dating from 989 AD, though it was probably created in 1465. In the bottom section of the basement are two cases containing the present queen's **crown jewels** and those of earlier monarchs, encrusted with jewels and precious stones. The largest piece, the Crown of the Absolute Monarchs, weighs in at over 2kg and includes a sapphire weighing over an ounce.

Kongens Have

Map 4, G7–H9. Daily 6am–sunset; free. Bus #5, #42, #43, #184, #185, #150S, #350S or Nørreport S-Tog.

Central Copenhagen's oldest and prettiest park, **Kongens Have** (Royal Gardens) was established in 1606 by Christian IV to provide Rosenborg Slot with a place in which to grow vegetables. The gardens still preserve much of their original layout, with a grid of wide lanes and narrower pathways – though the exact purpose of the seventeen large marble balls which surround the lawns opposite Rosenborg Slot remains a mystery. From the palace, it's a short stroll down to the park's southern entrance on Gothersgade, where two large plinths, topped with gold domes, neatly frame Kavalergangen (The Squire's Lane), originally used as a jousting run. Walk down here to the **Hercules Pavilion** – there's a small café here during the summer and, next door, a novel children's play area complete with large wooden dragons for clambering on. Look out, too, for the statue of a solemn-looking Hans Christian Andersen a couple of hundred metres east of here, towards Kronprinsessegade.

Botanisk Have

Map 4, D9–F7. Summer daily 8.30am–6pm; winter daily 8.30am–4pm. Bus #5, #7, #14, #16, #24, #40, #43, #84, #384 or Nørreport S-Tog.

Established on their present site in 1874, the **Botanisk**

ROSENBORG

Have (Botanical Gardens) occupy the levelled bastions of the old city fortifications – the zigzagging nature of the lakes inside reveals their original function as a protective moat. The gardens boast a small coniferous forest, rock gardens and waterfalls populated by herons, ducks and freshwater terrapins, while two greenhouses hold wonderful collections of citrus fruits, succulents and cacti. The largest is the circular **Palmehus** (daily 10am–3pm), where massive palms hang lazily in the steamy atmosphere over ponds festooned with waterlilies – a walkway runs around the top of the interior if you want to get up among the treetops. In the wings are collections of some economically and medicinally important plants from the tropics, including spices, cacao, coffee and coconut. Next to the Palmehus, the enthralling **Kaktushus** (Wed, Sat & Sun 1pm–3pm) contains around a thousand species of cacti and succulents, along with a section featuring over six hundred types of orchids, whose fragrant smells permeate the air.

Geological Museum

Map 4, F7. Tues–Sun 1pm–4pm; free; Ⓦ *www.geological-museum .dk.* Bus #184, #10 or Nørreport S-Tog.

The interesting if rather run-down **Geological Museum** (Geologisk Museum) has exhibits depicting how geological forces have shaped the Earth's landscape and life, a vast collection of minerals and, most interestingly, a startling collection of **meteorites** from a major fall thousands of years ago in Cape York, Greenland – some have been cut into enormous slices, creating strange, mirror-like effects. The collection's two biggest meteorites, "Savik" and "Agpalilik", are displayed outside – Savik, the smaller of the two, has pitted sides, the result of generations of Inuits hammering away at it to procure iron for knives and harpoons.

Royal Museum of Fine Arts

Map 4, F6. Tues & Thurs–Sun 10am–5pm, Wed 10am–8pm; 40kr
(combined ticket for permanent and temporary exhibitions, 50kr);
Ⓦ *www.smk.dk*. Bus #10, #14, #40, #42, #43, #72E, #79E, #150S,
#173E, #184, #185 or Østerport S-Tog.

Situated in the southern corner of Østre Anlæg park is the
Royal Museum of Fine Arts (Statens Museum for
Kunst) – not the most outstanding of Copenhagen's galleries, but worth a visit if you have the time. The museum's
wide-ranging exhibits are housed in two contrasting wings:
the older Dahlerup Building, a gloomy affair containing
classical works ranging from Tintoretto through to the
Danish Golden Age, and the bright and airy new wing,
devoted to contemporary works and a stimulating children's
museum.

Ascending the main stairs from the entrance hall of the
Dahlerup Building leads to an enormous collection of
works from all over Europe from the beginning of the
fourteenth century to the end of the nineteenth, including
rooms devoted variously to the almost photographic
images of the Dutch and Flemish masters, Italian religious
paintings (including a number of Tintorettos), and a smattering of lesser-known Breughels, Rembrandts and Van
Dycks.

The **new wing**, accessible via the ground floor or by
two footbridges from the Dahlerup Building, is an impressive architectural pile spread over five floors. Its light and
spacious design makes an excellent home for an extensive,
if rather lightweight, collection of contemporary art – you
may feel it's the building rather than the paintings that
grabs your attention. There's also an excellent **children's
museum** on the ground floor, with stimulating temporary exhibits drawn from the permanent collection,
thoughtfully hung at a lower, child-friendly height, and

ROSENBORG

●

63

paper and paint for kids to create their own works of art with.

The main body of the collection, on the second and third floors, highlights most major movements of the twentieth century. The **second floor** has a large sample of Danish and international work – the colourful postsurrealist abstractions of the Cobra movement (made up of mid-twentieth-century artists from *CO*penhagen, *BR*ussels and *A*msterdam – hence the name) are particularly well represented. Elsewhere, look for the enormous, quirky photographic self-portrait by Gilbert & George and, in an adjacent room, Dane Øyvid Nygaard's impressive *The Light Conductor* sculpture, reminiscent of the Silver Surfer. The rest of the second floor holds a largely uninspiring cache of works by contemporary German artists and a small collection of Danish and US sculpture.

The **third floor** features an important collection of modernist works, including a small selection of the Danish artist Asger Jorn's dramatic canvases, examples of works from twentieth-century movements such as Surrealism and Expressionism, and works by Picasso and Matisse – look out for the latter's *The Green Line*, in which a severe-looking Madame Matisse is unceremoniously bisected into contrasting halves by a noticeable green line.

Hirschsprung Collection

Map 4, E6. Wed 11am–9pm, Thurs–Sun 11am–4pm; 25kr, Wed free. Bus #10, #14, #40, #42, #43, #184, #185 or Østerport S-Tog. Crossing Østre Anlæg from the Royal Museum of Fine Arts brings you to the back of the Greek-inspired Neoclassical pavilion which houses the **Hirschsprung Collection**, the best collection of nineteenth-century Danish art in the city. The collection was donated to the Danish state in 1902 by second-generation German-Jewish immigrant and tobacco magnate Heinrich Hirschsprung – there's a large portrait of him smoking a cigar in the entrance hall.

Moving clockwise through the collection takes you through all the major periods of nineteenth-century Danish art. The **Golden Age** (roughly 1810–40) – an era when Danish cultural life flourished with the writings of Hans Christian Andersen and Søren Kirkegaard, the sculpture of Thorvaldsen and the paintings of C.W. Eckersberg – is initially reflected through a collection of Eckersbergs, one of Denmark's first professional artists, whose work was rooted firmly in romantic and idealistic traditions (*Woman Before a Mirror* is typical, with a poetic picture of a flesh-and-blood Venus de Milo), and his students, such as Christen Købke and William Bendz.

In room 13 are the remarkable historical paintings of Kristian Zahrtmann, a late nineteenth-century artist known for his colourful portrayals of eighteenth-century royal scandals, such as the ill-starred liaison between Princesss Caroline Mathilde, the English wife of the particularly mad Christian VII, and prime minister Count Struensee (Caroline Mathilde was sent into exile in Germany; Struensee was hung for treason). Room 15 contains one of the collection's most popular paintings, Harold Slott-Møller's *Spring*, a simple but engaging painting of a young girl, her hair garlanded with yellow flowers. The haunting symbolism of the almost pre-Raphaelite paintings of Ejnar Nielsen and Vilhelm Hammershøi takes centre stage in room 19 – Nielsen's *The Blind Girl* is particularly melancholy. Room 20 contains a large collection of works by painters from Skagen – a town on the northernmost tip of the country renowned for its bewitching light – some of whom Hirschsprung personally supported. P.S. Krøyer's depictions of the beaches around Skagen give a real feel for the qualities of its strange light.

ROSENBORG

Filmhuset

Map 4, H9. Tues–Fri 9.30am–10pm, Sat & Sun 1.30–10pm; free; Ⓦ *www.dfi.dk*.

Situated on Gothersgade just south of Rosenborg Slot, **Filmhuset** (The Film House) is a state-of-the-art complex dedicated to all things connected to the big screen. Occupying a restructured office block, the curious interior contains a large black sarcophagus-like edifice which encloses two of Cinemateket's (the in-house cinema; see p.202) screens. Other parts of the building are sometimes used as a gallery – expect to see cutting-edge, if not always interesting, Danish art. There's also a bookshop, café-bar and a film museum for temporary exhibitions, but the main attraction is the wonderful archives, with three libraries of books, posters, stills and videos (with free viewing facilities).

Davids Samling

Map 4, I8. Tues–Sun 1pm–4pm; free. Bus #10, #43 or Nørreport S-Tog.

Housed in an eighteenth-century house on Kronprinsessegade, the **Davids Samling** Islamic collection is an Aladdin's cave of Persian, Arabian and Indian antiques dating back to the sixth century (it also houses a less noteworthy collection of antique European furniture and ceramics). The well laid-out collection includes everything from delicate embroidered silks through to savage-looking daggers, and there's also an extensive collection of illuminated manuscripts and Korans, dating back to the thirteenth century, from all over the Islamic world.

Nyboder

Map 4, H6–J5. Bus #1, #6, #9 or Østerport S-Tog.

Further down Kronprinsessegade away from the city centre

are the striking cobbled streets and ochre cottages of the **Nyboder** district, built by Christian IV in the seventeenth century to provide free housing for his sailors. It's a pleasant enough place to wander about, even if it does all look a little bit too perfect to be true – in fact, all but one of the buildings here are nineteenth-century reconstructions. The solitary original building that does survive, dating from 1630, is now the small and reasonably interesting **Nyboders Mindestuer** museum (May–Aug Wed & Fri 11am–2pm, Sun 11am–4pm; Sept–April Wed 11am–2pm, Sun 11am–4pm; 10kr), containing a collection of furniture and domestic objects reflecting life at Nyboder.

FREDERIKSTAD

Commissioned by Frederik V and designed by Danish architect Nicolai Eigtved, the district of **Frederikstad** was intended as a royal quarter fit for a noble elite. Containing the residence of Danish royalty, **Amalienborg**, and the grandest place of worship in the city, **Marmorkirken**, Frederikstad raised Copenhagen to new levels of urban elegance.

Marmorkirken

Map 4, K7. Mon, Tues & Thurs–Sat 10.30am–4.30pm, Wed 10.30am–6.30pm, Sun noon–4.30pm; free. Bus #1, #6 or #9.

Topped by a large green dome modelled on – and intended to rival – St Peter's in Rome, the grandiose **Marmorkirken** ("The Marble Church"; officially called Frederikskirken) was commissioned by Frederik V to be a splendid centre of worship befitting his new royal quarter. Originally designed by Eigtved, Frederik V himself laid the church's first stone in a grand ceremony in 1749. After Eigtved's death in 1754, however, the scheme ran into difficulties, and in 1770 the exorbitant cost of the Norwegian marble being used in the church's construction forced Prime Minister Struensee to abandon the project. The building was then left in disarray for a century, while various plans were mooted as to what to do with it – one proposed turning it into a gasworks – until N.F.S. Grundtvig (see p.112) finally had it completed using cheaper Danish marble (there's a portrait of him in the church, unmissable with flowing white beard and bald head). The church was consecrated in 1894, 145 years after the foundation stone was laid.

Marmorkirken stages classical music concerts, normally on Wednesdays at 4.30pm and usually free – a full programme can be picked up in the church.

The **interior** of the church is grandly proportioned, if a bit drab – if you look at the walls you can see the materials change from expensive Norwegian to cheaper Danish marble about a quarter of the way up. The best reason to visit the church, however, is to climb the steep, twisting steps, all 260 of them, to the top of the bell tower, where the grand vista of Copenhagen is laid before you. The ascent involves entering the space between the inner and outer domes before climbing through a trap door and out into the elements. On a clear day you can see out to Malmö, Helsingør and across the city to Roskilde – look for the arrows on the bell tower. You can only make the climb from Monday to Friday at 1pm and 3pm (they are *very* precise about these times), when for 20kr a guide will take you through the passages and staircases that lead to the summit.

Next door to Marmorkirken are the gilded onion domes of the **Alexsander Nevsky Church**, Denmark's only functioning Russian Orthodox Church – look for the "weeping" icon, which from time to time allegedly sheds miraculous tears.

Amalienborg

Map 4, L6–M7. Bus #1, #6, #9 or #10.

Turn right down Frederiksgade from Marmorkirken to reach Slotsplads, a square surrounded by the four palaces of **Amalienborg**, the centrepiece of Frederikstad and the home of the Danish royal family since 1794. Designed by Eigtved, the four almost identical palaces are functional rather than sumptuous, and the whole ensemble is striking for its accessibility and openness rather than its grandeur – you're free to wander around Slotsplads, though you'll be challenged by the bearskin-hatted **Livgarden** (Life Guards) if you get too close to the palaces. Hang around long enough and you may even catch a glimpse of Denmark's first family.

Every day at noon the Livgarden perform a changing of the guard, during which they march back to their barracks beside Rosenborg Slot. A marching band is added to the procession if the queen or any other head of state is in residence.

The first palace on the left from Frederiksgade is home to the crown prince and the **Royal Danish Collection** (De Danske Kongers Kronologiske Samling; May–Oct daily 10am–4pm; Nov–April Tues–Sun 11am–4pm; 40kr, joint ticket with Rosenborg Slot 60kr), which includes a part of the royal family's living quarters that have been turned into what is basically a shrine to the monarchy. Queen Margerethe has had a sizeable input into designing the museum, as well as putting together the cover to the collection's catalogue – decide for yourself whether she got the job on merit. The museum itself is a mish-mash of family mementos, stuffed animals, garish military pictures and carefully preserved living quarters shielded from the

FREDERIKSTAD

hoi-polloi behind glass screens. The rooms of previous kings (the present queen is the first female monarch) do reveal something of their character – some are stuffed full of assorted regalia and military tackle; others are more homely affairs, with family portraits, pipes and slippers. There are also dull collections of jewellery and an absorbing Europe-wide royal family tree revealing the generations of inbreeding that have gone into producing the monarchs of today.

At the centre of Slotsplads is an enormous **equestrian statue** of Frederik V – it reputedly cost more than the four palaces combined thanks to sculptor, Jacques Saly, who, invited to Copenhagen to create the work, spent thirty years in the city living it up at the court's expense.

Medical History Museum

Map 4, L6. Guided tours: in English July & Aug Wed–Fri & Sun at 1pm; in Danish Wed–Fri & Sun at 11am & 1pm; free. Bus #1, #6 or #9. Returning to Bredgade and continuing north brings you to the **Medical History Museum** (Medicinsk-Historisk Museum), situated in a wing of what was originally the Danish Academy of Surgery, designed by Peter Meyn in 1787, and thus one of the few classical buildings in this area not designed by Eigtved. The museum's macabre account of Denmark's medical history features aborted foetuses, syphilis treatments, amputated feet, eyeballs and a dissected head, along with an original operating theatre complete with the dissecting table around which the gore-splattered pioneers of Danish surgery learnt their trade.

Danish Museum of Decorative Art

Map 4, L5. The collections from the middle ages to 1800: daily 1pm–4pm. Rest of the collection: Tues–Fri 10am–4pm, Sat & Sun noon–4pm; 35kr. Bus #1, #6, #9, #19, #29 or Østerport S-Tog.

The **Danish Museum of Decorative Art** (Kunstindustrimuseet) traces the development of European – and particularly Danish – design, as well as examining the influence of Eastern styles on Western design through a notable collection of Oriental furniture, ceramics and other exhibits. Most of the museum is used for displaying items from the permanent collection, which covers the period from the middle ages to 1800. One wing (on the right as you enter) is kept for later pieces, and temporary exhibits focusing on Danish design. Note that these two parts of the collection have slightly different opening hours.

The museum's excellent café, serving good-value Mediterranean-style food, is a nice place for lunch.

Oriental exhibits include a collection of early Japanese porcelains and sword-hilt decorations (*tsuba*s), along with some Chinese Ming vases, all displaying styles from which Europeans were to derive later designs. Early examples of styles borrowed from the East are shown through decorative work on Baroque furniture and the earliest glazed European porcelain from Meissen, Germany, while a section devoted to British design displays copies of Chinese lacquerware, Chippendale furniture and a toiletry set given to the unfortunate Princess Caroline Mathilde. The next part of the collection focuses on early Danish porcelain production in the district of Amager (Royal Copenhagen still make porcelain today in Frederiksberg, see p.96 – and it's possible to purchase exact copies of eighteenth-century pieces from their shop, see p.38). On a slightly more off-beat note are the ceramic pieces produced by Gauguin – who was married to a Dane – including a unique ceramic self-portrait.

The last part of the collection houses a disappointing assortment of twentieth-century furniture and design featuring the chairs of Wegner and other more abstract pieces – this section is scheduled for renovation.

Den Frie Udstilling

Map 4, H4. Mid-Aug to May daily 10am–5pm; 20kr; Ⓦ *www.denfrie.dk*. Bus #1, #6, #9 or Østerport S-Tog.

A rather strange-looking wooden building directly opposite Østerport station, at the northern tip of Nyboder, **Den Frie Udstilling** (The Free Exhibition) is *the* place to check out Denmark's budding young artists – note though that it's "free" as in free space rather than free entry. The exhibition hall was built in 1898 by an artists' collective looking for a place to exhibit and sell their work – the same collective still runs the hall today. Many of the big names of Danish art, such as Asger Jorn and Christian Lemmerz, have exhibited here at various times, but the exhibitions, as you might expect, can vary dramatically in quality. The building itself is virtually unchanged since 1898, with creaky old wooden floors and natural light spilling in through the glass roof – a great exhibition space, though unfortunately the greenhouse effect created by the roof makes it too hot to be used in high summer.

KASTELLET AND AROUND

At the far end of Bredgade, the straight streets of Eigtved's Frederikstad are replaced by the green open spaces of Churchillparken and **Kastellet**. There is a distinct military feel to this part of the city, with both the Resistance Museum, detailing Denmark's struggles against the Nazis during World War II, and Kastellet, Europe's oldest working fort, situated here. Nearby is that enduring symbol of the city, the Little Mermaid.

The Resistance Museum

Map 4, L4. May to mid-Sept Tues–Sat 10am–4pm, Sun 10am–5pm; mid-Sept to April Tues–Sat 11am–3pm, Sun 11am–4pm; free. Bus #1, #6, #9, #19, #29 or Østerport S-Tog.

Situated within Churchillparken – a small park named after the British wartime leader – the **Resistance Museum** (Frihedsmuseet) offers a comprehensive account of Denmark's role in World War II, using video displays (with English dubbed versions), personal accounts and exhibits such as resistance broadsheets, home-made weapons and printing presses.

The museum also grasps the thorny issue of the Danish government's **collusion** with German rule. Denmark, uniquely amongst the countries invaded by the Nazis, was afforded a kind of independence. The price of this was a large degree of collaboration: the Danish government was convinced that a Europe-wide Nazi victory was inevitable, and displays show the signed agreements between the two countries, while uniforms of the Danish Freikorps – volunteers who joined the German army – bear witness to the degree to which some Danes aligned themselves with the invaders.

Initially slow to offer armed resistance, the first acts of sabotage were carried out in 1942 by a group of teenage boys from Aarhus called the **Churchill Gang** (photographs and filmed interviews with them are on display). These acts of sabotage gave impetus to other groups, largely made up of illegal Danish communists, and the period of collusion ended with a number of uprisings in 1943, which led to the Germans imposing martial law, imprisoning hundreds and engaging in acts of terror against the Danish population. There are some dramatic photographs (and mundane police reports) of these first acts of sabotage, along with home-made printing devices, machine guns and bombs.

Another act that infuriated the Nazis was the mass

evacuation of Denmark's **Jewish population** – all but a tiny percentage were saved from the death camps by the Danish government's refusal to collaborate on this issue and the efforts of ordinary Danes, who helped Jews escape to neutral Sweden. Personal accounts, video interviews and original maps showing the escape routes attest to the courage shown during this episode of the war.

One of the most moving parts of the exhibition is just in front of the large stained-glass windows in a section called **"The Dead"**, showing the original wooden posts to which arrested resistance fighters were tied and shot, along with last letters to loved ones from those sentenced to death.

The Gefion Fountain

Map 4, M3. Bus #1, #6, #9, #19, #29 or Østerport S-Tog.

Just past the museum is the incongruous British St Alban's Church, beside which is the dramatic **Gefion Fountain**. The fountain is based on the story of the goddess Gefion who, according to legend, was promised as much land as she could plough in a single night. She promptly turned her four sons into oxen and ploughed out a chunk of Sweden (creating Lake Vänern), then picked it up and tossed it into the sea – where it became the Danish island of Zealand. Created in 1908 by Anders Bundgaard, the fountain is one of the largest public monuments in Copenhagen, depicting an enormous bronze Gefion engaging in her work, with water cascading down a series of steps from which huge snakes coil out of the bubbling water.

Kastellet

Map 4, J2–L3. Daily 6am–sunset; free. Bus #1, #6, #9 or Østerport S-Tog.

Just past Churchillparken are the unmistakable ramparts and

moats of **Kastellet** (The Citadel). Conceived by Christian IV as the key element in the city's defences, the fortress has been occupied by troops since 1660, making it the oldest still-functioning military base in Europe, and it remains the only part of the city's ancient defence system which is still in use. The star-shaped fortress is formed by five grass-covered bastions surrounded by a series of moats; it can be entered via one of two gates – Kongensporten, near Churchillparken to the south, and Norgesporten, at the opposite end near the Little Mermaid – which are linked by a thoroughfare flanked by barracks and storehouses. Due to its secure nature, Kastellet was also used as a prison – the windows in the west wall of the church were bricked-up so that those attending services did not have to look at the detainees in the prison building in front, although small holes were cut through, allowing prisoners to hear the words of the Lord.

Kastellet's church hosts free classical music concerts every Sunday at 2pm.

Kastellet's principal attraction is the chance for a bracing walk around its bastions and ramparts. Remember that this is still a working military complex – soldiers can be seen practising drill on the cobbled squares and pathways – and some parts are off limits to the public; keep an eye out for the *Adgang Forbudt* (No Entry) signs.

The Little Mermaid

Map 4, L1. Bus #1, #6, #9 or Østerport S-Tog.
Copenhagen's most famous symbol, the statue of the **Little Mermaid** (Den Lille Havfrue), was created in 1913 by Edvard Eriksen. A rather plain bronze figure on top of a pile of carefully positioned rocks by the harbour's edge, the statue has become the city's de facto emblem despite its

KASTELLET AND AROUND

LITTLE MERMAID VANDALISM

Over the years the Little Mermaid has been repeatedly vandalized, usually by artists or political protestors. The following are some of the most notable incidents:

1961: Bra and knickers painted on and hair painted red.

1963: Covered in red paint.

1964: Decapitated.

1976: Covered in paint (again).

1984: Right arm amputated.

1990: Attempted decapitation.

1998: Successful decapitation.

modest dimensions, and continues to hold a powerful sway over the imagination of Danes and visitors alike, conjuring up a period when Copenhagen was the fairy-tale capital of the world.

Inspired by the 1837 Hans Christian Andersen story of the same name, the statue was commissioned by Carlsberg brewery boss and art lover Carl Jacobsen after he had seen a performance of a ballet based on the Little Mermaid story at the Royal Theatre. The prima ballerina in that production, Ellen Price, was to have been the model for the statue, but her reluctance to pose nude for Eriksen forced him to use his wife as a model for the mermaid's body – only the face is Price's. Jacobsen originally wanted the mermaid to have the traditional fish's tail, but Eriksen noted that in Andersen's story the mermaid exchanges her golden hair and beautiful voice for legs – hence the final statue, with the outline of a mermaid's tail between two human limbs.

Tivoli and around

I mmediately to the west of Indre By, the **Tivoli area** is Copenhagen's entertainment zone, with virtually every kind of populist amusement you could imagine – if you want to ride one of the world's oldest rollercoasters or inspect a wax model of Hans Christian Andersen, this is the place to come.

The pleasure gardens of **Tivoli** themselves are synonymous with Copenhagen at its most innocently pleasurable, while mass-appeal amusements nearby include the mannequin celebrities of **Louis Tussauds**, the IMAX cinema and astronomical artefacts of the **Tycho Brahe Planetarium**, and the fun-packed square of **Axeltorv**. Entertainment of a more aesthetic variety can be enjoyed amongst the statues and assorted flora of the remarkable **Ny Carlsberg Glyptotek**, one of the jewels in Copenhagen's cultural crown, and the fascinating exhibits of the nearby **National Museum**.

The area covered by this chapter is shown in detail on colour map 3.

Tivoli

Map 3, D8–E8. Mid-April to Sept & first three weeks of Dec Mon–Thurs & Sun 11am–midnight, Fri & Sat 11am–1am; 39kr, mid-June to mid-Aug 49kr; Ⓦ *www.tivoli.dk*. Bus #1, #2, #6, #8, #28, #29, #550S, #650S, Vesterport S-Tog or Central Station.

Originally opened in 1843, **Tivoli** was inspired by London's Vauxhall Gardens, and this park of many bland amusements is now the most visited attraction in the city, claiming to pull in ninety percent of all foreign tourists to the city – as well as thousands of Danes – with its fairground rides, street performers, cafés, theatres and concert halls. Naturally it's overrated and overpriced, but an evening spent wandering among the revellers of all ages indulging in the mass consumption of ice cream is an experience worth having – once, at any rate – while on a fine summer's night, with all the fairy lights on and fireworks exploding overhead (every Wed, Fri and Sat at midnight) it can become almost magical.

The opening of Tivoli for the new season (second Friday in April) is one of Copenhagen's major annual celebrations, and anyone who is anyone will have booked tables at one of the garden's posh restaurants.

As one of the few still-functioning nineteenth-century pleasure gardens, Tivoli has its historical aspect too, with a number of playful and well-maintained period buildings, notably the Chinese-style, open-air **Pantomime Theatre**. Built in 1874, this now hosts the world's only regular performances of classical pantomime, a delicate art form, somewhere between ballet and mime – plus an element of farce – derived from Italian *commedia dell'arte*. Look out too for the striking *Nimb* restaurant, a large and slightly dilapidated white wood-and-plaster building in Moorish style. Some of the fairground rides are almost as old: don't miss a ride on the rickety wooden roller coaster (dating form 1914) – each train has its own brakeman – and the tiny Ferris wheel nearby, looking like a decorated museum piece.

TIVOLI AND AROUND

There are numerous other rides, with different sections of the park having different themes – Viking Valhalla is the most "authentically" Danish, featuring blonde waitresses with plaited hair and horned helmets. Music also plays a large part in Tivoli, with a renowned concert hall (see p.190), several smaller venues – the Sex Pistols once played in one of them – and an open-air concert area for rock and pop acts.

Tivoli is also open during the weeks around Christmas, but the generally bad weather and lack of fireworks, plus the fact that most of the rides are stored away and parts of the park closed, mean that the experience is somewhat diluted.

If you want to eat, *Divan 1* (℡ 33 11 42 42) is Tivoli's top dining option, with fine traditional Danish cuisine dished up in a genteel setting – though like everything else in the gardens it's overpriced.

Axeltorv

Map 3, C8–D8. Bus #1, #2, #6, #8, #28, #29, #550S, #650S, Vesterport S-Tog or Central Station.

Just opposite the main entrance to Tivoli is the small square of **Axeltorv**, complete with tacky fake classical statues and surrounded by a wealth of entertainment complexes, fast-food joints, bowling alleys and games arcades, among them the Scala shopping-and-cinema complex and the Axelborg entertainment centre. At one end of the square is the unmistakable **Palads Cinema** – a large and garishly paint-ed building resembling a huge Battenberg cake, resplendent in a variety of pink and orange pastel shades. Built in 1917 to replace the old central station, Palads acquired its distinc-tive decor in 1987, when artist Poul Gernes was brought in to redesign the exterior: the decoration survived the predictable storm of criticism and is now a Copenhagen landmark.

For further information about Copenhagen's cinemas, see p.201.

By far the most interesting building on Axeltorv is **Cirkus**, a circular, domed, pseudo-Roman auditorium with seating for 2000 people. Built in 1905, it was used as a proper circus until the 1960s, since when it's hosted everything from boxing matches to a talk by the Dalai Lama. The splendid auditorium has fanatastic acoustics and, despite its size, is surprisingly intimate; the striking painted frescoes of circus scenes which run round the interior frieze are originals from 1905.

Around Tivoli

You're likely to pass through **Central Station** (map 3, D9) sooner or later, given its excellent connections to both the airport and the rest of the Danish railway network. Built between 1904 and 1911, the exterior has a strikingly ecclesiastical appearance, rather like a red-brick neo-Gothic cathedral, topped with a green pyramidal roof. Inside, the huge main hall is nowadays fairly humdrum – only by looking up at the high ceilings and wooden beams do you get a sense of its former splendour.

On the north side of Tivoli, near the Rådhus, is the purpose-built **Danish Design Centre** (map 3, F8; Mon–Fri 10am–5pm, Sat & Sun 11am–4pm; 35kr; ⓦ *www.ddc.dk*), opened at the beginning of 2000 as a showcase for Denmark's outstanding design industry. Housing temporary exhibitions of Danish and international creations – anything from Bang & Olufsen stereo equipment to street furniture – it's been considered a bit of a flop, and is unlikely to appeal unless you're particularly fascinated by design. It does, however, have an excellent shop (see p.219).

If you've really exhausted every other option, then **Louis Tussauds** (map 3, E8), the Danish version of London's Madame Tussauds, is worth a look, but don't expect anything more than the usual collection of waxwork celebrities. The two most diverting areas are the pretty section dedicated to fairytales and Hans Christian Andersen, and the basement horror vault, where skeletons and ghouls rush towards you out of dark corridors – parts are *almost* scary.

Ny Carlsberg Glyptotek

Map 3, F8. Tues–Sun 10am–4pm; 30kr, Wed free;
Ⓦ *www.glyptoteket.dk*. Bus #1, #2, #5, #8, #10, #16, #28, #29 or Central Station.

The dazzling **Ny Carlsberg Glyptotek**, central Copenhagen's finest art gallery, was opened in 1897 by Carlsberg brewing magnate Carl Jacobsen as a venue for ordinary people to see classical art exhibited in amenable and accessible surroundings. At its centre is the glass-domed **winter garden** (*vinterhave*), its steamy interior filled with palm trees – Jacobsen correctly surmised that the warm tropical plantlife here would lure visitors who wouldn't be interested by the works of art alone, and even on a freezing winter's day a wander through these gardens and the museum's extensive collection of Etruscan, Greek, Roman, Egyptian, French and Danish artworks can prove both a physically and mentally warming experience. As Carl Jacobsen himself put it: "I called this collection Glyptotek to make clear that it was not a museum with the usual need for scientific order and completion, where works of art often stand freezing, alien to each other in heterogeneous company. No, it was to be a place where the statues are displayed in joy and harmony, to grace life for the living."

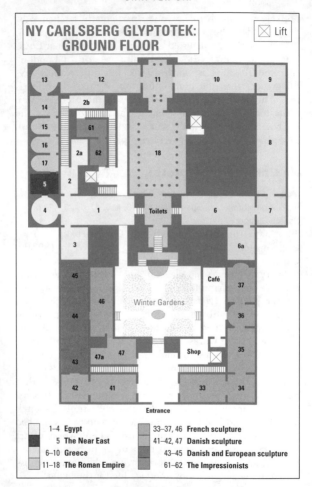

NY CARLSBERG GLYPTOTEK: GROUND FLOOR

⊠ Lift

13 | 12 | 11 | 10 | 9

14
15
16
17

2b
61
2a | 62
5
2

18

10
9

8

4 | 1 | Toilets | 6 | 7

3 | | | 6a

45
46 | Winter Gardens | Café | 37

44 | | | 36

47a | 47 | Shop | 35

43

42 | 41 | 33 | 34

Entrance

1–4 Egypt
5 The Near East
6–10 Greece
11–18 The Roman Empire

33–37, 46 French sculpture
41–42, 47 Danish sculpture
43–45 Danish and European sculpture
61–62 The Impressionists

The Glyptotek's highly rated restaurant (see p.164) makes a
perfect spot for lunch, particularly on a cold winter's day.

The Glyptotek is split into three sections centred on the
winter garden: the Dahlerup Building, the Kampmann
Building, and the new French wing. (The plan opposite
shows the Glyptotek's ground floor, on which most of the
collection is held, though be aware that a few exhibits are
housed on upper and lower levels.) The **Dahlerup
Building** at the front, completed in 1897, focuses mainly
on French and Danish sculpture, with some paintings from
the Danish Golden Age thrown in. The right-hand side is
devoted to the inspiring **French collection**, which features
a particularly fine collection of Rodins – the largest outside
France – including a version of *The Kiss* (there's also a version of *The Thinker* outside the back of the museum).
Other parts of this section include a dramatic collection of
white marbles: you'll find Marqueste's dramatic *Persus slay-
ing Medusa* set amidst a raft of huge, full-bodied women and
muscular men by various other artists, and a series of ornate
busts by nineteenth-century sculptor Carpeaux. Most of the
Danish collection is housed upstairs and is less stimulating, though it does provide a good reflection of Golden
Age painting, with some idealized landscapes by G.W.
Eckersberg, some more realistic paintings depicting the travails of Danish peasants by Marstrand, and a few decorative
frescoes by Herman Freund, a close colleague of
Thorvaldsen.

Pass through the winter gardens to reach the
Kampmann Building, which was added to the original
Glyptotek in 1906 (there's a good view of the exterior from
outside at the back, where a tiered pyramid looks dramatically down over Rodin's *The Thinker*). The interior is
refreshingly bare compared to the ornate Dahlerup Building,

though the floors are laid with exquisite mosaics, while clear sightlines down the interlocking corridors and exhibition spaces neatly frame views of distant statues. There's a fine collection of **Greek and Roman** portrait sculpture and statues on the upper ground floor – a portrait of Caligula, which still retains some of its original paint, and a large Alexander the Great are particularly striking – a small but excellent collection of **Egyptian** artefacts in the crypt, including several mummies, and, on the lower ground floor, an enormous and diverse haul of **Etruscan and Mesopotamian** works ranging from dozens of sarcophagi to weapons and jewellery. Unfortunately, the fake Roman colonnade in the Central Hall looks a bit tacky compared to the rest of the building, and its finest feature – a first-century AD Roman mosaic inlaid into the floor – is often covered up by chairs set out for concerts and other performances.

The last section of Glyptotek is the three-storey **French Wing**, opened in 1996 to house the museum's collection of French paintings and sculpture. The result – the exterior in particular – is an architectural triumph: a huge white vault in the most minimalist of contemporary architectural styles, which blends extraordinarily into its classical context. Linked to the other two buildings by arches and walkways, the wing's glimmering white surface creates a real sense of light and space, particularly when sunlight spills in through the glass roof.

Highlights here include a collection of charming Degas bronze figurines and an impressive collection of Gauguins – *Tahitian Girl*, a painting that really brings out the artist's unique style of flatly coloured shapes and heavy contours, is particularly eyecatching. Amongst other paintings on show are *The Lemon Grove* by Monet, a wonderful play of colour and technique, and Van Gogh's evocative *Pink Roses*. The ground floor of the French wing is given over to temporary exhibitions.

National Museum

Map 3, F7–G7. Tues–Sun 10am–5pm; 40kr, free Wed; Ⓦ *www
.natmus.dk*. Bus #5, #8, #10, #28, #29 or Central Station.

Heading back towards the city centre brings you to the well
thought-out **National Museum** (Nationalmuseet), home
to the country's finest collection of Danish artefacts, dating
from 10,000 BC to the mid-nineteenth century. There's
also a fantastic ethnographic collection containing one of
the most comprehensive displays of Inuit artefacts in the
world, a dull collection of Egyptian and Classical antiquities, and a programme of temporary exhibitions. Most of
the displays – the prolific ethnographic collection excepted
– are labelled in English. Attached to the main collection is
a superb **children's museum**, where kids can put on
armour, fire toy crossbows from model castles, and hide out
in Bedouin tents.

The **main collection**, spread over two floors on the
right as you enter (the ethnographic collections, temporary
exhibits and children's museum are all on the left), begins
with prehistoric artefacts and winds it way forwards
chronologically via a sequence of linked rooms – the quite
remarkable number of intact finds on display here is due to
the country's peat bogs, which acted as a preservative on
anything buried in them. The earliest moments of Danish
civilization are represented with a good number of carefully
crafted flint tools, stunning amber pieces and necklaces, and
a full-sized skeleton of an *auroch* – a very large (and now
extinct) indigenous buffalo – replete with stone-age hunting wounds. A good sense of the lives of the early settlers is
gained by a collection of 3500-year-old coffins, which contain domestic items along with the grisly remains of their
human occupants – the best preserved belongs to the
Egtved Girl, whose clothes, jewellery and blonde hair have
all survived intact. Another highlight is the Sun Chariot of

1400 BC. Made by Bronze Age sun-worshippers, it depicts a gold-leaf, spiral-decorated sun being drawn across the heavens by a magical horse.

Continue from here into the **Viking collection**. The idea that the Vikings were a distinct culture and people has been challenged in recent years – even some of the artefacts that are most closely associated with them, such as the characteristic horned helmets (examples of which are on display), pre-date them by centuries. Whatever the truth, the period from the birth of Christ to the triumph of Christianity in about 1100 AD saw the establishment of a sophisticated seafaring culture in Denmark, with extensive trade routes, military prowess, and colonies in France, Britain and Ireland. Many of the everyday tools and artefacts from this period, including clothes and weapons, are on display, and there's also a good collection of Viking coins and an enthralling section on runic lettering, featuring a number of original rune stones.

Moving on through the museum leads to several rooms dominated by the relics of **Danish Christianity**. Stern-looking late-Viking crucifixes give way to more naturalistic representations, while the Latin alphabet arrives to replace the runes. Further exhibits demonstrate the intricate crafts used to glorify Christ (and the church), with elaborate gold altars, wonderful ceremonial robes and grails. Other highlights include a fantastic collection of jewel-encrusted rings – made to be worn outside the gloves of the wearer – and an armoury that is a positive cornucopia of violent implements.

After this wonderful array of historical artefacts the collection continues through to the nineteenth century with a disappointing run of portraits of Danish worthies and a badly preserved royal apartment that formerly served as the home of various crown princes. The **ethnographic collection**, however, is worth investigating, though there are no labels and it can be hard to make sense of the displays. Of particular interest is the collection of **Inuit artefacts**, one of the largest in the world, with dozens of whale-bone carvings, harpoons and sealskin kayaks – the splendid body suit made entirely of bird feathers exemplifies human ingenuity in the face of a hostile climate. If you can be bothered to climb all the way to the top of the museum, the ethnographic collection also holds a small selection of **Egyptian** and **Classical antiquities**, with a few mummies and, more impressively, a good collection of glazed decorative pottery from the city states of Greece.

Tycho Brahe Planetarium

Map 3, B9. Mon & Fri–Sun 10.30am–9pm, Tues–Thurs 9.45am–9pm; 75kr including IMAX film; ⓦ *www.astro.ku.dk/tycho.html*. Bus #1, #14 or Vesterport S-Tog.

Situated at the southeastern corner of Skt Jørgens Sø (the southernmost of the lakes that enclose central Copenhagen), the **Tycho Brahe Planetarium** – named after the famous sixteenth-century Danish astronomer – is a distinctive cylindrical, sand-coloured brick affair which currently contains a disappointing astronomical collection and an equally uninspiring bookshop, although plans are afoot to create a brand-new hi-tech exhibition throughout. There's also a large IMAX cinema – the only one in the country. Entry is included with planetarium ticket, though the films screened here are more likely to cover topics like surfing or diving than anything astronomical – the only exceptions are *Cosmic Voyage* (shown daily), a cheesy look at the marvels of space travel, and the derisory five-minute show using the planetarium projector which is tacked onto the end of every film screening.

Vesterbro and Fuderiksberg

The two districts immediately west of the city centre, Vesterbro and Frederiksberg, couldn't be more different. **Vesterbro** has always been determinedly working class, and also has the city's highest multicultural mix – around seventy percent of kids in the local schools are bilingual. Despite encroaching gentrification, it's still one of the most colourful areas of the city, with the broadest selection of affordable ethnic restaurants and shops.

In stark contrast to Vesterbro's vibrant and colourful street life, **Frederiksberg**'s wealthy residents tend to stay behind the doors of their grand villas, and the district's spacious and leafy roads are relatively lifeless. Conservative to the core, Frederiksberg is renowned for its low taxes and expensive housing. Situated on the land leading up to Frederiksberg Slot, the king's summer residence, the area was originally used to grow crops and keep livestock to feed the royal household, and was ruled directly by the king. Even now the area retains a regal aura, and is still administered by its own council, independent of the city.

**The area covered by this chapter is shown in detail
on colour map 5.**

VESTERBRO

After the old city ramparts fell in 1851 and construction on areas outside the former defences took off on a massive scale, the **Vesterbro** area was quickly bought up by entrepreneurs, who crammed in as many housing blocks with minuscule flats as possible. Overcrowded and mismanaged for decades, it was not until the mid-1960s that the area's deplorable state was recognized by the city council. Wise from their experiences at Nørrebro a few years earlier – when local residents had clashed with police after historic buildings were torn down to make way for concrete housing blocks – it was decided to renovate rather than rebuild, and a long-term project to renew derelict areas of the city by the year 2010 was initiated. Large sections of Vesterbro have already been restored, though sadly the rapid gentrification that's followed has meant that many of Vesterbro's original inhabitants – and much of the area's immigrant community – have had to leave, unable to afford the hiked-up rents.

Vesterbro is crossed by the roughly parallel streets of **Vesterbrogade**, **Istedgade** and **Sønder Boulevard**, which run from Central Station at the eastern end of the district to the Carlsberg Brewery at the west. Vesterbrogade, the northernmost of the three, is the district's main artery and one of the city's main shopping streets, more affordable than Strøget, with speciality outlets selling everything from clothes to designer kitchenware, and with some of the best nightlife in the city and a broad range of bars and restaurants.

The area around Istedgade by Central Station is the only

VESTERBRO

89

part of the city where you might feel unsafe – this is home to what's left of the city's red-light district, and drunks, drug-dealers and junkies still roam the streets amidst numerous porn shops. Paradoxically, a constant police presence probably makes this one of the safest areas in the city but, that said, the sense of destitution can sometimes be a bit overwhelming.

In the same insalubrious area are the city's two so-called "hotel streets" – **Colbjørnsensgade** and **Helgolandsgade**. In a desperate attempt to avoid the district becoming a working-class stronghold, the city council decreed that all houses in these two streets were to have a minimum of four rooms. Their attempt had an unexpected outcome: shortly after they were built, many of the buildings were converted into the hotels which still exist here today.

DGI-byen and Øksnehallen

Map 5, N6–N7. Bus #10, #550S or Central Station.

Just behind Central Station, at the southern end of Colbjørnsensgade and signalled by a distinctive concrete climbing tower on the corner of Tietgensgade, the **DGI-byen** centre (Mon–Thurs 6.30am–9pm, Fri 6.30am–7pm, Sat & Sun 9am–5pm; ⓦ *www.dgi-byen.dk*) is the most visible evidence of the 2010 Vesterbro renovation project, offering superb sports and conference facilities – including the fantastic Swim Centre (Vandkulturhuset; see p.225) – and a top-of-the-range restaurant and hotel designed in classic Scandinavian minimalist style by the architects responsible for creating the Black Diamond. The centre is also the main venue of the **Images of the World** festival in August, a major country-wide event focusing on the cultures of Africa, Asia, South America and the Middle East. For a programme and information, ring Ⓣ 33 38 97 39 or visit ⓦ *www.images.org*.

Next door to DGI-byen, but with its main entrance around the corner on Halmtorvet, is the beautifully restored **Øksnehallen** (Tues–Sun 11am–6pm; Ⓦ *www.oeksnehallen.dk*). Located in the hall of a former cattle market of 1901, the enormous building preserves most of its original features, including the arched, wood-beamed ceiling typical of market places from the period. It's now used for temporary exhibitions, usually concentrating on contemporary culture, design (admission prices vary according to what's on), photography, art and fashion, though it's worth going inside irrespective of what's on simply to enjoy the hall's light and spacious interior.

The City Museum and around

Map 5, K6. Bus #6, #28 or #550S.

Fifteen minutes walk northwest of DGI-byen on Vesterbrogade is the small, triangular square of **Vesterbros Torv**. Popular in the summer with its outdoor bars and cafés, the square's main feature is an Italian-inspired church, the **Elias Kirken**, designed by Martin Nyrop, creator of the Rådhus, in 1908.

A bit further along Vesterbrogade at no. 59, the **City Museum** (Københavns Bymuseum; daily except Tues: May–Sept 10am–4pm; Oct–April 1–4pm; 20kr; Ⓦ *www.kbhbymuseum.dk*) is a slightly confusing, but interesting, introduction to the city's chaotic history. The fifteenth- and sixteenth-century city is brought to life through reconstructions of ramshackle house exteriors and tradesmen's signs. Looking at these, the impact of Christian IV becomes resoundingly apparent, and there's a large room recording the form and cohesion that this monarch and amateur architect gave the city, including a few of his own drawings. The rest of the city's thousand-year history is told by an array of paintings, photos, miniature models of the town, and items from daily life in various periods. Try to catch the free half-hour slide-show (daily except Tues May–Sept in English at 11.15am, 12.45 & 2.15pm), which presents a good, clear introduction to the city's history. Head upstairs for the room devoted to **Søren Kierkegaard** (see box below), filled with bits and bobs – furniture from his home, paintings of his girlfriend Regine Olsen, jewellery, books and manuscripts – that form an intriguing footnote to the life of this nineteenth-century Danish writer and philosopher, and much the most interesting part of the museum.

The museum is housed in the distinguished building of 1787 which was formerly home to the Royal Shooting Brotherhood. Outside, it backs onto the brotherhood's old firing range, Skydebanen, now a children's playground and unremarkable apart from its curious back wall,

SØREN KIERKEGAARD

The name of Søren Kierkegaard is inextricably linked with Copenhagen, yet his championing of individual will over social conventions and his rejection of materialism did little to endear him to his fellow Danes. Born in 1813, Kierkegaard believed himself set on an "evil destiny" – partly the fault of his father, who is best remembered for having cursed God on a Jutland heath. Kierkegaard's first book, *Either/Or*, published in 1843, was inspired by his love affair with one Regine Olsen; she failed to understand it, however, and married someone else. Few other people understood *Either/Or*, in fact, and Kierkegaard, though devastated by the broken romance, came to revel in the enigma he had created, becoming a "walking mystery in the streets of Copenhagen" (he lived in a house on Nytorv). He was a prolific author, sometimes publishing two books on the same day, and often writing under pseudonyms. His greatest philosophical works were written by 1846 and are often claimed to have laid the foundations of existentialism.

Skydebanemuren, a massive, twelve-metre-high red-brick wall adorned with the brotherhood's logo. It was erected in 1887, allegedly to protect passers-by from stray bullets, though rumours suggest that its real purpose was to protect the snobbish brotherhood from the distracting sight of Vesterbro poverty.

Continuing west for a couple of minutes along Vesterbrogade brings you to the right turn into **Værnedamsvej**. Dubbed "Little Paris", this street is haven for the food connoisseur, packed with no fewer than 66 speciality shops, most of them devoted to food and drink, and including an impressive selection of traditional butchers, a French bakery (boasting the best croissants in Scandinavia), a chocolate manufacturer, fishmongers, cheesemakers and ethnic fruit-and-veg shops.

Carlsberg Brewery Visitor Center

Map 5, D8–F9. Mon–Fri 10am–4pm; free. Bus #6 or #18.

It's a twenty-minute walk west from Værnedamsvej along Vesterbrogade, then left along Pile Allé, to the new **Carlsberg Brewery Visitor Centre**. Carlsberg sadly no longer offer tours of the brewery itself, having replaced them with this decidedly less inspiring centre, which takes you through the history of beer brewing and Carlsberg's chequered past, complete with models of old workers' quarters, some ancient brewing machinery and a selection of photos and diagrams – it's all perfectly interesting, but, when push comes to shove, not nearly as exciting as a noisy brewery in full action, though Carlsberg have at least retained the tradition of handing out free beer at the end of your visit. While you're in the vicinity, have a look at the **Elephant Gate** behind the visitor centre on Ny Carlsberg Vej: four elephants carved in granite supporting the building that spans the road.

VESTERBRO

From the Carlsberg Brewery, it's only a short walk to
the Bakkehus Museum (see p.98) and Frederiksberg
Have (see p.96) in Frederiksberg.

FREDERIKSBERG

"A city within the city" is how Frederiksbergers like to
describe their independent district. Positioned between the
districts of Vesterbro and Nørrebro, it covers a large area –
almost twice the size of Indre By – and with its own industry, shopping streets and city hall, tries to be completely
self-contained. Away from the main roads you'll find street
after street of the district's distinctively grand **villas**, quite
unlike the apartment blocks characteristic of residential
areas in other parts of the city. The first one was erected in
1846, and between them they represent the work of some
of Denmark's most distinguished architects, from
Functionalists to Neoclassicists.

Frederiksberg Allé and Runddel

Map 5, E5–I5. Bus #28.

Just beyond the City Museum (see p.91), **Frederiksberg
Allé** branches off Vesterbrogade to the right. Lined by rows
of trees, this wide boulevard was originally built by
Frederik IV as a private road to his summer residence,
Frederiksberg Slot (see p.97). Along it you'll find an
impressive array of old apartment buildings, a number of
theatres and the new ABC entertainment complex. At
Frederiksberg Runddel (Circus) the road joins Pile Allé
and Allegade and becomes the main entrance to
Frederiksberg Have. Look out here for the **Frederiksberg
Kirke** – a 1734 Dutch-style octagonal church built by

Dutch farmers coerced here by Frederik III to grow vegetables and care for the royal livestock – and the open-air **ice-skating rink** on the *runddel*, popular with all ages during winter.

The Light Theatre and Storm P. museums

Map 5, E5. Bus #28 or #18.

Just inside the Frederiksberg Have gates in a yellow building to your left, the **Museum of Light Theatre** (Morskabs-Museet; Tues–Sun 11am–4pm; free, but donations welcome) houses a unique collection of pictures, theatrical props, costumes, posters and other artefacts associated with the Frederiksberg entertainers who used to amuse – and ridicule – rich city folks on their weekend outings to the countryside.

While you're here, you could also call in at the entertaining **Storm P. Museum** (May–Sept Tues–Sun 10am–4pm; Oct–April Wed, Sat & Sun 10am–4pm; 20kr), to the right of the gate facing Frederiksberg Allé, packed with the satirical cartoons that made "Storm P". (Robert Storm Petersen) one of the most popular bylines in Danish newspapers during the 1920s. Even if you don't understand the Danish captions, you'll leave the museum with an insight into the national sense of humour.

Around Frederiksberg Have

Allégade, north of Frederiksberg Runddel, is the original main street of the now vanished village of Ny Amager, which housed Dutch immigrant farmers in the seventeenth century. It leads to Gammel Kongevej – Christian IV's main road to Frederiksberg Slot, replaced by Frederiksberg Allé a hundred years later – and Frederiksberg Town Hall, on the corner of Smallegade. One of the city's biggest and most

FREDERIKSBERG

colourful flea markets takes place in the car park behind the town hall on Saturdays from May to October.

Some 500m west of the town hall along Smallegade is the **Royal Copenhagen Porcelain** factory (map 5, B3; one-hour guided tours Mon–Fri at 9am, 10am, 11am, 1pm and 2pm; 25kr; bus #1, #14 or #39), founded by Dowager Queen Juliane Marie in 1775. Two unique types of porcelain design have made the factory world famous: "Flora Danica", a multicoloured wildflower pattern – no two pieces the same – and "Mussel Malet", with blue decorations based on Messien models. On their surprisingly interesting factory tours you'll witness the painfully delicate process of making both, showing the way the porcelain is shaped, fired, handpainted, re-fired and re-painted (sometimes with gold) – you're not allowed to talk on sections of the tour to avoid disturbing the artists. Pieces are sold at reduced prices in the factory shop.

Pile Allé, south of Frederiksberg Runddel, is famous for its many small gardens. The Royal Danish Horticultural Society is based here – just south of the main entrance to Frederiksberg Have – and boasts a garden (sunrise–sunset; free) stuffed with an amazing mishmash of intriguing plant environments. During the summer the garden also hosts concerts, mainly jazz. Further along, amidst a few so-called "family gardens" – popular restaurants formerly catering for palace staff, these days renowned for their sublime traditional Danish lunches accompanied by the obligatory schnapps – is the **maze**, shaped in the form of a Tuborg beer label. There are great views of Frederiksberg Slot from hereabouts.

Frederiksberg Have

Map 5, B4–D6. Bus #1, #6, #14, #18, #28.

From the main entrance on Frederiksberg Runddel, the

expansive gardens of **Frederiksberg Have** (daily 6am–sunset; free) stretch north toward Smallegade and south towards Frederiksberg Slot amidst a network of pathways, lakes and canals that criss-cross the lime-tree groves. Throughout the eighteenth century, the city's top nobs came here to mess about in boats, though nowadays you'll have to settle for one of the inexpensive tours in the large, manned rowing boats which depart regularly from in front of Frederiksberg Slot. Look out for the colourful **Chinese Folly** on one of the park's picturesque islands – it was built in 1799 and used for Frederik VI's tea parties – and the Neoclassical **Temple of Apis**, west of the palace near the zoo, from 1804 – a real architectural gem. The gardens are also a popular weekend picnic spot.

Frederiksberg Slot

Map 5, C6. One-hour guided tours at 11am on the last Sat of every month; 20kr. Bus #18 or #28.

At the southern end of Frederiksberg Have is the palace of **Frederiksberg Slot**, built by Frederik IV in the early eighteenth century on top of Valby Bakke hill, from where it would originally have commanded an uninterrupted view of the city ramparts and the Swedish coastline. Extended many times since, it acquired its present shape under Christian VI in 1735. The palace was the royal family's summer residence until the mid-1800s, when it was taken over by the Danish Officers' Academy. It's worth joining a guided tour to see the palace's evocative interior, with its imposing stucco work and ceiling paintings, along with the secret passageway leading down to an enormous marble bathtub (supposedly a secret meeting place of Queen Caroline Mathilde and her lover Count Struensee) and the black-and-white chequered kitchen, where she used to make pancakes. Have a look, too, at the exquisitely

FREDERIKSBERG

fashioned Baroque decorations in the adjacent, recently restored palace chapel.

City Zoo

Map 5, A5–B6. March Mon–Fri 9am–4pm, Sat & Sun 9am–5pm; April, May & Sept Mon–Fri 9am–5pm, Sat & Sun 9am–6pm; June–Aug daily 9am–6pm; Oct daily 9am–5pm; Nov–Feb daily 9am–4pm; 70kr. Bus #28, #39 or #550S.

Bordering the southwest corner of Frederiksberg Have is Copenhagen's **Zoo**, one of the oldest and largest in Europe, with over 2500 animals, ranging from pandas to polar bears. The zoo tries to keep its animals in enclosures which reproduce their natural environments as closely as possible – their reputable breeding results testify to their success. Check out the newest acquisition, a hot and humid tropical house that takes you straight into the jungle, or the African savannah in the section south of Roskildevej. The zoo also has a special **children's section** where kids can touch domestic animals such as goats, sheep, cows and horses.

Bakkehus Museum

Map 5, E7. Wed, Thurs, Sat & Sun 11am–3pm; 10kr. Bus #6, #18 or #38.

Southeast of Frederiksberg Have, and just north of the new Carlsberg Visitor Centre (p.93), the **Bakkehus Museum** (Bakkehus Museet) is located in what is claimed to be the oldest house in Frederiksberg – from the eighteenth century – and commemorates Denmark's literary Golden Age. The Rahbæk family lived here from 1802 to 1830, hosting a popular salon for Danish literary personalities – Hans Christian Andersen and Adam Oehlenschläger (author of the Danish national anthem) were frequent guests. The peaceful museum preserves the house more or less as the

Rahbæk left it, and provides an interesting insight into the literary milieu of the Golden Age – look out for Rahbæk's study, with his diary open on the desk and papier mâché replicas of the cakes served at the famous salon.

Nørrebro and Østerbro

To the north and east of the city centre are the districts of **Nørrebro** and **Østerbro** ("North Bridge" and "East Bridge"), built in the mid-nineteenth century on land outside the old city defences. Their similar age apart, the two districts have deeply contrasting histories: Nørrebro's is one of deprivation and social struggle followed by recent immigration and gentrification; Østerbro's is one of traditional wealth and privilege – hence the rather smug feel of the district today, though its leafy ambience makes it a pleasant enough place.

The area covered by this chapter is shown in detail
on colour map 6.

NØRREBRO

Working-class **Nørrebro** is synonymous with Copenhagen at its most militant. As the city expanded beyond the old ramparts during the 1850s, huge slum tenements began to

AN ARENA FOR PROTEST

The Danes are well known for their political and social toler-
ance, but in the 1980s the activities of a radical squatting
movement, the **BZ** (a shortening of the Danish word *besæt*,
meaning "to occupy"), led to massive and violent street con-
frontations with the authorities. Based mainly in Nørrebro –
then a very run-down area – the BZ's initial aim, apart from
alleviating a chronic housing shortage, was to establish an
autonomous youth centre outside the control of the city
council. After gaining widespread public support, they were
given Ungdomshuset (literally "The Youth House" –
see p.192). Even so, increasing confrontation followed, particularly during the eviction of a large squat in Ryesgade in
1985, when thousands of police – the country's biggest ever
peacetime deployment – faced down a large group of squatters armed with petrol bombs and sticks. By the early 1990s,
most of the city's squatters had been evicted, often after violent street clashes.

This violence reached a peak in 1993 when, following
Denmark's decision to sign the Maastricht Treaty, the police
lost control of an anti-EU protest organized by the BZ on
Nørrebrogade. In the ensuing chaos, several officers fired into
the crowd: eleven demonstrators were shot – some in the back
– in the worst incident of civil violence in Denmark's history.
Fortunately, no one was killed.

Nowadays, the BZ lacks the popular support they once had,
and Nørrebro faces new problems, such as the perceived
exclusion of immigrants from Danish society. In November
1999, after a number of incidents, a large-scale riot developed
along Blågårdsgade following the threatened explusion from
Denmark of a second-generation Turkish immigrant, during
which young locals hurled petrol bombs at the police from
hastily erected barricades.

AN ARENA FOR PROTEST

101

spring up to house Copenhagen's newly industrialized working class, and by the end of the nineteenth century Nørrebro had established itself as one of the country's most politicized areas – local residents were later instrumental in forming both the Danish trade union movement and the Social Democratic Party, Denmark's biggest political party.

Nørrebro militancy was expressed in more dangerous circumstances when local residents led the fight against the Nazis during World War II – you can see pictures of them on the barricades at the Resistance Museum (see p.73). The immediate post-war period was rather quiet, but by the 1960s Nørrebro residents were again challenging authority, first in anti-Vietnam War protests, later in protesting about local issues such as housing and public parks. By the 1980s this had transformed into one of Europe's most radical squatting movements, the BZ (see box on previous page).

More recently, an influx of immigrants has arrived in Nørrebro, bringing some much-needed cultural diversity to the city, while large numbers of Danish yuppies have also moved in, taking advantage of low property prices in an "authentic" area. Their arrival has been accompanied by a proliferation of sometimes pretentiously groovy cafés, bars and clubs, though the resulting – and much needed – economic boost for the district hasn't, so far at least, completely priced out the original inhabitants.

Skt Hans Torv and the Police History Museum

Map 6, D8–E7. Bus #3, #5, #16, #350S or Nørreport S-Tog.

At the heart of Nørrebro is the small square of **Skt Hans Torv**, formerly working-class, now transformed into a hub of gentrified cafés and bars. The trendy home of Copenhagen's annoyingly young and gifted – or at least rich – this is a favourite hangout of Denmark's "dynamic" thirty-something crown prince, Frederik.

Just down Fælledvej from Skt Hans Torv is the much more interesting **Police History Museum** (Tues & Thurs 10am–4pm, first Sun of every month 10am–3pm; 25kr), a fascinating – if somewhat macabre – document of crime, detection and incarceration, housed in the city's first purpose-built police station. On the ground floor, the exhibits initially focus on the gruesome methods of social control employed in medieval times, as well as the uniforms and brutal cudgels of the city's early nightwatchmen. There are grim old holding cells (in which you can temporarily lock yourself up, if you fancy), and a pair of impressive antique Nimbus police motorbikes, amongst dozens of other exhibits.

The stairwell contains an array of fake artworks, while the second floor is dedicated almost solely to crime and criminals. One room delves into the history of the various facets of the city's once illegal sex industry – there's a large collection of porn discreetly held in drawers under the display cases – while another concentrates on forgery and smuggling, and a third on murder. Each exhibit here is cross-referenced to drawers holding disturbing photographs of the crime scene from which they were taken – best not to look in them unless you have a *very* strong stomach.

The well-preserved streets around Skt Hans Torv still capture the flavour of how life must have been in this old working-class district, with narrow streets of dark, brick tenements. Heading south from the police museum down Fælledvej brings you to the large intersection with **Blågårdsgade**, a pleasant, pedestrianized street that is now at the heart of Copenhagen's immigrant and alternative communities, with south Asian and Middle Eastern immigrants rubbing shoulders with ex-squatters and protestors – there's also an intriguing multicultural blend of restaurants

NØRREBRO

and bars along here, and a pleasant tree-fringed square, **Blågårds Plads**, surrounded by al fresco dining spots.

Assistens Kirkegård

Map 6, B5–C6. May–Aug daily 8am–8pm; Sept & Oct 8am–6pm; Nov–April 10am–4pm; free. Bus #5, #16, #18, #350S or Nørrebro S-Tog and then a ten-minute walk.

Head north from Blågårdsgade, either through the back streets or up Nørrebrogade, and you'll eventually arrive at the unmistakable, graffiti-covered yellow walls of Copenhagen's most famous cemetery, **Assistens Kirkegård**. Originally positioned in open countryside outside the city's northern gate, the cemetery was founded as a place in which the city's poorer inhabitants could enjoy a decent Christian burial – it wasn't until much later that it became the eternal resting place of choice for Copenhagen's wealthier gentlefolk.

The Kapelvej entrance, where you'll find an information office with free maps, is the best place to start. Close to here (and well signposted) are the cemetery's two most famous graves, those of **Hans Christian Andersen** and **Søren Kierkegaard**, though don't expect anything grand: both graves, though well maintained, are pretty nondescript. Rather more imposing is the owl-topped tomb of the Bohr family, where Noble Prize-winning Danish physicist Niels Bohr is interred. Also keep an eye out for the grave of Martin Andersen Nexø, the famous Danish communist and author of *Pelle the Conqueror* (subsequently turned into an Oscar-winning film), and for the "Jazz Corner", where the American musician Ben Webster is buried alongside several lesser-known Danish jazz players.

Assistens' open green spaces offer a welcome respite from the confined streets of Nørrebro, and during the summer many locals can be seen sunning themselves amongst the gravestones – if you want to join them, avoid the garden of remembrance, where the ashes of the departed are scattered over inviting grassy lawns.

ØSTERBRO

Stretching from the fringes of Fælled Park in the west through to the commercial docks, warehouses and wealthy residences along the Øresund coast to the east, the salubrious suburb of **Østerbro** stands in marked contrast to the narrow streets and tenements of Nørrebro. Originally a watering hole full of taverns en route to the hunting grounds of Dyrehaven and the amusements at Bakken (see p.114), Østerbro is nowadays home to Copenhagen's moneyed classes, who luxuriate in the expensive houses along the coastal fringes. Nearer to the city centre, the district's broad avenues are home to ornate apartment blocks and most of the city's embassies.

Fælled Park and Parken Stadium

Map 6, H7–K5. Fælled Park: bus #1, #3, #42, #43, #184, #185 or #150S; Parken Stadium: bus #1, #6 or #14.

At the western edge of Østerbro are the wide open spaces and tree-lined avenues of **Fælled Park** (Community Park), an enormously popular swathe of greenery that has its roots firmly in Copenhagen's social-democratic history. Originally founded in 1900 as a recreation space for the city's workers, Fælled Park still does its bit for the good of the city, hosting workers' fairs, free live concerts and carnivals (see box on p.106).

On the eastern fringe of Fælled Park is the 41,000 all-seater **Parken Stadium**. There has been a football stadium on this site for almost a hundred years – five of Copenhagen's football clubs played here at one time – and it's

ØSTERBRO

FÆLLED PARK FESTIVALS

Fælled Park is the site of two of Copenhagen's main festivals. On **May Day** (May 1), trade unions march through the city to the park, where there's a rock concert-cum-political rally. Most Danish political parties are represented, and although the speeches go on forever, most people are more interested in the stalls selling ethnic delicacies, the Danish bands that perform between speeches and, especially, the enormous quantities of beer. The **Whitsun Carnival** (June), basically Copenhagen's answer to a Brazilian carnival, is a weekend extravaganza featuring 24-hour live world music with a predominantly Latin flavour, dancing and some offbeat costumes which their wearers optimistically liken to those found in Rio.

now the home of the Danish national team and FC Copenhagen (usually known as FCK), while big-name acts like Bruce Springsteen and Tina Turner also show up from time to time. Next door is the much smaller **Østerbro Stadium**, home to athletics meetings and football team B93 – look out for the splendid entrance on Østerbrogade, topped with bronze figurines engaging in miscellaneous sporting activities.

Further details about football matches at Parken and Østerbro are given on pp.222-223.

Zoological Museum

Map 6, H4. Tues–Sun 11am–5pm; 25kr; Ⓦ *www.zmuc.dk* or *www.zoologiskmuseum.dk*. Bus #18, #42, #43, #184, #185 or #150S. The area immediately to the west of Fælled Park is occupied by Copenhagen's main hospital, Rigshospitalet, and by various departments of the university, amongst which is the **Zoological Museum**, on the fifth floor of a modern building – look out for the metallic cockroach on the roof of the entrance. Walk inside, past the stuffed polar bear, and catch the lift up to the museum. First founded in 1622 (and thus the oldest museum in Denmark), the collection is presently being restored and expanded – improvements, planned to be finished by spring 2001, are expected to include a display on the post-ice age period with life-size woolly mammoths and ice effects.

The present collection is made up mainly of an impressive selection of **stuffed animals**, starting with Danish wildlife and moving on through the fauna of rain forests, savannahs, ice floes and deserts: the close-up views of exotic, beautiful – and dead – animals such as armadillos, anteaters and various apes are educational, if a bit creepy. Particularly impressive are the stuffed sea elephants and walruses, which are immense – as are the skeletons of sperm and Greenland whales. The museum also has a very popular **children's section**.

Experimentarium

Map 2, F1. Mon & Wed–Fri 9am–5pm, Tues 9am–9pm, Sat & Sun 11am–5pm; 79kr; ⓦ *www.experimentarium.dk*. Bus #6, #21, #650S or S-Tog to Hellerup or Svanemøllen then a 10min walk.

Designed to make the sciences more accessible to the masses, **Experimentarium** – sited in the old Tuborg brewery bottling hall on the northeastern edge of Østerbro – makes for an educational and entertaining few hours, particularly if you've got children (if not, try to visit during a weekday afternoon, as the place tends to get overrun with kids in the mornings).

Not strictly a museum, Experimentarium describes itself as a "science centre" where everybody can get hands-on

ØSTERBRO

experience of the physics, biology and chemistry which shape our lives. Most of the exhibits – such as the "emotion tester", which judges your reaction to pictures of fluffy kittens, naked men/women and sweaty feet – are great fun. There are also lectures giving simple explanations of scientific topics illustrated by down-to-earth experiments using things like bubbles and prisms. Further scientific demonstrations are conducted throughout the museum by guides (called "pilots"), who introduce you to processes ranging from cheese-making to dissection – you can have a go at cutting up a cow's heart or lung yourself, if the fancy takes you.

The suburbs

Copenhagen's suburbs are relatively characterless, though there are a few attractions dotted about here and there, along with a number of surprisingly good beaches and refreshing tracts of open park and woodland within easy reach of the city centre. To the north of the city are the determinedly populist attractions of the **Danish Aquarium** and the brash **Bakken** amusement park, along with the idyllic **Frilands Museum** and the curious **Grundtvigs**

COPENHAGEN BEACHES

Denmark has a surprising number of excellent beaches, including several within easy reach of Copenhagen's city centre. The water year round is generally pretty cold, although it can get as high as 20°C in summer. The most popular beaches are **Bellevue** (p.114) and **Charlottenlund** (p.111) to the north of the city, and **Ishøj** (p.118) and **Amager** (p.115) to the south. The most popular beaches operate a flag system on busy days: red means danger and no swimming; yellow: bathe with caution; green: bathe freely. Toplessness is tolerated pretty much everywhere; if you want to swim in the nude, find a very quiet spot or go to the designated nudist bathing spot at Helgoland bathing pier (see p.115).

Kirke, commemorating one of the nation's most celebrated priests and scholars. South of the city you'll find the large island of **Amager**, with its pleasing mixture of beaches, parkland and nature reserve, and the controversial **Arken** museum of modern art. All the places listed here are fairly easily reached by public transport from central Copenhagen.

FRILANDS MUSEUM

Map 1, C4. Kongevejen 100. Tues–Sun: mid-April to Sept 10am–5pm, Oct 10am–4pm; 40kr, Wed free. Bus #184 from the city centre stops outside the main entrance, or take the S-Tog to Sorgenfri, from where it's a ten-minute walk.

Twenty minutes north from the city centre is the open-air **Frilands Museum** (Frilandsmuseet), a wonderful mixture of heritage park, city farm and woodland retreat; if the weather's good it's worth bringing a picnic – you could spend hours here amidst the wild flowers and thatched and sod-roofed cottages. Established on its present site in 1901, the museum displays over a hundred buildings dating back to the seventeenth century from all over Denmark, southern Sweden and the Faroe Islands, furnished according to various trades – bakers, potters, blacksmiths, and so on – and offering a vivid picture of how rural communities lived in northern Europe in times past. The lopsided ochre cottages and farmsteads are grouped together according to region; the ticket office provides a map. The museum also runs a number of well-planned events, with staff in period costume engaging in arts and crafts such as weaving and folk dancing – the programme varies from week to week, so visit for details.

- -

A horse-drawn carriage circles the Frilands Museum every thirty minutes (Tues–Thurs & Sun 10am–3pm, leaving from near the ticket office; 20kr).

- -

FRILANDS MUSEUM

At the far end of the museum, the **Brede Museum** (same opening hours, and entrance with same ticket) preserves parts of the industrial community – factory workers' cottages (many with their original interiors) and vegetable allotments – that grew up around the large clothes mill that existed here from 1831 to 1956, when it was handed over to the National Museum.

GRUNDTVIGS KIRKE AND UTTERSLEV MOSE

Map 2, A1–B2. Bus #10, #16, #43, #69 or Emdrup S-Tog, then a ten-minute walk.

Five kilometres north of the city centre, **Grundtvigs Kirke** (Mon–Sat 9am–4pm, Sun noon–1pm, April–Oct Sun until 4pm) was designed by Peder Vilhelm Jensen-Klint in 1913 as a monument to the Danish theologian and pedagogue N.F.S. Grundtvig (see box overleaf). Resembling a kind of enormous church organ, with parallel yellow-brick buttresses running upwards, the church dwarfs the neighbouring housing, which was built using similar motifs. Inside, the cavernous, unadorned space and large high windows provide a suitably reverential atmosphere, with wonderful acoustics and beautiful natural lighting.

About one kilometre west of the church – head along På Berget and then Mosesvinget – is the large lake and park of **Utterslev Mose**, an excellent place for biking, walking, sunbathing and picnics. The park stretches about 3km west to the old outer defences at Husum, where you reach a cycle path which circumnavigates the city centre, running almost solely through green areas.

CHARLOTTENLUND AND THE DANISH AQUARIUM

Map 1, D5. Bus #6 or Charlottenlund S-Tog.

A twenty-minute S-Tog ride north of the city is the

N.F.S. GRUNDTVIG
AND THE FOLKEHØJSKOLE

Although less well known internationally than his contemporaries Søren Kierkegaard and Hans Christian Andersen, N.F.S. Grundtvig left the most indelible mark on Danish history and culture. As a man given to manic bouts of frenzied activity – he is still the most prolific Danish author ever – Grundtvig forged a career as a priest and scholar, developing the grand humanist vision that would go on to shape almost every aspect of Danish cultural and social life. To many, his lasting legacy was the establishment of the uniquely Danish "Folkehøjskole" (People's High School) system, residential colleges for adults offering courses in arts, crafts and, more recently, computers and the media. In these schools, Grundtvig's philosophy of equality, democracy, participation and the pursuit of knowledge was put into practice. The first school opened in 1844, and they soon spread throughout the country and abroad – there are now schools as far afield as the US, India and Nigeria.

One of the main principles of the Folkehøjskole is to provide an education which eschews the usual authoritarian teacher–pupil relationship in favour of shared experience and knowledge. Schools also avoid competitiveness (there are no exams) and vocational training – the aim is to produce rounded human beings rather than good little workers. If you're interested in attending one, contact the International People's College in Helsingør (Montebello Alle 1, 3000 Helsingør ☎ 49 21 33 61), the only place in Denmark where courses are taught in English. They run a variety of courses varying in length from two to eight weeks; expect to pay about 1250kr a week, including board and lodging.

notoriously snooty suburb of **Charlottenlund**. From the train station – walk up the station concourse and turn right – it's a ten-minute walk through some woods to the immaculate lawns and tree-lined avenues of **Charlottenlund Palace** and its gardens – an excellent spot for a picnic. There's been a palace here since the seventeenth century: the present one dates from 1731, though it's of no particular interest and now houses the fish research unit of the Danish Ministry of Agriculture. You can't go into the palace itself, but the gardens (free) are open 24 hours a day.

A short walk beyond the palace towards the sea is the functional white building which houses the **Danish Aquarium** (mid-Feb to mid-Oct daily 10am–6pm; mid-Oct to mid-Feb Mon–Fri 10am–4pm, Sat & Sun 10am–5pm; 60kr; ⓦ *www.danmarks-akvarium.dk*), home to over 300 species of fish, plus crocodiles, turtles, frogs and a tank of mudskippers – remarkable creatures, half-fish, half-reptile, which hop between land and water (the bigger ones sometimes hop straight out of their tank into the crocodile pool below, never to return). The tropical collection is an exotic and enticing blend of colourful creatures and rare corals, along with some sharks and a vicious-looking shoal of piranhas, which you can watch being fed at 2pm on Wednesday, Saturday and Sunday. Look out too for the coelacanth preserved in alcohol, a mysterious, prehistoric-looking fish thought to have been extinct for sixty million years until a live specimen was netted in the Indian Ocean in 1938 – further examples have continued to turn up occasionally off the coast of southern Africa.

Carry on out towards the sea from the aquarium and you'll arrive at a nice flat, green area leading to a small sandy **beach**. On hot days you can hardly move here for exposed flesh, and even in winter some hardy souls like to take a dip in the sound. On the left of the beach there's a

CHARLOTTENLUND AND THE DANISH AQUARIUM

small private bathing pier (20kr) with showers, toilets and a small café. To the right is an old fort, now part of the excellent Charlottenlund Fort campsite (see p.149).

KLAMPENBORG AND BAKKEN

Map 1, D4. Bus #6, #185 or Klampenborg Station.

The final destination on the northbound S-Tog C-line is the wealthy suburb of **Klampenborg**. Turning right out of the station brings you to the attractive and very popular **Bellevue Beach**, the preferred spot for Copenhagen's poseurs, where beautiful young things lounge around on the sand pretending to read French existential novels.

Turn left out of the station and walk for ten minutes through some woods to reach the **Bakken** amusement park (April–Aug daily noon–midnight; free; ⓦ *www.bakken.dk*). Compared to the supposedly genteel Tivoli, Bakken is a strictly blue-collar affair, with dozens of brash beer halls, cheap restaurants and fairground rides whose colourful trashiness provides a welcome contrast to the staid atmosphere of many of Copenhagen's other attractions. It also boasts of being the oldest surviving amusement park in the world – a claim the park's antiquated wooden rollercoaster would seem to bear out. The third weekend of March, when the park opens for the new season, is a big annual event, with Copenhageners congregating en masse to sample the latest attractions, and a mass rally of city bikers turning up to mark the occasion.

You can take a horse-drawn carriage from Klampenborg station to Bakken for 60kr.

Almost entirely surrounding Bakken is the enormous **Dyrehave** (Deer Park), a former royal hunting ground which is still home to large numbers of deer and whose cool oak and beech woods are a wonderful spot for walking, picnicking and relaxing. In the middle of the park, and at its highest point, is a Rococo hunting lodge, Eremitagen (closed to the public), built in 1736 by Christian VI and still used by the royals today.

AMAGER

Just southeast of the city centre, and connected to it by a series of lifting bridges, is the large island of **Amager** (pronounced *Ama*). Although within walking distance of the city, the area feels quite separate, and the locals – the so-called "Ama'rkaner" – have a reputation for being rougher and tougher than their "mainland" counterparts.

Even so, recent developments have linked Amager more closely with the city, and the atmosphere of the island is gradually beginning to change. In particular, the brand new **Øresund Bridge**, connecting Copenhagen via Kastrup airport on Amager to Malmö in Sweden, has turned the island upside-down, and connecting trains and a new metro network – due for completion in 2004 – mean that most corners of Amager are now (or will shortly become) accessible by fast public transport. In addition, the **Ørestad** area, south of the motorway on the way to the airport, is being rapidly developed and is expected to house some 70,000 people in the future, as well as (possibly) the city's major new concert hall (see p.198), though for the time being most of the area is still ploughed field.

The island's main attraction is the string of excellent **beaches** along its eastern coastline (bus #12 or #13; ask for Helgoland). Far less pretentious than those to the north of the city, they're mostly family oriented, with large sections of pebble, though there are patches of sand here and there. During summer weekends, music lovers in their thousands are drawn to the section of the beach called **Femøren** (named after the five-øre coin) for inexpensive open-air rock concerts – check with Use It for what's on.

Kalvebod Fælled

Map 1, D6. Bus #31, #36 or #71E.

Amager's other big draw, the enormous **Kalvebod Fælled** nature reserve on the island's western side, is remarkable for its proximity to the city – no other European capital has a reserve of this size so close to its centre. Reclaimed from the sea during World War II in an effort to create work for unemployed Danes who might otherwise have been deported to Germany, it's now home to an amazing number of predatory birds, including kestrels, blue hawks and buzzards. Up until recently, the reserve was a military firing range, and as large areas are still being cleared for potentially explosive debris, it's strongly recommended that you stick to the marked paths.

The **Naturcenter Vestamager**, at the fringe of the reserve, offers free bike rental (call ☏ 36 13 14 15 if you want to book in advance – a good idea during school holidays) and free camping for one night in a designated campsite.

Dragør

Map 1, E6. Bus #30, #36, #73E or #350S.

East of Kalvebod Fælled, at the southeastern corner of Amager, lies the atmospheric fishing village of **Dragør**, departure point for ferries to Limhamn in Sweden and home to a couple of good local history museums. The first of these, the **Amager Museum** (May–Sept Tues–Sun noon–4pm; Oct–April Wed & Sun noon–4pm; 20kr), at Store Magleby village on the road leading into Dragør, is housed in two of Amager's old four-winged farmhouses. In the early sixteenth century, Christian II invited a group of farmers from Holland – at the time, a more agriculturally advanced nation than Denmark – to settle here to produce food for the royal household. Twenty-four families arrived, and they and their descendants stayed for three centuries, continuing to live in the Store Magleby and Dragør area and leaving only for their weekly trips to the Amagertorv market in Indre By – amongst their many other achievements they were responsible for introducing the carrot to Denmark. The museum comprises two working farms, complete with livestock and vegetable patches, their interiors kept as they would have been at the time. Museum staff demonstrate how the Dutch grew their crops and kept their animals, as well as explaining the distinctive dress and cultural traditions they introduced to Denmark.

The Dragør Music Festival (last weekend in July),
featuring mostly Danish mainstream pop bands, is
a good opportunity to experience a real village festival,
with lots of good food and a splendid habourside view.

The summer-only **Dragør Museum** (May–Sept Tues–Fri 2–5pm, Sat & Sun noon–6pm; 20kr joint ticket with Mølsteds Museum), by Dragør harbour, is devoted to the maritime history of the village, from the thirteenth-century herring trade to the arrival of the Dutch. Loads of outdoor activities, including trips out to sea, mainly oriented towards kids, give you a real taste of what it meant to live off the sea. There's also a large display of model ships, navigation instruments, and curios collected by sailors during their travels to distant parts of the world. **Mølsteds Museum** (May–Aug Sat & Sun 2–5pm; 20kr joint ticket with Dragør Museum), in the centre of the old village on Dr Dichs Plads, displays paintings by local celebrity Christian Mølsted (1862–1930), known for his atmospheric

AMAGER

and colourful paintings of the land- and seascapes around Dragør.

ARKEN

Map 1, C6. Ishøj S-Tog, and then bus #128 or a 25-minute walk. Tues–Sun 10am–5pm; 50kr; Ⓦ *www.arken.dk*.

Situated 17km southwest of the city centre on a lonely, windswept beach near the rundown suburb of Ishøj is the controversial **Arken** museum of modern art. The obscure location seems almost wilfully perverse for a museum that aspires to be an internationally recognized showcase for the contemporary arts, but it's worth the trouble of getting there, and you'll also find a decent beach right on the museum's doorstep.

Arken has a reasonable, nautical-themed restaurant with great views over the bay.

It was originally intended to build Arken ("The Ark") actually *in* the sea, though environmental concerns prevented this, and it was finally placed on the seafront instead. The building resembles a beached sailing ship – a striking sight when seen from across the dunes, with its large, white, angled expanses and steel wings. The interior, formed by an intersecting hall and a narrower corridor, is slightly bewildering, and the unusual character of the building and its location can tend to overwhelm the exhibits themselves. The museum is used for temporary exhibitions devoted to contemporary art; it's intended to expand the permanent collection too, though the museum's only acquisitions on permanent display at present are the massive Asger Jorn abstracts by the ticket desk. Check out the steel-and-marble toilets in the basement – a work of art in themselves.

Day-trips

The area around Copenhagen is steeped in history, with a plethora of castles, museums and sites of natural beauty, and with fast public transport links reaching into virtually every corner of Zealand and southern Sweden, there are dozens of possible destinations for day-trips. Heading north up the coast from Copenhagen will take you past the **Karen Blixen Museum** and the excellent collection of modern art at **Louisiana** to the town of **Helsingør**, and its magnificent castle. Nearby is the even grander castle of **Frederiksborg** at Hillerød, while heading inland brings you to the ancient Danish capital of **Roskilde**. In summer, bring a picnic or sample the freshly baked goods from local *konditoris* – many of the places listed here also have fine cafés and restaurants.

The 24-hour ticket (see p.11) and Copenhagen Card (see p.10) are both valid for travel to all the places covered in this chapter. The Copenhagen Card also gives free entry to all the following sights, with the exception of Kronborg.

KAREN BLIXEN MUSEUM

Map 1, D3. May–Sept daily 10am–5pm; Oct–April Wed–Fri 1pm–4pm, Sat & Sun 11am–4pm; 30kr. Local train to Rungsted Kyst from Central Station or Nørreport S-Tog and then a fifteen-minute walk.

A visit to the **Karen Blixen Museum** is easily combined with a trip further up the coast to Louisiana and Helsingør, though unless you're a big fan of this writer's work you might find it all a bit underwhelming. While long a household name in Denmark for her short stories (often written under the pen-name of Isak Dinesen) and outspoken opinions, Blixen enjoyed a resurgence of international popularity during the mid-1980s when the film *Out of Africa* – based on her 1937 autobiographical account of running a coffee plantation in Kenya – won seven Oscars.

The museum is set in the Blixen family home, where Karen lived after her return from Africa until her death in 1962, and much of the house is maintained as it was during her final years. Lining the walls are texts describing Blixen's eventful life – her father committed suicide and she married the twin brother of the man she loved, among other things – while exhibits include a collection of first editions and the tiny typewriter she used in Africa, along with audiovisual displays, old radio recordings, some nice furniture and personal effects and temporary exhibitions relating to her life and work. The **living quarters** (note that you'll only be allowed into this section at the time printed on the back of your ticket) house a small collection of paintings and drawings by Blixen – the smaller room at the back was where she wrote most of her books.

You might find the museum's surroundings at least as interesting as the museum itself, facing onto the seafront and backed by delightful woodlands – now a bird sanctuary established by Blixen and also her final resting place; the ticket office can provide a map.

LOUISIANA

Map 1, D3. Gamle Strandvej 13. Daily 10am–5pm, Wed until 10pm; 60kr; Ⓦ *www.louisiana.dk*. Local trains to Humlebæk every from Central Station (departures every 20min), then a seven-minute sign-posted walk.

Situated right on the coast about 30km north of Copenhagen is one of Europe's most intriguing galleries, **Louisiana**. With its compelling mixture of unusual architecture and outstanding modern art, set in a memorable natural setting, it's worth at least half a day, though be prepared for huge crowds at weekends during summer. Most of the displays are permanent, although the museum also hosts top-notch temporary exhibitions, plus regular concerts of chamber music and solo recitals, often featuring internationally renowned performers.

> Louisiana has an imaginative children's wing where kids can paint and hear stories. Outside, an adventure playground, designed by renowned Italian nature-artist Alfio Bonnano, features enormous birds' nests and playful houses made of boats.

Divided between the museum buildings and the sculpture garden outside, the collection reflects most of the important art movements of the twentieth century. Exploring the gallery's confusing array of nooks and crannies requires time and persistence, though, while finding your way around is further complicated by the fact that, with the exception of the Giacometti and Cobra sections, all the collection's displays get moved from place to place to make way for the many touring exhibitions that stop off here.

The museum's **interior** is entered through an 1855 villa (built by a man whose three wives were all called Louise – hence the museum's name), beyond which stretches a twisting

LOUISIANA

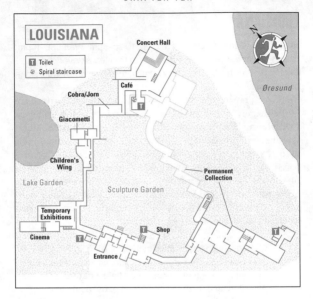

and sometimes bewildering array of glass corridors, laid out in a roughly circular shape, through which loom the intriguing shapes of the sculptures in the grounds outside. Start walking clockwise around the gallery, through a section which usually houses temporary exhibits, to reach a wonderfully lit, purpose-built wing containing several of **Giacometti**'s gaunt bronze figures and many of his original sketches. Corridors connect from here to a collection of work by artists of the **Cobra** movement (named after the cities of *C*openhagen, *Br*ussels and *A*msterdam), a left-wing collective of artists characterized by their distinctive and colourful abstracts. Henry Heerup's odd wood sculptures, including the bizzare *Ironing Board Madonna*, and some large and characteristically tortured abstracts by

Asger Jorn, former Cobra member and one of the country's most renowned artists. You'll also find small rooms dedicated to the bright, Constructivist works of Rodchenko and Delaunay, with their straight lines and simple colours, and large spaces filled with German Anselm Kiefer's energetic canvasses and the large-scale model of a bomber plane he made from lead. There's also a fine collection of Pop Art, with works by Warhol sitting alongside Oldenburg's models of oversized cigarette butts and a lunch box.

The grounds **outside** are dotted with small copses and carefully tended lawns overlooking an old harbour – part of the Danish fleet fled here to escape British cannons during the Napoleonic War – scattered amongst which is a fantastic array of world-class sculpture, most of it specifically designed for this site. Here you'll find the strange, flat, abstract sculptures of Alexander Calder rubbing shoulders with Max Ernst's surreal creations, and Henry Moore's dramatic *Bronze Woman* perched on a small hill, with the Øresund and distant Sweden providing a stunning backdrop.

HELSINGØR

Map 1, D2. Local train (departures every 15–20min) from Central Station or Nørreport S-Tog.

Some 45km north of Copenhagen, on the coast facing Sweden, is **Helsingør**, one of the most popular day-trips from the capital. Most people head straight for the dramatic fortress of Kronborg, the "Elsinore Castle" of Shakespeare's *Hamlet*, but there's also an atmospheric old quarter in the small town centre – for in-depth information, contact the **tourist office** (June–Aug Mon–Sat 9am–7pm, Sun 9am–noon; Sept–May Mon–Fri 9am–5pm, Sat 9am–1pm; ℡49 21 13 33, ⓦ *www.helsingorturist.dk*), just opposite the train station. The town is also a busy port, with 24-hour ferries bringing in hordes of Swedes from Helsingborg looking for (to them) cheap Danish booze. Note that the Copenhagen Card is not valid for entry to Kronborg.

Kronborg

May–Sept Tues–Sun 11am–4pm; Oct–April Tues–Sun 11am–3pm; 45kr.

The castle of **Kronborg**, a fifteen-minute walk from the train station, completely dominates the town. Originally constructed in the fifteenth century by Erik of Pomerania, the fortress was for hundreds of years the key to control of the Øresund – the narrow strip of water that divides Denmark from Sweden – enabling the Danish monarchs to extract a toll from every ship that passed through it, a practice that continued until the nineteenth century. The castle was turned into a grand fortress by Frederik II around 1600, before being largely destroyed by a massive fire in 1629. The cost of rebuilding it almost bankrupted the Danish state, and shortly afterwards the hapless castle was bombarded and overrun by the Swedes, who carted off many of its treasures. Three relatively uneventful centuries followed, until in 1924 the military moved out and a major restoration programme began.

Even now, walking through the lines of gates, moats and earthen and brick defences still gives you a sense of the fortress's former invincibility, with antique cannons pointing out across the narrow sound. The main keep is rather ornate, with plenty of Renaissance features, two spindly towers roofed with green copper jutting out into the usually blustery sky, and another tower providing a fully functioning lighthouse. The **interior** doesn't really live up to the grandeur of the outside. There are some massive rooms, such as the main banqueting hall, collections of period furniture in the royal bedrooms and some splendid tapestries from 1590 (housed in a disconcertingly dark room) depicting battle scenes, but apart from this not much remains of the original fixtures and fittings. The castle is also home to the **Danish**

KRONBORG AND HAMLET

The origins of the story of a tragic Danish prince stretch back far beyond Shakespearean times. The earliest mention of a character called Amled can be found in a story, derived from Icelandic and Celtic sagas, written around 1200 by one of Bishop Absalon's scribes, a certain Saxo Grammaticus. An earlier Elizabethan version of the Hamlet story, thought to have been written by Thomas Kyd, had already appeared on the London stage twenty years before Shakespeare's *Hamlet* was produced in 1602. Quite how the semi-mythical Danish prince and the very real Danish castle became connected isn't entirely clear, though it's probable that Elizabethan England got wind of Kronberg from sailors who had passed through the Øresund, returning with stories of the mist-shrouded fortress that subsequently metamorphosed into Shakespeare's Elsinore.

Maritime Museum, a briefly diverting collection of detailed model boats, with a few nautical paintings and a number of old ship figureheads, including several of busty Viking maidens.

Three ferry lines cross from Helsingør to Helsingborg in Sweden (around 30kr return). On a sunny day it's very enjoyable to rent a bike (40kr a day) from the courtyard behind the tourist office and cross to Helsingborg for a day's cycling along the Swedish coast.

The medieval quarter

Away from Kronborg and the harbour area, Helsingør has a well-preserved **medieval quarter**. Stengade is the main

HELSINGØR

pedestrianized street, linked by a number of narrow alley-ways to Axeltorv, the town's small market square and a good spot to linger over a beer – alternatively, stroll into nearby Brostræde, a street that's famous for the immense ice creams made with traditional ingredients sold here. Near the corner of Stengade and Skt Annagade, the spired Skt Olai's Kirke is connected to the Karmeliterklosteret Monastery, which served originally as a hospital, during which time it prided itself on its brain operations. The unnerving tools of this profession are still on show next door at the **Town Museum** (daily noon–4pm; 10kr), together with diagrams of the corrective insertions made into patients' heads. For something less disturbing, seek out the oddball **Journeymen's Club** (Naverhulen) in a nearby courtyard, cluttered with souvenirs of world travel, such as crab puppets and armadillo lampshades. Act interested and you might get a free guided tour.

For eating in Helsingør, there's fine Danish food in the small, atmospheric *Bixen*, Hovedvagtsstræde 7, across from the train station (☏ 49 21 67 54), and a good café, the *Kronborg Havbad*, right next to Kronborg Slot.

FREDERIKSBORG SLOT

Map 1, B3. Daily: April–Oct 10am–5pm; Nov–March 11am–3pm; 45kr; ⓦ *www.frederiksborgmuseet.dk*. Hillerød S-Tog, and then bus #701, #702 or a twenty-minute walk.

The town of **Hillerød** is half an hour by train from Helsingør and a similar distance from Copenhagen. Here is a castle, **Frederiksborg Slot**, which easily pushes the more famous Kronborg into second place. Lying decorously across three small islands within an artificial lake, it was originally the home of Frederik II and birthplace of his son

Christian IV, who, at the turn of the seventeenth century, began rebuilding the castle in an unorthodox Dutch Renaissance style. It's the unusual aspects of the design – a prolific use of towers and spires, Gothic arches and flowery window ornamentation – that still stand out, despite the changes wrought by fire and restoration.

The Hillerød tourist office is at Slotsgade 52 (June–Aug Mon–Fri 9am–6pm, Sat 10am–5pm; Sept–May Mon–Fri 9am–4pm, Sat 10am–1pm; ☎ 42 26 28 52).

You can see the exterior of the castle for free simply by walking through the main gates, across the seventeenth-century S-shaped bridge, and into the central courtyard. Since 1882, the interior has functioned as a **museum of Danish history**, largely funded by the Carlsberg brewery magnate Carl Jacobsen in an attempt to create a Danish Versailles, and to heighten the nation's sense of history and cultural development. It's a good idea to buy the illustrated guide (25kr) to the museum, since without it the contents of the sixty-odd rooms are barely comprehensible. Many of the rooms are surprisingly free of furniture and household objects, and attention is drawn to the ranks of portraits along the walls – a motley crew of flat-faced kings and thin consorts who between them ruled and misruled Denmark for centuries, giving way in later rooms to politicians, scientists and writers.

Two rooms deserve special mention. The **chapel**, where Denmark's monarchs were crowned between 1671 and 1840, is exquisite, its vaults, pillars and arches gilded and embellished, and the contrasting black marble of the gallery riddled with gold lettering. The shields, in tiered rows around the chapel, are those of the knights of the Order of the Elephant, who sat with the king in the late seventeenth century. The **Great Hall**, above the chapel, is a

FREDERIKSBORG SLOT

reconstruction, but this doesn't detract from its beauty. It's bare but for the staggering wall and ceiling decorations: tapestries, wall reliefs, portraits and a glistening black marble fireplace. In Christian IV's day the hall was a ballroom, and the polished floor still tempts you to some fancy footwork as you slide up and down its length.

There's a great restaurant in one of the castle gatehouses, *Slotsherrens Kro* (April–Oct) which serves fantastic *smørrebrød* for about 70kr a piece – try the air-dried beef and fresh horseradish.

Away from the often crowded interior, the **gardens**, on the far side of the lake, have some photogenic views of the castle from their stepped terraces and are a good spot for a rest. The quickest way to them is through the narrow Mint Gate to the left of the main castle building, which adjoins a roofed-in bridge leading to the King's Wing. In summer you can also cross the lake on the hourly *M/F Frederiksborg* ferry (May–Sept daily).

Though Frederiksborg is the main reason to come to Hillerød, while here you could also visit the **Money Historical Museum** (open during banking hours; free) at Slotsgade 16–18. During the reigns of Frederik II and Christian IV, all Danish coins were minted in Hillerød. Besides samples of these, the place displays currencies from all over the world.

ROSKILDE

Map 1, A6. Local train from Central Station (departures every 20min). A visit to Copenhagen is incomplete without a trip to the ancient Danish capital of **Roskilde**, the seat of the country's ecclesiastical and royal power from the eleventh to the fifteenth centuries. There's been a community here since

THE ROSKILDE FESTIVAL

Held over four days and nights during the last weekend of June, and attracting crowds of 80,000 people from all over Europe, the **Roskilde Festival** (Ⓦ *www.roskilde-festival.dk*) is one of Europe's largest rock events. When the festival began in the 1970s the good burghers of Roskilde were not particularly amused, but nowadays the festival is seen as a massive boost to the local economy, while all profits go to community projects.

The Roskilde Festival's darkest moment came on June 30, 2000, when nine young people died as a result of a crowd surge during a performance by US rock band Pearl Jam. The whole incident is currently under police investigation, though organizers are confident that the festival will continue in future years and are currently looking into dozens of recommendations to improve safety – something they will have to do if they are to regain their status as one of the best festivals in Europe. **Tickets** for the entire four days of the festival with a place in the campsite cost about 900kr; tickets are sometimes sold for the Sunday only (about 300kr) – they're available via Billetnet (see p.197).

prehistoric times, and the Roskilde Fjord later provided a route to the open sea that was used by the Vikings. But it was the arrival of Bishop Absalon in the twelfth century that made the place the base of the Danish church – and, as a consequence, the national capital. Roskilde's importance waned after the Reformation, and it came to function mainly as a market for the neighbouring rural communities – much as it does today, as well as serving as dormitory territory for Copenhagen commuters. Nowadays, it's probably as well known for its summer **rock festival** (see box above) as for its cathedral. There's enough to fill a day here, and quick transport connections to the centre of Copenhagen.

THE ROSKILDE FESTIVAL

Roskilde's tourist office (July & Aug Mon–Fri 9am–6pm,
Sat 9am–3pm, Sun 10am–2pm; Sept–June Mon–Thurs
9am–5pm, Fri 9am–4pm, Sat 10am–1pm; ⓣ 46 35 27 00,
ⓦ *www.destination-roskilde.dk*) is at Gullandsstræde 15,
a ten-minute walk from the railway station.

The cathedral

April–Sept Mon–Fri 9am–4.45pm, Sat 9am–noon, Sun
12.30pm–3.45pm; Oct–March Tues–Fri 10am–3.45pm, Sat
11.30am–3.45pm, Sun 12.30pm–3.45pm; 12kr.

The major pointer to the town's former status is the fabulous **Roskilde Domkirke**, the burial place of Danish royalty and one of Scandinavia's most important religious sites. The cathedral was originally founded by Bishop Absalon in 1170 on the site of a tenth-century church erected by Harald Bluetooth and finished during the fourteenth century, although portions have been added right up to the twentieth. The result is a mishmash of architectural styles, though one that hangs together with surprising neatness. The interior is dominated by the grandiose tombs of twenty Danish kings and seventeen queens in four large **royal chapels**. The most richly endowed chapel is that of Christian IV, a once austere resting place jazzed-up – in typical early nineteenth-century Romantic style – with bronze statues, wall-length frescoes and vast paintings of scenes from his reign. (The most recently interred monarch, Frederik IX, the father of the present queen, lies outside in a small contemporary tomb which looks strangely out of place against the historic cathedral.) Look out, too, for the massive altarpiece: made in Antwerp in 1560, and depicting the various travails of Christ, it was taken as payment for the Sound Toll.

The Viking Ship Museum

Daily: May–Sept 9am–5pm, 50kr; Oct–April 10am–4pm, 42kr.

Ten minutes' walk north of the cathedral there's another slice of Danish history at the **Viking Ship Museum**, situated directly on the waterfront of Roskilde Fjord. The museum is split into two parts: workshops in the newer buildings on the left, open during summer, make full-sized working replicas of Viking longboats; the older buildings contain the rather rotten-looking wooden hulls of five Vikings boats – a deep-sea trader, a merchant ship, a man-of-war, a ferry and a longship – each retrieved from the fjord, where, according to one theory, they had been sunk to block invading forces. Together, they give an impressive indication of the Vikings' nautical versatility, their skills in boat-building, and their far-ranging travels to places as various as Paris, Hamburg, and North America. The material here tries hard to convince you that the Vikings sailed abroad not only to rape and pillage, but also to find places where they could quietly settle down and farm. Try to catch the film downstairs first (shown in English on request), which goes into fascinating detail about the project to restore the ships, helping to bring the main exhibits alive.

For eating, the Viking Museum cafeteria is one of the best spots in town for a quick and inexpensive bite, while *Havne Caféen* at Havne Vej 43, on the waterfront north across the docks from the Viking Museum, has pizza and fish specials from 50kr.

LISTINGS

Accommodation

Accommodation in Copenhagen is varied but relatively expensive, with prices on a par with other Western European capitals. Most of the hotels in the city centre are aimed either at tour groups or business travellers – they generally have great service and amenities but tend to be pricey and a bit characterless. Rooms rates are generally most expensive in summer, though in the majority of big hotels prices rise and fall on a daily basis year-round according to demand; discounts can sometimes be negotiated in smaller hotels or if you book via the Internet. Note that prices at business-oriented hotels fall at weekends; those at tourist-oriented hotels fall during winter. Rooms fills up quickly during the summer high season and around Christmas – book ahead during these times.

ACCOMMODATION PRICE CODES

All the hotels in this guide have been graded according to price bands given below, based on the cost of each hotel's **cheapest double room** in summer.

❶ Under 350kr   ❸ 600–900kr   ❺ 1200–1500kr
❷ 350–600kr   ❹ 900–1200kr   ❻ Over 1500kr

There's a **hotel reservations desk** right by arrivals at the airport (daily 6am–11pm; 50kr per reservation), and another at the Wonderful Copenhagen office in front of Tivoli (see p.8) – you can only book in person, and must pay a commission (50kr) plus deposit. They have all the latest room rates, and in low season or when things are a bit quiet may be able to find you a really good deal. If you want to book accommodation before you arrive, Wonderful Copenhagen runs a telephone booking line (Mon–Sat 10am–4pm ☎ 33 25 38 44).

A smaller and more affordable **guesthouse** sector is slowly starting to develop, but numbers are presently very low and rooms fill quickly in the busier summer months. Another option is to contact the Wonderful Copenhagen tourist office (☎ 70 22 24 42, ⓦ *www.visitcopenhagen.dk*) or Use It (☎ 33 73 06 20, ⓦ *www.useit.dk*) and ask about **private rooms** in local homes. Some of these are in as good a location as the best hotels, and prices are very reasonable – roughly 350kr per double. If you're on a budget, there are a number of **hostels** scattered around the city centre and suburbs. **Campsites** provide a good alternative if you're really watching the pennies.

HOTELS

Most of Copenhagen's classier hotels are concentrated in the desirable canalside area **around Nyhavn**, on the eastern side of Indre By, and there's also a smattering around the western side of Indre By. There are dozens of cheaper, though sometimes seedy, hotels in the streets **around Central Station**, Helgolandsgade and Colbjørnsensgade in particular, plus a further selection of places slightly further out in the district of **Frederiksberg**.

We've divided our hotel listings into the following areas: Nyhavn and around (p.137), Western Indre By (p.139), Around Central Station (p.140), and Vesterbro and Frederiksberg (p.144).

NYHAVN AND AROUND

Admiral

Map 3, J2. Toldbodgade 24–28

ⓣ 33 74 14 14
ⓕ 33 74 14 15
ⓦ *www.admiral-hotel.dk*
Bus #550S

Housed in a converted 200-year-old granary in a great location right by the harbour, the *Admiral* is geared mainly towards the business traveller, with comfortable wood-beamed, en-suite rooms, all with TV. Breakfast not included. ❺

D'Angleterre

Map 3, H3. Kongens Nytorv 34

ⓣ 33 12 00 95
ⓕ 33 12 11 18
ⓦ *www.remmen.dk*
Bus #1, #6, #9, #10 or #29

Dating back to 1755, this prestigious five-star hotel is one of Europe's oldest hotels

– guests have included Winston Churchill and Michael Jackson. The ultra-stylish classical rooms contain every conceivable amenity, and there's also a luxurious spa and fitness centre and two gourmet restaurants, though breakfast isn't included in the extravagant price, and parking costs extra too. ❻

City

Map 3, J4. Peder Skramsgade 24

ⓣ 33 13 06 66
ⓕ 33 13 06 67
ⓦ *www.hotelcity.dk*
Bus #550S

Three-star Best Western hotel in a quiet street near Nyhavn which is aiming to become the most environmentally friendly hotel in Copenhagen – look out for the range of organic products at breakfast. Rooms are comfortably furnished in modern Danish style, though a bit on the small side. ❹

HOTELS: NYHAVN AND AROUND

Esplanaden

Map 4, K5. Bredgade 78

ⓣ 33 48 10 00

ⓕ 33 48 10 66

ⓦ *www.neptun-group.dk*

Bus #1, #6, #9, #10 or #29

Set in a nice location near Churchillparken, this pleasant hotel has decent en-suite rooms, all with TV, a good restaurant and free parking. ❺.

Maritime

Map 3, J4. Peder Skramsgade 19

ⓣ 33 13 48 82

ⓕ 33 15 03 45

ⓦ *www.hotel-maritime.dk*

Bus #550S

Located in a former seamen's home, this is one of Nyhavn's more affordable hotels – rooms are nothing special, but perfectly adequate. You might be able to negotiate some good deals out of high season if you're staying for a few days. ❹.

Neptun

Map 3, J2. Skt Annæ Plads 14–20

ⓣ 33 13 89 00

ⓕ 33 96 20 66

ⓦ *www.neptun-group.dk*

Bus #550S

Expensive hotel housed in a renovated nineteenth-century townhouse, and aimed mainly at business travellers. You're paying above-average prices for the prime location near Nyhavn, though all the cosy and old-fashioned rooms are en suite and come with cable TV. ❻.

71 Nyhavn

Map 3, K3. Nyhavn 71

ⓣ 33 43 62 00

ⓕ 33 43 62 01

ⓦ *www.71nyhavnhotel copenhagen.dk*

Bus #550S

Located on the corner of the harbour and Nyhavn canal, this wooden-beamed, nineteenth-century warehouse has been transformed into one of the city's classiest hotels. The small but stylish rooms have superb views of the harbour and there's an excellent restaurant, the *Pakhuskælderen*, famous for its traditional Danish cuisine. Reductions possible at weekends. ❻.

Sømandshjemmet "Bethel"

Map 3, J3. Nyhavn 22

ⓣ 33 13 03 70

Ⓕ 33 15 85 70

Bus #550S

Old seamen's hostel, with bare and basic rooms, some with and some without en suite – you pay over-the-odds for the fantastic location on hip Nyhavn. ❸.

Sophie Amalie

Map 3, J2. Skt Annæ Plads 21

Ⓣ 33 13 34 00

Ⓕ 33 11 77 07

Bus #550S

One of the Nyhavn area's better-value hotels, with large and luxurious en-suite rooms, all with cable TV and Internet access (60kr for 30mins), plus a sauna (free to guests) and solarium (25kr) in the basement. Breakfast not included. ❹.

WESTERN INDRE BY

Ascot

Map 3, C7. Studiestræde 61

Ⓣ 33 12 60 00

Ⓕ 33 14 60 40

Ⓦ www.ascothotel.dk

Vesterport S-Tog

The arched reception hall with black granite pillars and reliefs of bathing men and women is the only surviving evidence of the *Ascot*'s former incarnation as a public bath. Now serves a mainly business clientele, with pleasant and comfortable en-suite rooms outfitted with modern Danish furniture. Free parking. ❺.

Ibsens

Map 3, B4. Vendersgade 23

Ⓣ 33 13 19 13

Ⓕ 33 13 19 16

Ⓦ www.ibsenshotel.dk

Bus #5 or #40

Set between Nørreport and the lakes, the recently upgraded, three-star *Ibsens* has comfortable and attractively outfitted rooms. Each floor is themed – the fourth is "romantic", the fifth "bohemian" – and the downstairs *Brasserade* brasserie is equipped with a children's play area. ❹.

Kong Arthur

Map 3, A4. Nørre Søgade 11

Ⓣ 33 11 12 12

Ⓕ 33 32 61 30

Ⓦ www.konyarthur.dk

Bus #5 or #16

Located in a largely residential area by the Peblinge Lake,

Kong Arthur sells itself as a family hotel, with luxurious, individually designed rooms, some non-smoking, and a comfy "King Arthur" bar (open 24hr), with King Arthur-related curiosities from around the world, including a Danish version of the Round Table. Free parking. **⑤**.

Palace

Map 3, E7. Rådhuspladsen 57
ⓣ 33 14 40 50
ⓕ 33 14 52 79
ⓦ *www.palace-hotel.dk*
Bus #5 or #29

Elegant and historic hotel, conveniently located for the city centre and Strøget. Rooms are lavishly and tastefully decorated with flowery English designs, and there's a good, though pricey, restaurant downstairs. **⑥**.

Park

Map 3, C6. Jarmers Plads 3
ⓣ 33 13 30 00
ⓕ 33 14 30 33
Bus #14, #16 or #150S

Each of the small, bright rooms here is different, so be specific about what you want (tub or shower, old or new, overlooking the street or the back courtyard), and note that those overlooking busy Jarmers Plads are noisy. Good parking facilities. **④**.

AROUND CENTRAL STATION

Absalon

Map 5, M6. Helgolandsgade 15
ⓣ 33 24 22 11
ⓕ 33 24 34 11
ⓦ *www.absalon-hotel.dk*
Bus #16

On the corner of Istedgade, this large but friendly family hotel offers a choice of rooms with or without en suite, plus a number of deluxe suites (**⑤**) on the top floor equipped with Louis XVI-style furniture – some also have their own kitchenettes. Facilities are clean and modern, while sound-proofing keeps things nice and quiet. **③**–**④**.

Ansgar

Map 5, N6. Colbjørnsensgade 29
ⓣ 33 21 21 96
ⓕ 33 21 61 91
ⓦ *www.ansgar-hotel.dk*
Bus #16

Former Danish Mission hotel at the far end of Colbjørnsensgade, near Halmtorvet, with small, neat, basic en-suite rooms. ❹.

Bertrams

Map 5, I6. Vesterbrogade 107
ⓣ 33 25 04 05
ⓕ 33 25 04 02
Bus #6 or #550S
This cosy and good-value hotel is a haven of peace, and handy for a night out in lively Vesterbro. Rooms, decorated in brown and green, are fairly large, and some are en suite. ❷–❸.

Centrum

Map 5, M6. Helgolandsgade 14
ⓣ 33 31 31 11
ⓕ 31 23 32 51
ⓔ centrum.hotel@adr.dk
Bus #16 or Central Station
On the corner of Istedgade, this large hotel offers a range of no-frills but clean rooms, some en suite, at a range of prices. The in-house restaurant, the *Borobudur*, serves authentic Indonesian food. You might be able to wangle a discount if they're not too busy and you're staying a couple of days. ❸.

Cosmopole

Map 5, M5. Colbjørnsensgade 7–11
ⓣ 33 21 33 33
ⓕ 33 31 33 99
ⓦ www.hotelcosmopole.com
Bus #16 or Central Station
Enormous hotel a stone's throw from Central Station. It's often used by large international tour groups, and so isn't particularly quiet, but its size means there are almost always rooms available. ❹.

DGI-byens Hotel

Map 5, N6. Tietgensgade 65
ⓣ 33 29 80 50
ⓕ 33 29 80 59
ⓦ www.dgi-byen.dk
Bus #10, #550S or Central Station
Part of the DGI-byen centre (see p.90), this is one of the newest hotels in town and a beautiful example of minimalist Scandinavian design. Rooms are large and immaculate, and have Internet access. Rates drop at weekends. ❺.

Euroglobe

Map 5, J3. Niels Ebbesens Vej 20
ⓣ & ⓕ 33 79 79 54

Ⓦ *www.hoteleuroglobe.dk*
Bus #29
Exceptionally good-value hotel, occupying an old villa on one of Frederiksberg's characteristically elegant streets. Rooms are simple, with shared showers, and there's also a kitchen for guests' use. Seven nights for the price of six. ❷.

Grand
Map 3, C9. Vesterbrogade 9
Ⓣ 33 31 36 00
Ⓕ 33 27 69 01
Bus #550S or Central Station
Very popular with British travellers, the big, old-fashioned *Grand* hotel is a little bit overpriced for what you get, but excellently located close to both the Tivoli Gardens and a row of British- and American-style pubs and restaurants. Rooms all come with bathroom and cable TV. ❻.

Mayfair
Map 5, M5. Helgolandsgade 3
Ⓣ 33 31 48 01
Ⓕ 33 23 96 86
Ⓦ *www.dkhotellist.dk/mayfair.htm*
Bus #16 or Central Station
Right in the centre of the

hotel street of Helgolandsgade, with olde English-style rooms complete with all mod-cons – including clothes-press, fridge and Internet access – plus carved wooden beds, frilly curtains and oodles of floral decoration. ❺.

Missionshotellet Nebo
Map 5, M6. Istedgade 6
Ⓣ 33 21 12 17
Ⓕ 33 23 47 74
Ⓦ *www.nebo.dk*
Bus #16 or Central Station
Next door to Central Station – take the back exit – this well-run Danish Mission hotel is one of the best deals this close to the centre. Rooms – most of them en suite – are simple but adequate and clean, and staff are friendly. Parking costs 25kr a day. ❷–❸.

Saga
Map 5, M6. Colbjørnsensgade 18–20
Ⓣ 33 24 49 44
Ⓕ 33 24 60 33
Ⓦ *www.sagahotel.dk*
Bus #16 or Central Station
Friendly and laidback family hotel at the grotty, but cheap,

end of Colbjørnsensgade, near Halmtorvet. Simple rooms – mostly en suite – and a friendly bar where you can get the latest info on what's happening in town from the owners. Rates fall at weekends. ②.

Scandic Hotel Webers

Map 5, M5. Vesterbrogade 11b

ⓣ 33 31 14 32

ⓕ 33 31 14 41

ⓦ www.scandic-hotels.com

Bus #6, #28 or #550S

Elegant hotel – plush, cosy and full of charm – on busy Vesterbrogade, around the corner from Central Station. Ask for rooms facing the courtyard if you want to avoid street noise, though the soundproofing is good. Much cheaper at weekends and during the summer. ⑤.

Top Hotel Hebron

Map 5, M5. Helgolandsgade 4

ⓣ 33 31 69 06

ⓕ 33 31 90 67

ⓦ www.hebron.dk

Bus #6, #29 or #550S

Good-value Danish Mission hotel at the quiet end of Helgolandsgade, near

Vesterbrogade, popular with Danish business travellers. Rooms (all en suite) are large and comfortable, if a bit nondescript. ③.

Triton

Map 5, M5. Helgolandsgade 7–11

ⓣ 31 31 32 66

ⓕ 31 31 69 70

ⓦ www.phg.dk

Bus #6, #29 or #550S

At the nice end of Colbjørnsensgade, *Triton* is soon to become part of the Ibis hotel chain, which could mean a welcome makeover for this attractive but slightly run-down hotel, a good example of light and simple Danish design. Rooms are functional but comfortable, with enormous bathrooms. ③.

Valberg

Map 5, K8. Sønder Boulevard 53

ⓣ 33 25 25 19

ⓕ 33 25 25 83

ⓦ www.valberg.dk

Bus #10

On the fifth floor of an apartment building on the corner of Dybølgade, the large rooms here all come with TV, sink and fridge; bathroom facilities are shared. Cheap weekly rates. ❸.

FREDERIKSBERG

Avenue

Map 6, A7. Åboulevard 29
ⓣ 35 37 31 11
ⓕ 33 37 34 86
ⓦ *www.avenuehotel.dk*
Bus #67, #68 or #69
Comfortable and welcoming hotel on the border between Frederiksberg and Nørrebro, with en-suite rooms (all with TV), breakfast buffet (served outdoors in the summer) and free parking. Rates often fall at weekends. ❹.

Cab-Inn Copenhagen

Map 5, J3. Danasvej 32–34
ⓣ 33 21 04 00
ⓕ 33 21 74 09
ⓦ *www.cab-inn.dk*
Bus #29
The flip-up tables and tiny showers here will make you feel like a passenger on an overnight boat, but it's clean and safe, and the pleasant staff and unbeatably low

price make this one of the top budget hotels in town. Closed October to March, though there's a second *Cab-Inn* around the corner on Vodroffsvej which is open all year (see below). Wheelchair accessible; breakfast not included. ❷.

Cab-Inn Scandinavia

Map 5, K2. Vodroffsvej 57
ⓣ 35 36 11 11
ⓕ 35 36 11 14
ⓦ *www.cab-inn.dk*
Bus #29
The second and larger *Cab-Inn*, open all year round. Inspired by passenger cabins on the Oslo ferry, the rooms here also feature flip-up tables and tiny showers. Clean and very good value if you don't suffer from claustrophobia. Wheelchair accessible. ❷.

Josty

Map 5, E5. Pile Allé 14
ⓣ 38 86 90 90
ⓕ 38 34 78 50
Bus #18 or #28
Classic hotel with just seven rooms – book well in advance – on the edge of Frederiksberg Have.

Primarily used for large dinner functions, *Josty* was built as a restaurant in 1813 by sculptor Agostino Taddei, and still preserves its original romantic Italian style. The rooms are all en suite, and the beautiful location by the park makes it an ideal spot for a romantic break. ❸.

Skt Jørgen
Map 5, K1. Julius Thomsens Gade 22

ⓣ 35 37 15 11
ⓕ 35 37 11 97
ⓦ *www.hotellist.dk/st.jorgen*
Bus #8, #13 or #69

Peaceful and easygoing family hotel in an old Frederiksberg apartment building, on the corner of Gyldenløvsgade near the lakes. Rooms – all with shared bathrooms – are large and bright and, as there's no restaurant, breakfast is served in your room. ❸.

HOSTELS AND GUESTHOUSES

There are a number of **hostels** – often called **"sleep-ins"** – in and around Copenhagen, mostly aimed at the hordes of young Swedes who descend on the city during the summer months looking for cheap alcohol and thrills. Some are more relaxed and quieter, however, and have private rooms which can work out good value if you're in a small group. Prices are roughly the same throughout the city; sheets and breakfast cost around an extra 20kr each. At hostels run by Danhostel (the Danish branch of Hostelling International) you'll also have to pay for temporary membership of HI if you're not already a member – about 30kr per night, or 160kr for annual membership.

We've divided our hostel listings between inner-city hostels (p.146) and those in the suburbs (p.148).

INNER CITY

City Public Hostel Vesterbro Ungdomsgård

Map 5, K6. Absalonsgade 8, Vesterbro

ⓣ 31 31 20 70

ⓕ 31 23 51 75

Bus #6 or #28

Easygoing and handily placed hostel, ten minutes' walk from Central Station between Vesterbrogade and Istedgade. There's a noisy sixty-bed dormitory on the lower floor, and less crowded four- to twenty-bed rooms on other levels, plus a kitchen. No curfew. Open May–Aug; 100kr per person.

Inter Point

Map 5, I6. Valdemarsgade 15, Vesterbo

ⓣ 33 31 15 74

Bus #3, #6 or #16

Run by the Danish YMCA/YWCA, with cheap dorm beds, though there are only 28 of them to be had and there's a 12.30am curfew. Open late June to early Aug; 80kr per person.

Jørgensen

Map 3, C4. Rømersgade 11, Indre By

ⓣ 33 13 81 86

ⓕ 33 15 51 05

Bus #5, #14, #16, #40, #150S, #154 or Nørreport S-Tog

Gay-friendly hostel-cum-hotel offering dormitory accommodation in three rooms of six to twelve beds, with a television in each room and breakfast included. It also has a few cheap and newly decorated doubles (❷). You can rent sheets for 30kr if you don't have a sleeping bag. Very central, near both Nørreport Station and Købmagergade; 115kr per person.

Løven

Map 5, L5. Vesterbrogade 30, Vesterbro

ⓦ 33 79 67 20

Bus #6, #28 or #550S

One of central Copenhagen's real bargains, this affordable guest house has spacious and pleasantly decorated rooms (all with shared bathroom), plus the use of a large and well-equipped kitchen. The major drawback is the noise – if you take a room on Vesterbrogade the din of traffic is horrendous, whilst those overlooking Stengade are battered at 8.30am every morning by church bells. Rooms facing the courtyard inside are quieter, though a bit pokey. ❷

Sleep-In
Map 6, I8. Blegdamsvej 132, Nørrebro
ⓣ 35 26 50 59
ⓕ 35 43 50 58
ⓦ www.sleep-in.dk
Bus #3, #10, #42 or #43
Vast hall divided into four-bed compartments, with a nice, if busy, atmosphere, young and friendly staff and sporadic free gigs by local bands; no curfew. Open July & Aug; 90kr per person.

Sleep-In Green
Map 6, D8. Ravnsborggade 18, Nørrebro
ⓣ 35 37 77 77
Bus #5, #16, #81N or #84N
Ecological hostel right in hip Nørrebro, featuring bright rooms of 10, 20 and 38 beds, good all-volunteer staff, and organic snacks. It also looks onto a pretty interior court-

yard, which is unfortunately off-limits to guests. Extra charge for bedding (20kr) and breakfast (30kr); noon–4pm lockout. Open late May to Sept; 85kr per person.

Sleep-In Heaven
Map 6, B6. Struenseegade 7, Nørrebro
ⓣ 35 35 46 48
ⓦ www.sleepinheaven.com
Bus #8, #12, #13 or #85N
Big hostel, next to Assistens Kirkegaard, with two large dorms, subdivided into four- and eight-bed sections, plus two tiny new self-contained "bridal suites" (though you still have to share a bathroom; ❷). Also has lockers, Internet access, and takes credit cards. 100kr per person.

Susanne's
Map 4, D7. Gammeltoftsgade 8, Indre By
ⓦ 33 11 83 74
Bus #14, #40 or Nørreport S-Tog
Excellent, tiny guesthouse with a homely atmosphere, centrally located in an apartment block just across the road from the Botanisk Have. Breakfast isn't included,

though there are cooking facilities if you want to make your own. Fills up quickly, so book ahead. ❶.

THE SUBURBS

Danhostel Copenhagen Amager

Map 1, D6. Vejlands Allé 200, Amager

ⓣ 32 52 29 08

ⓕ 32 52 27 08

ⓦ *www.danhostel.dk/amager*

Bus #46 or S-Tog to Sjælør, then #100S towards Sundbyvester Plads – a 20min journey. HI hostel on Amager, a twenty-minute journey from the city centre, with cheap but basic two- and five-bedrooms, plus laundry and kitchen. Tends to be crowded and noisy, though there's no curfew. HI members 90kr, non-members 120kr.

Danhostel Copenhagen Bellahøj

Map 1, C5. Herbergvejen 8, Brønshøj

ⓣ 38 28 97 15

ⓦ *www.danhostel.dk/bellahoej*

Bus #2, #11 or #82N to Herbergsvejen. Buses #8, #63 and #68 also stop close by. More homely than its rivals, situated in a residential part of the city a fifteen-minute bus ride from the centre, with cheap beds. Reception is open 24hr and there's no curfew, although there's a dormitory lockout from 10am–1pm. Closed Dec. HI members 90kr, non-members 120kr.

Danhostel Ishøj Strand.

Map 1, C6. Ishøj Strandvej 13, Ishøj

ⓣ 43 53 50 15

ⓦ *www.danhostel.dk/ishoj*

Ishøj S-Tog

Out near Arken and Ishøj beach, but within a ten-minute walk of Ishøj S-Tog station, this spanking new hostel has every facility imaginable, with great four-person rooms and dormitory beds, plus a decent café and shop. No curfew. Also near to Ishøj beach. Open all year. HI members 100kr, non-members 130kr.

CAMPSITES

The Danes' love affair with camping is evident from the quality of their **campsites**, which are mostly very well run and have excellent facilities. Some of the campsites near Copenhagen are in peerless locations by beaches or in woodlands, whilst all are easily accessible by public transport. Most also have full hook-ups for trailers and campervans, and some also have **cabins** – usually basic huts without bedding, though pleasant enough. Some campsites may ask for a **Danish Camping Pass** (45kr), available at most sites and valid for a year, though most don't.

Absalon

Map 1, C5. Korsdalsvej 132, Rødovre

☎ 36 41 06 00

Brøndbyøster S-Tog

Friendly campsite a ten-minute walk from Brøndbyøster S-Tog Station, about 9km to the west of the city. Good facilities for campers or those with caravans, and pleasant cabins for rent (2-6 people). Open all year.

Bellahøj

Map 1, C5. Hvidkildevej, Bellahøj

☎ 38 10 11 50

Bus #2, #8, #63 or #68

The cheapest of Copenhagen's campsites, and the nearest to the city centre, Bellahøj is rather grim, with temporary facilities and little cover from the elements. One plus point is its proximity to the excellent open-air Bellahøj public baths. Open June to August.

Charlottenlund Fort

Map 1, D5. Strandvejen 144B, Charlottenlund

☎ 39 62 36 88

Bus #6

Situated in the old fort at beautiful Charlottenlund beach, this excellent campsite is the best within easy striking distance of the city centre (bus #6 stops right outside). The excellent facilities are actually built inside the fort, and there

CAMPSITES

are also sites for camper vans and trailers. If you're camping, try to get a pitch around the back, where there's greater protection from the elements. Open May to September.

Nærum

Map 1, D4. Ravnebakken, Søllerød
☎ 45 80 19 57
Nærum Station
Fifteen kilometres north of the city centre (S-Tog to Jægersborg, then private train – InterRail and Eurail not valid – to Nærum), though in a very pleasant setting beside some woods. Very much family-oriented, with great play areas for the kids, though the staff can be slightly unfriendly. Cabins are also available (340kr for up to 4 people). Open mid-April to mid-Sept.

Tangloppen

Map 1, C6. Ishøj Havn, Ishøj
☎ 43 54 07 67
Ishøj S-Tog, then bus #128 or a 25min walk.
Right next door to Arken (see p.118), and facing onto a lagoon, Tangloppen is a wonderful place if you want a beach, modern art and not much else – shelter is minimal, and tents take a battering here in bad weather. There's also a cheap café selling grilled food and a number of cabins (225kr for up to 4 people; 350kr for up to 6) and hookup points for trailers and campervans.

Eating

In recent years, the number of **restaurants** of all descriptions in Copenhagen has increased dramatically, with a burgeoning array of designer places aimed at the city's young and wealthy alongside a raft of old-fashioned establishments offering expensive but excellent Danish fare. Traditionally, Danish cooking has been based on meat or fish plus two veg, though today it can encompass anything from delicious cuts of lean meat accompanied by wild mushrooms and berries to stodgy plates of grisly sausage. An affordable, if somewhat hit and miss, way to sample

PRICE CATEGORIES

The categories used to code our restaurants are based on the cost of a **single main course without drinks**.

Cheap Under 30kr

Inexpensive 30–60kr

Moderate 60–100kr

Expensive 100–150kr

Very expensive Over 150kr

DANISH MENU READER

Basics

Bread	Brød
Ice Cream	Is
Coffee (with cream)	Kaffe (med fløde)
Tea	Te
Milk	Mælk
Frankfurters/ sausages	Pølser
Cheese board	Ostebord
A selection of spiced and pickled herring	Sildebord
Sugar	Sukker
Noodles	Nudler
Rice	Ris
"Danish" pastry	Wienerbrød

Egg (æg) dishes

Boiled egg	Kogt æg
Fried eggs	Spejlæg
Omelette	Omelet
Scrambled eggs	Røræg

Fish (Fisk)

Cod	Torsk
Herring	Sild
Prawns	Store rejer
Salmon	Laks
Trout	Forel

Meat (Kød)

Beef	Bøf
Chicken	Kylling
Ham	Skinke
Lamb	Lam
Pork	Svinekød
Venison	Vildt

Vegetables (Grøntsager)

Beans	Bønner
Brussel sprouts	Rosenkål
Carrots	Agurk
Cucumber	Salatgurk
Lettuce, salad	Salat
Mushrooms	Champignoner
Onions	Løg
Peppers	Peberfrugt
Potatoes	Kartofler
Sweetcorn	Majs

Fruit (Frugt)

Apples	Æbler
Bananas	Bananer
Blueberries	Blåbær
Cherries	Kirsebær
Grapes	Vindruer
Melon	Melon
Orange	Appelsiner
Pineapple	Ananas
Raspberries	Himbær
Strawberries	Jordbær

traditional Danish food is to look for the chalk boards outside the city's *kros* (bars) offering *dagens ret* ("dailymeal"), set lunches or dinners where the emphasis is on affordable and nourishing home cooking. Another Danish speciality is the **smørrebrød** (see box on p.162), or open sandwich, normally a tiny piece of ryebread heaped with toppings such as cold meats, beef tartar or herring, to name but a few. If your Danish is a bit rusty, be aware that nearly all cafés and restaurants in Copenhagen have English-language menus, though you may have to ask for one.

For snacks or cakes, there's an amazing selection of **cafés**, often doubling as bars, many of which spill out onto the city pavements during summer. With large, cheap sandwiches available in most, they offer great value for money. Another Danish speciality is its excellent, and ubiquitous, **konditorier** (bakeries), which sell affordable pastries, cakes and bread. If you're really on a shoestring there are dozens of takeaway **pizzerias**, most of a reasonable standard, along with the ubiquitous **grill stands**, which offer a variety of sausages and burgers. Though not exactly cordon bleu, they can provide welcome pitstops on a long walk around the city. The immigrant community's impact is also being increasingly felt, with a large array of **kebab** and **curry** houses – probably Copenhagen's cheapest eating-out options – along with a good selection of (slightly pricier) **Thai** restaurants. **Vegetarians** are reasonably well catered for in Copenhagen – most restaurants will have at least a couple of meat-free dishes (see box on p.156 for a list of the best). We've given phone numbers for restaurants in all cases where it's advisable to book in advance.

If you're self catering, there are many good **health food shops** in the city. Three of the best places are *Naturpoteket* Torvegade 36, Christianshavn (Map 3, K6), *Solhatten*, Istedgade 85 (Map 5, K7), in Vesterbro and *Solsikken*, Blågårdsgade 33, Nørrebro (Map 6, C8).

EATING

●

We've divided our listings into the following areas: Indre By (p.154), Tivoli and around (p.164), Christianshavn (p.164), Vesterbro (p.166), Frederiksberg (p.168), Nørrebro (p.169) and Østerbro (p.170).

INDRE BY

Atlas Bar

Map 3, D6. Larsbjørnstræde 18 ☎ 33 15 03 52. Bus #14 or #16.
Mon–Fri 11am–10pm, Sat noon–10pm. **Moderate.**

On trendy Larsbjørnstræde in the basement underneath *Flyvefisken* restaurant, the *Atlas Bar* was originally a vegetarian restaurant which now also features non-vegetarian dishes (around 100kr) of an international – and usually spicy – nature, like Mexican chilli or Bali chicken. Portions are large and the menu is chalked up on a bar column – one side meat, the other fish and vegetarian. Always packed at lunchtime, when it's a good idea to book in advance.

Bankeråt

Map 3, B4. Ahlefeldtsgade 29. Bus #40.
Mon–Fri 9.30am–midnight, Sat & Sun 10.30am–midnight.
Inexpensive.

On the corner of Nansensgade, cosy *Bankeråt* is renowned for its affordable, quality dishes – mostly Asian, Italian and Mexican – and its free movie screenings on Sunday evenings in winter.

Café & Ølhalle "1892"

Map 3, C3. Rømersgade 22 ☎ 33 93 25 75. Nørreport Station.
Daily 11.30am–4pm, Nov–June closed Mon. **Moderate.**

In the basement of the Workers' Museum, the *1892* is the only restaurant in Copenhagen in a listed building, complete with 1930s decor and unique glass ceiling. Specializing in food from the period, such as traditional Danish *bidesild* (strongly flavoured pickled herring) washed down with schnapps. Lunchtime is always very busy – book in advance.

Dan Turéll

Map 3, G3. Store Regnegade 3.
Bus #31, #42 or #43.
Mon–Wed 10am–midnight,
Thurs 10am–2am, Fri & Sat
10am–4am, Sun 11am–midnight. Moderate.
French-style café off
Gothersgade devoted to the
memory of popular Danish
author Dan Turéll. French
and English breakfasts, sandwiches and wok meals are all
good, while the Dan Turéll
burger (beef or chicken; 90kr)
is big and tasty, and comes
with heaps of salad.

Davids

Map 4, D6. Sølvgade 91
℡ 33 13 80 56. Bus #10.
Tues–Fri 6pm–8.30pm.
Inexpensive.
Selling a single, set takeaway
meal (changes daily), *Davids* is
probably the best place in
town to get a carry out
(there's no in-house seating).
The food is a delightful blend
of Mediterranean and Danish
influences, such as scallops in
a creamy sauce with pesto and
cous-cous, and its proximity
to various parks means there's
no shortage of places to eat.

The price (60kr) includes a
loaf of freshly baked bread.
Call ahead, as meals are made
individually and take thirty
minutes to prepare.

Eastern Corner

Map 4, D7. Sølvgade 85A.
℡ 33 11 58 35. Bus #10.
Mon–Thurs & Sun 5pm–11pm,
Fri & Sat 5pm–midnight.
Moderate.
Affordable and reasonable Thai
restaurant. The red and green
curries are tasty and wellspiced, and there's a small barcafé attached if you fancy an
after-dinner coffee and cake.

L'Education Nationale

Map 3, D6. Larsbjørnsstræde
12 ℡ 33 91 53 60. Bus #14 or
#16.
Mon–Sat 11.30am–midnight,
Sun 4pm–midnight. **Moderate.**
Paris in Copenhagen: everything in this café comes from
France – even the butter on
the table – and the tipple of
choice is French wine by the
glass rather than the usual
Danish beer. The food is
well-made French country
cooking in large portions;
110kr for the meal of the day.

VEGETARIAN COPENHAGEN

Most Copenhagen restaurants have at least a couple of vegetarian options on the menu. The following places are some of the best:

Altas Bar (p.154)
Base Camp (p.164)
Den Grønne Kælder (p.157)
Hackenbusch (p.166)

Morgenstedet (p.165)
Picnic (p.169)
Spiseloppen (p.165)

Etcetera

Map 3, H3. Hovedvagtsgade 8
ⓣ 33 33 99 97. Bus #1, #6 or #9.
Tues & Wed 4pm–midnight,
Thurs 4pm–1am, Fri 4pm–3am,
Sat 6pm–3am. **Expensive.**
In a small street just off the west side of Kongens Nytorv, ultra-hip *Etcetera* is full of model types and men in poloneck jumpers sampling reasonable Tunisian/North African-inspired food. The seating on deep sofas is comfortable, though getting to your food on the table can prove a bit of a pain.

Europa

Map 3, F5. Amagertorv 1. Bus
#1, #6 or #29.
Mon–Wed 9am–midnight,
Thurs–Sat 9am–1am, Sun
10am–midnight. **Moderate.**

Overlooking Amagertorv and the Storkespringvand Fountain, the traditional, glass-fronted *Café Europa* is a welcome halfway point down Strøget for a cup of coffee, a superior slice of cake or a snack or light meal. Outdoor service is very efficient, so if you're in a hurry, this is the place to go.

Flyvefisken

Map 3, D6. Larsbjørnsstræde
18 ⓣ 33 14 95 15. Bus #14 or
#16.
Mon–Sat 5.30pm–midnight.
Moderate.
In the same building as the *Atlas Bar*, on the corner of Studiestræde and with a good view of goings-on in trendy Larsbjørnstræde, *Flyvefisken* offers up to 100 excellent

DANISH PASTRY AND BAKERIES

Bread- and pastry-making is a thriving business in Denmark, and you'll find a bakery around almost every corner in Copenhagen. Danes generally eat freshly made bread from the local bakers rather than sliced and packaged supermarket loaves. Try the *rundstykke* (literally "round piece"), a crispy bread roll baked with different combinations of seeds and grain, and eaten fresh at breakfast with butter and jam or cheese. Follow this with a piece of freshly made pastry and a cup of coffee and you have the traditional Danish breakfast. And don't expect the Danish pastries made in Denmark to resemble those you'll find abroad, however: they're less sweet and sticky, and much more flaky and crispy (in Denmark, Danish pastry is actually called *Wienerbrød*, "Viennese bread", because the art of making flaking pastry was learnt from bakers in Vienna).

Two of the city's best bakeries are *Kræmmerhuset*, Christianshavns Torv (Map 3, K6), which produces amazing bread baked in traditional stone ovens, plus great pastries and cakes, and *Reinh. Van Hauen*, Frederiksberggade 23 (Map 3, E7), which has over 27 years of organic baking to its credit and serves up mouthwatering *rundstykker* and pastries. For sit-down cakes and pastries, try *Café Europa* (opposite), *Konditoriet* (p.159), *La Glace* (p.160), *Norden* (p.160) and *Salonen* (p.169).

Thai dishes (around 100kr each) – try the excellent deli or deluxe menus (148kr and 210kr respectively).

Den Grønne Kælder
Map 3, G4. Pilestræde 48 ☎ 33 93 01 40. Bus #31, #42 or #43.

Mon–Sat 11am–10pm.
Moderate.
Cosy vegetarian place with a large selection of scrumptious dishes from a lunchtime buffet and an a la carte menu in the evening – try the beetroot roesti and garlic-roasted leeks.

Also serves organic wines and homemade bread.

Huset Med Det Grønne Træ

Map 3, E6. Gammeltorv 20 ⓣ33 12 87 86. Bus #5. April–Aug Mon–Fri 11am–3pm; Sept–March Mon–Sat 11am–3pm. **Expensive.** Frequented mostly by lawyers and solicitors from the nearby law courts, the "House with the Green Tree" offers some of the finer Danish lunches in the downtown area. The spread of *smørrebrød* leaves little to be desired; neither do the fourteen different types of schnapps.

Ida Davidsen

Map 4, J8. Store Kongensgade 70 ⓣ33 91 36 55. Bus #1, #6, #9, #10, #29 or #650S. Mon–Fri 10am–4pm. **Moderate.** Situated in an atmospheric cellar, this is one of the best places in town to sample the traditional Danish *smørrebrød*, with toppings including smoked salmon, herring and roast beef with powerful horseradish, all topped with a raw egg yolk, if you like.

Look out for members of the Danish royal family: they live just around the corner and often pop in for a quick bite.

Klaptræet

Map 3, E4. Kultorvet 13. Nørreport Station. Mon–Wed 10am–1am, Thurs 10am–3am, Fri & Sat 10am–5am, Sun 1pm–midnight. Inexpensive. Frequented during the week by backgammon-playing locals and exhausted shoppers, *Klaptræet* transforms during weekends to a busy hangout for the local high-school kids. Breakfasts are cheap and there are good-value light meals – quiche, pizza and suchlike – throughout the day. The enormous sandwiches – smoked turkey, brie, and roast beef (all 41kr) – are worth a try.

Klimt

Map 3, C3. Frederiksborggade 29 ⓣ33 11 76 70. Bus #5 or #16. Mon–Wed 10am–midnight, Thurs–Sat 10am–2am, Sun 10am–11pm. **Moderate.**

A small and cosy place on the busy thoroughfare from Indre By to Nørrebro, *Klimt* serves scrumptious fusion cuisine, focusing on high-quality fresh produce, at affordable prices (main courses 50–100kr), plus a large selection of choice teas, coffees, fruit juices and cognacs.

Konditoriet

Map 3, G5. Amagertorv 6. Bus #1, #6 or #29.
Mon–Thurs 11am–5pm, Fri 11am–6pm, Sat 10am–4pm.
Inexpensive.
Inside the Royal Copenhagen Porcelain shop (see p.38), *Konditoriet* is the place for a genteel cup of coffee or cocoa, or a Danish pastry or finger sandwich served up on the shop's own beautiful porcelain and silverware.

Kong Hans

Map 3, H4. Vingårdsstræde 6
☎33 11 68 68. Bus #1 or #6.
Mon–Sat 6pm–midnight. Very expensive.
One of Denmark's best restaurants, this classic French restaurant, boasting a Michelin star, is housed in a historic fifteenth-century vaulted basement that was once King Hans's wine cellar. The French menu with an Asiatic twist couldn't be more enticing, but reckon on around 600kr for a five-course meal.

Konrad

Map 3, G4. Pilestræde 12
☎33 03 29 29. Bus #31, #42 or #43.
Mon–Wed noon–1am, Thurs noon–2am, Fri & Sat noon–4am.
Expensive.
Serving fantastic Scandinavian food in an ultra-chic setting, *Konrad* pulls in the power-lunchers and business diners in their droves. Portions are small, prices are high and the service can be a little over fussy, but if you want to be seen this is one of the places to be – at least for the moment. Book ahead.

Krasnapolsky

Map 3, E6. Vestergade 10. Bus #5.
Mon–Wed 10am–2am, Thurs–Sat 10am–5am, Sun 2pm–midnight. Moderate.

EATING: INDRE BY

Spacious café off Strøget that caters for a broad range of customers, from suburban housewives on shopping sprees to hip techno freaks, with its almost round-the-clock service of chic, French-style café food. Brunch (40–75kr) is served until 2pm, or try the excellent Krasnapolsky burger.

Krogs Fiskerestaurant

Map 3, G5. Gammel Strand 38 ⓣ 33 15 89 15. Bus #29.
Mon–Sat 11.30am–4pm & 5.30pm–midnight. **Very expensive.**

One of the city's oldest, best and most expensive fish restaurants, located along the canalside where fisherwomen used to sell their catch. The classic interior, with high stucco ceilings, white tablecloths, golden mirrors, and eighteenth-century paintings, is kept as it was when the restaurant first opened in 1910. The delicious, five-course *menu gastronomique* costs 465kr; the equally mouthwatering traditional bouillabaisse with Danish fish and shellfish costs 200kr. Book in advance.

La Glace

Map 3, E5. Skoubogade 20. Bus #5.
Mon–Thurs 8am–5.30pm, Sat 9am–5pm, Sun 11am–5pm.
Inexpensive.

Time seems to have stood still here, with primly dressed waitresses ministering to a genteel clientele who come for the beautifully sculpted, cream-heavy layered cakes and real hot chocolate. It's just south of Vor Frue Kirke, on a tiny street between Strøget and Skindergade.

Norden

Map 3, G5. Østergade 61. Bus #1, #6 or #29.
Mon–Sat 9am–midnight, Sun 10am–midnight.
Moderate.

On the corner of Købmagergade and Strøget, with a fine view of the hectic shoppers below from the first floor. The café-style food – soups, sandwiches, quiches and pasta dishes – is good value, considering the location, and the mouthwatering cakes are freshly made every day.

Nyhavns Færgekro
Map 3, J3. Nyhavn 5 ⊤ 33 15
15 88. Bus #1, #6, #9 or #10.
Daily 11.30am–11.30pm.
Expensive to very expensive.
Located on the sunny side of
Nyhavn, *Færgekro* – the "ferry
inn" – serves unpretentious
and tasty traditional food,
either from the fish-laden
lunchtime open buffet (80kr)
or the a la carte restaurant
upstairs. Choice dishes
include the entrecôte and
pomme frites (155kr) and tit-
bits from the vast dessert table.

Pasta Basta
Map 3, F4. Valkendorfsgade 22
⊤ 33 11 21 31. Bus #5.
Mon–Thurs & Sun 1.30pm–3am,
Fri & Sat 11.30am–5am.
Inexpensive.
Open very late, and offering
an array of fish and meat pasta
plus a buffet of nine cold pasta
dishes, this is a favourite final
stop for all-night groovers,
and extremely popular with
young locals at all times.

Peder Oxe
Map 3, F5. Gråbrødretorv 11
⊤ 33 11 00 77. Bus #5.
Daily 11.30am–12.30am.

Expensive.
Very popular French-inspired
steakhouse on the small
Gråbrødretorv square, busy
both at lunch and dinner. The
main attraction is the salad buffet (109kr), including a juicy
organic Oxeburger, made of
finest beef. The only drawback
is the lack of space – it can be a
tight squeeze, and intimate
conversation is impossible.

Sommersko
Map 3, F4. Kronprinsensgade
6. Bus #31, #42 or #43.
Mon–Thurs 8am–midnight, Fri
8am–2am, Sat 9am–2am, Sun
10am–midnight. Moderate.
Busy, Parisian-style café off
Købmagergade serving simple
and filling food, like delicious
pasta with wild mushrooms,
daily until 11pm. Popular
meeting spot for Sunday
brunch (62–79kr).

Sporvejen
Map 3, F5. Gråbrødretorv 17.
Bus #5.
Daily 11am–midnight. Cheap.
Housed in the last of
Copenhagen's old trams – the
rest are now in Egypt – parked
up on Gråbrødretorv, inside

SMØRREBROD

The most characteristic, and perhaps the most appetizing, feature of Danish cuisine is the open sandwich, or **smørrebrød**, basically a thin slice of rye bread covered in fresh butter and heaped with an array of delicious foodstuffs. The traditional meal starts with a fish *smørrebrød*, followed by a meat *smørrebrod* and then a cheese *smørrebrod* (each washed down with a small glass of ice-cold schnapps). To the uninitiated, it can be a bit of a mystery which toppings go well together, though café and restaurant staff will always be pleased to introduce you to the mysteries of this Danish artform.

Smørrebrød come in one of three forms: either you order your toppings from a list of ingredients, or you construct your own sandwiches from a buffet, or you have your *smørrebrød* served up ready made. The first two can be difficult for the *smørrebrød* novice, as neither order forms nor buffet tables give much indication of which things can be mixed and which can't – as a general rule, don't combine different types of meat on the same slice of bread until you really know what you're doing.

Good restaurants for ready-made *smørrebrød* are *Ida Davidsen* (p.158) and *Café & Ølhalle "1892"* (p.154), while at *Huset Med Det Grønne Træ* (p.158) and *Hansens Gamle Familiehave* (p.168) you'll be ordering from a list of toppings. Fantastic and amazingly varied *smørrebrød* buffets can be found at *Traktørstedet på Rosenborg* (opposite) and *Kanalen* (p.165).

which you can sample some of the city's best burgers (omelettes for vegetarians) served up with egg and chips. There are blankets available to keep you warm if you want to sit outside on a chilly summer's night.

Sticks 'n' Sushi
Map 3, B4. Nansensgade 59
☏ 33 11 14 07. Bus #5 or #16.
Mon–Sat 6–11pm, Sun 6–10pm.
Moderate.

This classy sushi bar is among the city's favourite Japanese eateries. The menu changes according to the fresh fish of the season (try the *yakitori* sticks) and there are six different set menus (170–200kr). There's a second, takeaway, branch (open until 9pm) further down Nansengade.

Thorvaldsen Gourmetbar & Café

Map 3, G5. Gammel Strand 34 ⓣ 33 32 04 00. Bus #29. Mon–Thurs 10am–midnight, Fri & Sat 10am–2am, Sun 11am–11pm. **Moderate.**
Popular canalside café, serving a strange combination of Danish and Spanish food that somehow works well – try some spicy Danish herring with Spanish salad. There's a great view of the colourful frescoes of the Thorvaldsen's Museum from the seats outside, which get packed during summer.

Traktørstet på Rosenborg

Map 4, F8. Øster Voldgade 44 ⓣ 33 15 76 20. Bus #184 or #150S.
Daily 11am–3pm, closed Mon Oct–April. **Moderate.**
Just by the gatehouse of Rosenborg Slott and open only for lunches and early afternoon cake and coffee, *Traktørstet* focuses on traditional Danish fare – the *smørrebrod* and herring are exceptional. It's often crowded with tourists visiting the palace and it can be hard to find a seat – book a table or, on a warm day, sit outside on the lawn.

Tyvenkokkenhans-koneoghendeselsker

Map 3, F6. Magstræde 16 ⓣ 33 16 12 92. Bus #5.
Tues–Sat 6pm–1am. **Very expensive.**
Named after the Peter Greenaway film *The Cook, the Thief, his Wife and her Lover*, this cosy and charming restaurant (on a small street running east off Rådhusstræde near the Use It office) offers a fantastic selection of set menus (from 350kr), ranging from four to twelve courses and featuring traditional Scandinavian fare with a modern twist. Individual a la carte dishes are also available, along with a

EATING: INDRE BY

great wine list, and service is excellent.

TIVOLI AND AROUND

Glyptoteket

Map 3, F8. Dantes Plads. Bus #8, #10 or #34.

Tues–Sun 11am–4pm.

Moderate.

The Ny Carlsberg Glyptotek's restaurant, set in the gallery's incomparable Winter Gardens, makes for one of the best lunchtime settings in town – even in the middle of winter the atmosphere is warm and uplifting. The food is excellent – try the pickled herring (*sild*), one of the best in town, served with dollops of sour cream, fresh bread and chives. Also has great homemade cakes and wonderful coffee.

CHRISTIANSHAVN

Base Camp

Map 3, N2. Halvtolv bygningen 148, Holmen ⊤ 70 23 23 18. Bus #8.

Mon–Wed & Sun 11am–1am, Thurs–Sat 11am–5am, kitchen closes at 11pm. Moderate.

Gigantic combined eaterie, nightclub and live-music venue located in the Danish Navy's old artillery hall on the Arsenaløen island part of Holmen. Though there's room for up to 750 diners, the place never appears empty, and the fusion food with an oriental twist is good. The enormous and delicious all-you-can-eat Sunday brunches (80kr; served until 3pm) tempt diners here from all over the city.

Bastionen og Løven

Map 3, M6. Voldgade 50, Christianshavn ⊤ 32 95 09 40. Bus #31 or #37.

Mon–Thurs & Sun 10am–midnight, Fri & Sat 10am–1am.

Moderate.

Set in the miller's house next to the Løven windmill, this is a superb spot for a bite of traditional Danish food – try the house speciality, fish meatballs on rye bread covered in *remoulade* (a sort of tartare sauce and mayonnaise with chopped pickles). The large buffet brunch is also popular. There's peaceful outdoor seating in summer, with

EATING: TIVOLI AND AROUND • CHRISTIANSHAVN

a pretty view of the old city moat.

Era Ora

Map 3, L6. Torvegade 62, Christianshavn ☎ 32 54 06 93. Bus #2, #8 or #9.

Mon–Sat 6pm–midnight. **Very expensive.**

Top-flight new-Italian cuisine – more fish, less pasta – good enough to earn a Michelin star and priced accordingly, with a five-course set menu costing 550kr. Popular with power-lunchers and expense-account executives. Book well in advance.

Kanalen

Map 3, L5. Wilders Plads 31, Christianshavn ☎ 32 95 13 30. Bus #2, #8 or #9.

Mon–Sat 11.30am–midnight. **Expensive.**

Intimate, romantic canalside restaurant in an eighteenth-century building which was formerly the police photographer's dark room – there's outdoor service under a canopy too. The lunchtime menu consists of a delicious traditional *smørrebrød* buffet; the evening a la carte menu is mostly French.

Månefiskeren

Map 3, N5. Fremtidsskoven, Christiania. Bus #8.

Tues–Sun 10am–1am. **Cheap.**

Impossible to miss (look for the large, colourful sign painted on a bright-red cast-iron gate), off Pusherstreet heading north towards the bike shop, *Månefiskeren* is a reliable and informal café renowned for its morning servings of eggs and bacon, followed later in the day by excellent sandwiches and home-made cakes. No alcohol, but joints are welcome.

Morgenstedet

Map 3, N5. Langgaden, Christiania. Bus #8.

Mon & Wed–Sun noon–9pm. **Cheap.**

Vegetarian and vegan buffet food from a mainly organic kitchen – there are usually five dishes, such as salad, curry and ratatouille. The tables are decorated with pots of fresh rosemary and you can help yourself to pickled ginger and chilli. No alcohol is served, but you can bring your own.

Spiseloppen

Map 3, N5. Christiania

⊤ 32 57 95 58. Bus #8.
Tues–Sun 5–10pm. Inexpensive.
Upstairs from the music venue
Musikloppen, this award-
wining restaurant serves superb
food that won't break the
bank. The frequently changing
but always appealing menu
includes a variety of vegetarian
dishes along with specialities
such as venison roast with
raspberry compote (150kr).
Very popular, so book ahead.

VESTERBRO

Bang & Jensen
Map 5, J7. Istedgade 130. Bus
#16.
Mon–Fri 8am–2am, Sat
10am–2am, Sun 10am–mid-
night. Moderate.
At the quieter end of
Istedgade – no sex shops
here – this popular café
serves brunch daily until 6pm,
featuring a wide range of
unusual foods which you can
combine in novel ways – try
the *ymer* (a mild, creamy
yoghurt) with maple syrup.
Sandwiches, pasta and quiches
are offered from lunch
onwards, before the place

transforms into a cocktail bar
in the evening.

Boyesen
Map 5, J5. Værnedamsvej 10
⊤ 33 31 70 55. Bus #1, #14 or
#28.
Mon–Fri & Sun noon–11pm, Sat
11am–11pm. Expensive.
One of the city's most
renowned restaurants, the offbeat *Boyesen* offers an excellent menu of both Danish and
international fish and meat
dishes. Afterwards, try some
of the incredible homemade
chocolate, flavoured with outlandish ingredients including
curry powder.

Hackenbusch
Map 5, H6. Vesterbrogade 124
⊤ 33 21 74 74. Bus #6 or #550S.
Mon–Wed 10am–2am, Thurs
10am–4am, Fri & Sat 10am–5am,
Sun 10am–midnight, kitchen
closes at 10pm. Inexpensive.
Long-established place with a
bar in front and an excellent
Mediterranean-style restaurant
at the back. Try the spicy and
delicious "frog burger" – its
ingredients are a well-kept
secret (but don't be put off by
the attention-grabbing name,

it's actually made of beef) –
on offer on Tuesdays (25kr) in
the restaurant.

K-2

Map 5, L6. Abel Cathrinesgade
21. Bus #6, #16 or #28.
Daily noon–11pm. **Inexpensive.**
Very good-value north Indian
restaurant ten minutes' walk
from Central Station serving
standard curry-house staples
like tandooris and biryanis.
The three-course set meal is a
real bargain, and actually
cheaper than an à la carte
main course.

Merhaba

Map 5, M6. Abel Cathrinesgade
7 ⓣ33 22 77 21. Bus #6, #16 or
#28.
Mon, Tues & Sun noon–midnight,
Fri & Sat noon–1am. **Moderate.**
Scandinavia's first Turkish
restaurant, *Merhaba* still serves
up good Anatolian cuisine,
including a three-course set
meal for 79kr – there's belly
dancing at weekends, too, if
you can stomach it.

Shezan

Map 5, L6. Viktoriagade 22.
Bus #16.

Mon–Sat 11.30am–midnight, Sun
11.30am–11.30pm. **Inexpensive.**
Copenhagen's first Pakistani
restaurant, popular with sub-
continental expats, and still
going strong. The fiery dishes
come in mild, medium and
strong – be warned, even
medium burns your tongue
off. Choose a table overlooking Istedgade if you want free
entertainment watching the
infamous red-light district
street.

Thai-Esan

Map 5, M6. Lille Istedgade 7
ⓣ33 24 98 54. Bus #16 or
Central Station.
Tues–Sun noon–11pm.
Inexpensive.
Exceedingly popular Thai
restaurant serving cheap, hot,
no-frills food in a fairly
authentic Thai atmosphere,
with plastic dishes and dan-
gling, fake-gold decorations.
Always very busy, so book
ahead.

Zugar Baby

Map 5, H6. Vesterbrogade 113.
Bus #6 or #28.
Daily 9.30am–12.30am.
Inexpensive.

EATING: VESTERBRO

Slap-bang in the middle of lively Vesterbro, *Zugar Baby's* speciality is its burgers (40kr), though you can also get English and French brunches (eggs and bacon, and croissants and jam respectively) here until 3pm. Convenient for a late snack too – the kitchen's open until 11.30pm.

FREDERIKSBERG

Café den Blå Hund
Map 2, B8. Godthåbsvej 28
T 38 87 46 88. Bus #2, #11.
Mon–Sat 10.30am–2am, Sun 11am–1am, kitchen closes at 10pm. Inexpensive.
Mediterranean-style café-restaurant featuring enormous sandwich platters and tapas. Speciality main courses include grilled goat's cheese with crab tails, or chicken salad with bacon and cold curry sauce (both 52kr). During summer, tables are moved across the road to Axel Møllers Have and a small stage erected for live jazz. It's just north of Frederiksberg S-Tog: walk north up Falkoner Allé and turn left into Godthåbsvej.

Hansens Gamle Familehave
Map 5, E6. Pile Allé 10–12
T 36 30 92 57. Bus #18 or #28.
April–Sept daily 11am–midnight.
Moderate.
On the edge of Frederiksberg Have, this historic, summer-only outdoor restaurant dishes up some of the city's most stunning, open sandwiches, with a fantastic spread of herring, cold meats and cheeses, all lavishly decorated with fresh salad, pickles, fried onions and other *smørrebrod* essentials.

Café Sokkelund
Map 5, C3. Smallegade 36e.
Bus #1 or #14.
Mon–Wed 9am–midnight, Thurs & Fri 9am–1am, Sat 10am–1am, Sun 10am–8pm. Inexpensive.
Midway between the Royal Copenhagen porcelain factory and Frederiksberg Town Hall, *Sokkelund* is a convenient watering point after a factory tour or a visit to the Saturday flea market on the town hall parking lot, with a selection of coffee, snacks and light meals. The small monthly concerts – at the better end of

the Danish pop-rock scale –
are worth seeking out.

NØRREBRO

- - - - - - - - - - - - - - - - - - -

Floras Kaffebar

Map 6, C8. Blågårdsgade 27.
Bus #5 or #16.
Mon–Wed & Sun 10am–midnight, Thurs–Sat 10am–1am.
Inexpensive.
Situated on one Nørrebro
best-kept streets, *Floras* has
outdoor seating on sunny days
and daily specials, plus soups
and cakes, all served in an
easygoing atmosphere. Come
back at night for cheap beer.

Kashmir

Map 6, D6. Nørrebrogade 35
℡ 35 37 54 71. Bus #5 or #16.
Daily 5pm–midnight. Inexpensive.
One of Nørrebro's best bargains, with decent Indian
food at affordable prices, and
conveniently located on the
area's main thoroughfare.

La Mer

Map 6, C8. Blågårds Plads 10
℡ 35 37 22 24. Bus #5 or 16.
Daily noon–10pm, closed July.
Inexpensive.

Set on one of the city's most
laidback squares – a delightful
spot in the summer – this is
one of city's best fish restaurants, and affordably priced,
with fish and chips (42kr),
plus more elegant meals of
grilled fish.

Picnic

Map 6, D7. Fælledvej 22b. Bus
#3.
Mon–Fri 11am–10pm, Sat & Sun
noon–10pm. **Cheap.**
Tiny and friendly sandwich
and lunch place near Skt Hans
Torv. Not much seating, but a
great pit stop, particularly if
you're heading to Fælled Park
for an afternoon's lazing.
Huge sandwiches cater to
most appetites and budgets.

Salonen

Map 6, C9. Peblinge Dossering
6. Bus #5 or #16.
Daily 10am–11pm. Inexpensive.
This super-hip Nørrebro
coffeehouse provides a genial
atmosphere in which to quaff
excellent coffee and munch
your way through ice cream,
cakes and light meals. Has
outdoor tables with lakeside
views and a waterside terrace

on a floating dock too, and also rents paddleboats for cruising the Peblinge Lake.

ØSTERBRO

Amokka

Map 4, F3. Dag Hammarskjolds Allé 38–40. Bus #6 or #14.
Mon–Wed 11am–11pm, Thurs & Fri 11am–midnight, Sat 10am–11pm, Sun 10am–10pm.
Inexpensive.
Popular Østerbro coffeehouse serving wonderful pastries, some of the best coffee in the city, plus an eclectic mix of Danish- and international-inspired sandwiches and lunches, a special children's menu and speciality chocolates.

Circus

Map 6, J8. Rosenvængets Allé 7 ⓣ 35 55 77 72. Bus #6 or #14.
Mon–Thurs & Sun 11am–1am, Fri & Sat 11am–2am. Moderate.
An eccentric mix of delicatessen, hairdresser and restaurant, *Circus* is one of Copenhagen's most original and popular places to eat. Booking is advised, particular-

ly at weekends, though in fine weather the seating spills out onto the pavement. The menu changes weekly, but expect a varied selection of international cuisine – one permanent fixture are the superb mussels, delicately marinaded in white wine.

Guldanden

Map 6, I8. Sortedam Dossering 103 ⓣ 35 42 66 06. Bus #6 or #14.
Mon–Sat 5.30pm–9pm.
Expensive.
One of Østerbro's best restaurants, with great views over the lakes, magical on a moonlit evening. Serving both themed fixed menus ("Spanish", "wild food", "spring") and a la carte dishes, prices are high, but it's well worth a splurge. Excellent wine list.

Park

Map 6, K7. Østerbrogade 79 ⓣ 35 42 62 48. Bus #6 or #14.
Mon–Wed & Sun 11am–midnight, Thurs–Sat 11am–5am.
Moderate.
A very popular French-inspired restaurant with a café

atmosphere and a relaxing roof garden, *Park* offers everything from simple, though tasty, burgers through to large beef steaks with all the trimmings. Book ahead, particularly at weekends, when it becomes a nightclub after midnight.

Drinking

Drinking is a favourite pastime for many Danes, with
liberal licensing laws, a relaxed attitude to alcohol
and the lowest prices in Scandinavia (a combination
which has proved irresistible to the hundreds of thirsty
Swedes who pile off the ferry each weekend and drink
themselves senseless in Copenhagen's bars). Denmark's
drinking holes come under a bewildering variety of names:
a *vinstue* (literally "wine room"), is an old and traditional
venue, while a *værtshus* tends to be a small, dimly lit and
smoke-filled place, populated with locals playing dice and
billiards. *Bodegas* are generally neighbourhood drinking
holes, while the French café aspires to the hip and fashionable – most also serve some kind of light food. The newest
introductions, British and Irish pubs, haven't really caught
on outside Indre By. The Danish *kaffebar* is the equivalent
of the British greasy spoon, but serving beer instead of tea,
and with less food on the menu. Bars are more neutral and
cover just about everything not mentioned above.

The choice of drink in Copenhagen's bars has traditionally been quite limited, though this is gradually changing.
Lager-style **beer** is still without doubt Denmark's staple
drink. The two most common brands are Tuborg and the
ubiquitous Carlsberg, usually sold by the bottle, less frequently in 250ml or 500ml draft measures – bottled beer is

DANISH DRINKS

Beer	Øl	Red wine	Rødvin
Export beer (very strong lager)	Eksport-Øl	White wine	Hvidvin
		Apple juice	Æblemost
		Orange juice	Appelsin juice
Draught beer	Fadøl		
Strong beer	Guldøl	Carbonated soft drink	Sodavand
Christmas beer	Juleøl		
		Buttermilk	Kærnemælk
Easter beer	Påskeøl	Soda water	Mineralvand
Wine	Vin	Tomato juice	Tomatjuice
House wine	Husets vin		

cheaper than draft (20–30kr per bottle; draft beer can cost up to 80kr for half a litre). During Christmas and Easter the breweries also brew "Christmas" and "Easter" beers – a bit stronger than normal beer and a lot more festive. The two days when they are released – "J-Day" and "P-Day" (J for *Jul* and P for *Påske* – Christmas and Easter respectively) see beer enthusiasts all around the country venturing out to taste the latest offerings. Guinness and draft British and Irish ales can generally only be found in British- and Irish-themed pubs, and are quite pricey. **Wine** is also usually available in most bars, though in Denmark it's still predominantly drunk with meals and you won't usually have the same choice as in restaurants. **Cocktail bars** are the newest trend in Danish nightlife, and are worth checking out for their tasty specialities.

Opening hours vary according to police licensing and the bar owner's inclination, though you'll be able to find somewhere to drink at any time of the day or night – it's generally always possible to find a bar open within walking distance of your last venue and so-called "death routes" have been mapped out, walking from bar to bar to ensure all-night drinking. As the evening moves on, more lively dancing venues are selected, often ending before breakfast in a traditional *værtshus* with billiards and a jukebox. If you're shopping for wine or beer, note that shops aren't allowed to sell alcohol after 8pm.

We've divided our listings into the following areas:
Indre By (p. 174), Tivoli and around (p.178), Christianshavn (p.178), Vesterbro (p.180), Frederiksberg (p.182), Nørrebro (p.183) and Østerbro (p.185).

INDRE BY

Bo-Bi Bar
Map 3, F4. Klareboderne 14. Bus #31, #42, #43 or Nørreport S-Tog. Mon–Sat noon–2am, Sun 2pm–2am.
Home to Copenhagen's oldest bar counter – an idea first introduced to the city by a New York-returned sailor in 1917 – this small and cosy drinking hole is now patronized by inner-city professional types, students and artists.

Café Dan Turéll
Map 3, G3. Store Regnegade 3. Bus #31, #42 or #43. Mon–Wed 10am–midnight, Thurs 10am–2am, Fri & Sat 10am–4am,

Sun 11am–midnight.
Named after the popular Danish author, this swanky café-bar, covered in steel and mirrors, sports Turéll book covers above the bar and an arty but sociable student crowd. During summer the large front opens out onto the street.

Café Floss
Map 3, D6. Larsbjørnstræde 10. Bus #5, #14 or #16. Daily noon–2am.
Small and lively café-bar which manages to be hip and homely at the same time. Guldøl (Tuborg's strong gold beer) and tequila are on special offer during happy hour between 10pm and 11pm.

THE HØCKER BEER

In the warm summer months the cold *høcker* beer – the generic name for any beer bought in a shop and drunk outside – can't be beaten. In Denmark, drinking al fresco – on beaches, parks, or simply catching a ray of sun on a city bench – isn't frowned upon as a sign of homelessness and alcoholism, but rather seen as an appreciation of life and the great outdoors. So do what the locals do: stock up at a corner shop, find a spot you like and settle down with your own bag of supplies.

Foley's Irish Pub
Map 3, E5. Lille Kannikestræde 3. Nørreport S-Tog.
Daily 11am–4am.
Dim lighting and a superabundance of candles give this place an almost ecclesiastical feel (an effect only slightly spoilt by Sky Sports above the bar). Often the final stop for local Irish after a night of pub-crawling. Decent food too.

Globe Irish Pub
Map 3, D5. Nørregade 45. Bus #5.
Mon, Tues & Sun 1pm–1am, Wed 1pm–2am, Thurs & Fri 1pm–3am, Sat noon–5am.
Loud, flashy and spacious Irish pub, with lots of televised sports, although your fellow drinkers are more likely to be tourists or Danish theatre folk than expats from the Emerald Isle.

Hviids Vinstue
Map 3, H3. Kongens Nytorv 19. Bus #1 or #6.
Mon–Thurs & Sun 10am–1am, Fri & Sat 10am–2am.
Old-fashioned *vinstue* dating back to 1723 – Hans Christian Andersen may have been a regular, since he lived just around the corner – whose many crowded rooms are patrolled by uniformed and respectful waiters. Outdoor seating in summer.

Krasnapolsky
Map 3, E6. Vestergade 10. Bus #5.
Mon–Wed 10am–2am, Thurs–Sat

10am–5am, Sun 2pm–midnight.
Hip and hi-tech, this trend-setting establishment features Copenhagen's longest bar counter and Danish avant-garde art on the walls. Yuppies and techno freaks hang out here side by side with ritzy shoppers from nearby Strøget, while from Thursday to Saturday a DJ delivers techno and house in the back room dancing area. The bartenders can be difficult, but don't let this put you off.

Musen og Elefanten
Map 3, D6. Vestergade 21. Bus #14 or #16.
Mon–Thurs, Fri 3pm–5am, Sat & Sun 5pm–2am.
Personable bar set up in homage to its owner's twin obsessions: Carlsberg Elephant Beer – one of the strongest in Denmark – and traditional rock music. Draught Elephant flows from a carved trunk into the glasses of the rock fiends who sit around having their ears blown off.

Nyhavn 17
Map 3, I3. Nyhavn 17. Bus #9, #10 or #29.

Mon–Thurs & Sun 10am–2am, Fri & Sat 10am–4am.
Located on fashionable Nyhavn, this is a cross between a British pub and a maritime museum, with old iron diving helmets, ships' figureheads, anchors and rudders scattered around the dimly lit interior – the gleaming brass bar fittings are the only bright feature. Popular among tourists and Danes alike, with moderately priced draught beers and ciders.

Sabines Cafeteria
Map 3, C6. Teglgårdsstræde 4. Bus #14 or #16.
Mon–Sat 10am–2am, Sun 2pm–2am.
Small and easygoing café-bar where the city's young and good-looking begin their evening's drinking. During the day, a more sedate clientele comes here to drink coffee and read the newspapers.

Café Smash
Map 3, D6. Skt Peders Stræde 24a. Bus #5, #14 or #16.
Mon 10am–5pm, Tues & Wed 10am–11pm, Thurs 10am–midnight, Fri & Sat 10am–1am.

BARS WITH OUTDOOR SEATING

Alléenberg (p.182); al fresco drinking in a tranquil garden in smart Frederiksberg.

Barbar Bar (p.180) and **Café Obelix** (p.181): outdoor seating on cobbled Vesterbro Torv.

Base Camp (p.178): soak up the atmosphere by a peaceful and picturesque canal on the island of Holmen.

Café Den Blå Hund (p.182): sit outside on Axel Møllers Have – you may catch one of the jazz concerts which are sometimes held here.

Front Page (p.183): enjoy a view of the waters of Sortedams Sø lake with the city in the distance.

Hviid's Vinstue (p.175): traditional old *vinstue* which spills out onto busy Kongens Nytorv in good weather.

Nemoland (p.179): at the heart of the "free city" of Christiania and a good place to people-watch.

Park Café (p.186): rooftop seating looking out over Fælledparken and busy Østerbrogade.

Pussy Galore's Flying Circus (p.184) and **Sebastopol** (p.185): right on trendy Skt Hans Torv square – *the* place to be seen.

Plush bar with Denmark's largest selection of cocktails. Tell the bartender your favourite colour and flavour and he'll mix you a delicious blend of rainbow liquors. A tad pricey, but good fun. The café also serves reasonable food.

Café Sommersko
Map 3, F4. Kronprinsensgade 6. Bus #31, #42 or #43.
Mon–Thurs 8am–midnight, Fri 8am 2am, Sat 9am–2am, Sun 10am–midnight.
Popular and spacious French-style café on two levels with

bright red plastic sofas and waiters with attitude. On summer Sunday afternoons, there's free live music to soothe away hangovers.

Stereo Bar
Map 3, C4. Linnésgade 16a. Nørreport S-Tog.
Wed–Sat 8pm–3am.
Almost invisible from the road, but a few steps up from street level lead you into a dark, smoke-filled and usually overcrowded bar where music takes first priority, with DJs in the cellar playing jazz-oriented world music.

TIVOLI AND AROUND

Bryggeriet Apollo
Map 3, C9. Vesterbrogade 3. Bus #6, #8, #12 or #28.
Mon–Thurs 11am–midnight, Fri & Sat 1.30pm–2am, Sun 3pm–midnight.
Freshly brewed on the premises, *Bryggeriet*'s organic beer is served up amidst gleaming vats, copper kettles and heavy wooden tables; food is available in the bright upstairs section. If you want

you can have your beer served in a Belgian "Kwak", similar to a short-yard glass – if you're not careful, you end up pouring beer all over yourself. Not surprisingly, it's all a tad pricey, but worth it.

The Old English Pub
Map 3, D8. Vesterbrogade 2b. Bus #6 or #28.
Mon–Fri noon–3am, Sat & Sun 10am–5am.
One of the fancy Anglophile drinking establishments outside the Scala entertainment complex, this English theme pub is so thoroughly and lavishly kitted out with British paraphernalia that it's impossible not to be impressed. Also boasts the widest selection of beers in Copenhagen, including a couple of British ales.

CHRISTIANSHAVN

Base Camp
Map 3, N2. Halvtolv bygningen 148, Holmen. Bus #8.
Mon–Wed & Sun 11am–1am, Thurs–Sat 11am–5am.
Hip and happening, this gigantic naval shed, located in

out-of-the-way Holmen, houses a combined restaurant (see p.164), bar, concert hall and nightclub (see p.190) – an unusual venue for all-night drinking. There's bungee jumping by the canal and other outdoor activities like wall climbing during summer.

Eiffel Bar

Map 3, L5. Wildersgade 58. Bus #2, #8, #9, #19, #28, #31 or #37. Daily 9am–2am.

Next door to smart *Café Wilder* (see below), though this traditional drinking den couldn't be more different. Rumours of its shifty past, featuring assorted sailors and can-can girls, add to the serious drinking atmosphere, while the old carved mirrors and the tricolour hanging outside takes you back to raucous Paris in the 1930s. Prices are very reasonable.

Nemoland

Map 3, N5. Christiania. Bus #8. Mon–Thurs & Sun 10am–2am, Fri & Sat 10am–3.30am.

One of Christiania's two main watering holes, and among Copenhagen's most popular

open-air bars during summer, when it's often packed with tourists and shoppers tasting their purchases from nearby Pusherstreet. It's quieter during winter, with regulars playing backgammon or billiards.

Rabes Have

Map 3, J8. Langebrogade 8. Bus #5, #11 or #30. Daily noon–midnight.

Supposedly the oldest bar in Copenhagen – it has a documented history dating back to 1632 – this bohemian venue offers everything a local pub should: beer at reasonable prices, a selection of traditional Danish food and the obligatory billiard table. Popular among the rich and famous.

Café Wilder

Map 3, L5. Wildersgade 56. Bus #2, #8, #9, #19, #28, #31 or #37. Daily 9am–2am.

Old-time favourite among trendy Christianshavners (Helena Christiansen supposedly comes here), this slightly run-down but always busy corner café sells good, though pricey, food and drink. Look out for *Wilder*'s trademark painting in the bar: an abandoned naked woman left with a pile of empty beer bottles.

Woodstock
Map 3, N5. Pusherstreet, Christiania. Bus #8.
Daily 9am–5am.
Housed in a ramshackle former military barracks on Pusherstreet, easygoing *Woodstock* is the place to enjoy a laidback drink in an unpretentious bar kitted out with old garden furniture and full of 1960s spirit.

VESTERBRO
- - - - - - - - - - - - - - - - - - - -

Bang & Jensen
Map 5, J7. Istegade 130. Bus #16.
Mon–Fri 11am–2am, Sat & Sun 10am–2am.
Vesterbro's newest in-place has high stucco ceilings and a mahogany counter left over from its former incarnation as a pharmacy. The classic old shop front has been maintained, along with the period wall decorations. It's usually packed with students, especially on Saturday nights.

Barbar Bar
Map 5, K6. Vesterbrogade 51. Bus #6 or #28.
Mon–Wed 10am–1am, Thurs–Sat 10am–2am, Sun 11am–6pm.
Located on Vesterbro Torv near the City Museum, this unassuming place is a favourite of up-and-coming musicians and a relaxing spot for a quiet drink. There's al fresco service on the square during summer.

Hackenbusch
Map 5, H6. Vesterbrogade 124. Bus #6.
Mon–Thurs 10am–2am, Fri & Sat 10am–5am, Sun 10am–midnight.
One of Vesterbro's older and more eccentric cafés, frequented by a mixed set. The popular and slightly pricey restaurant attracts wealthy trendsetters, while the crazy front bar, furnished with high steel-wire sofas and an ancient Portuguese table football, caters to more alternative types. The music selection, however, doesn't seem to have changed much since the place opened in the 1980s.

Keegans Bar

Map 5, L5. Stenosgade 1. Bus #6 or #28.

Daily 4pm–5am.

A scuzzy but lively late-night/early-morning drinking den with an Anglophone clientele – beer is served in pints rather than half litres. A selection of stouts, such as Guinness and Kilkenny, is sold at very reasonable prices, and it's a cheap place for a late-night drink. There's also Sky Sports and late-night pool games.

Café Ludwigsen

Map 5, H6. Sundesvedsgade 2. Bus #6.

Mon, Tues & Sun noon–2am, Wed noon–3am, Thurs–Sat noon–5am.

Outrageously popular late-night bar (despite the "café" in the name, there's no food) where the young, free and extremely desperate congregate en masse after hours.

Café Obelix

Map 5, K6. Vesterbrogade 53. Bus #6 or #28.

Daily 8.30am–2am.

This winsome tribute to the large, menhir-wielding Breton pulls in Vesterbro's yuppies, who drink amongst themed decorations based on the Gaulish cartoon village. During summer, tables are moved outside and gas heaters make even cool nights bearable.

Pinden

Map 5, N5. Reventlowsgade 4. Central Station.

Daily 10am–2am.

Across the road from Central Station, *Pinden* (The Stick) is a traditional, smoky drinking den where local old-timers hang out on worn-out furniture playing the odd game of dice – a much more entertaining meeting point than the station's cold platforms and shiny cafés.

Café Sorte Hest

Map 5, H6. Vesterbrogade 135. Bus #6.

Mon–Thurs 11am–midnight, Fri 11am–1am, Sat 10am–1am, Sun 10am–9pm.

Once a stronghold of BZ squatters during their battles with the police, *Sorte Hest* is now a swanky café

DRINKING: VESTERBRO

181

where you can enjoy a quiet beer without fear of hurled cobblestones or tear gas – look out for the peculiar small glass-floor art exhibit. A pianist plays music from Chaplin movies every Sunday lunchtime and there are live bands one weekend a month.

FREDERIKSBERG

90eren
Map 5, H4. Gammel Kongevej 90. Bus #1 or #14.
Mon–Wed 11am–1.30am, Thurs–Sat 11am–2am, Sun 1pm–1am.
Famous for its painstakingly pulled draught beer, an operation which can take up to twelve minutes, *90eren* is the only bar in Copenhagen serving un-carbonated beer (it's brewed at the nearby Carlsberg brewery). The strong hops flavour is reminiscent of English real ale and – supposedly – very similar to the original Carlsberg beer produced in the mid-nineteenth century.

Alléenberg
Map 5, E4. Allégade 4. Bus #18.
Mon–Sat 10pm–5am.
Decorated with Danish theatre memorabilia, this lively bar is the preferred watering hole of the local Frederiksberg theatre crowd of wannabes and will-bes – they'll probably give you a tune on the piano at some point – and the last stop for the neighbourhood's high-school students after late nights on the town.

Café Den Blå Hund
Map 2, B8. Godthåbsvej 28. Bus #2 or #11.
Mon–Sat 10.30am–2am, Sun 11am–1am.
By day, people come here to drink coffee, read newspapers and chat. After sunset, the draught beer begins to flow and, on a few nights a week, there's live jazz. During summer, the café spills out across busy Godthåbsvej to Axel Møllers Have, where covered seating is available, serviced by tray-balancing white-aproned waiters. Good food, too (see p.168)

Café Svejk

Map 5, C3. Smallegade 31. Bus #1 or #14.

Mon–Thurs 3pm–2am, Fri & Sat noon–2am, Sun 1pm–8pm.

Near Frederiksberg Have, Svejk's claim to fame is its Czech draught beer, Bohemia Regent, a refreshing change if you've had enough of Danish brands. There's also live jazz at weekends, and a 42-inch screen showing football matches at other times.

NØRREBRO

- -

Barcelona

Map 6, D7. Fælledvej 21. Bus #3, #5 or #16.

Mon–Thurs & Sun 11am–2am, Fri & Sat 11am–5am.

Located close enough to Skt Hans Torv to be considered part of the hip Nørrebro café scene, this swanky, two-level hangout – restaurant upstairs, café-bar downstairs – is converted during weekends into the *Bar'Cuda* night club, when the back-room dance floor becomes a sweaty cavern of funk and soul. The restaurant serves well-prepared

Danish and southern European dishes, and the tapas in the downstairs café are tasty accompaniments to a vast array of drinks.

Café Blågård's Apotek

Map 6, C8. Blågårds Plads 20. Bus #5 or #16.

Daily 3pm–2am, in summer open from noon.

Homely bar, still patronized by some of the left-wing activists who used to clash on this square with the police during the 1970s. They're now joined by a less commit-ted crowd who come to sam-ple the bar's many wines and Urquell draught beer. Gets jam-packed during weekends, when there's also live jazz, blues or rock.

Front Page

Map 6, E8. Sortedam Dossering 21. Bus #5 or #16.

Mon–Wed & Sun 11am–1am, Thurs–Sat 11am–1am.

Attractive lakeside café-bar, especially popular in summer, when tables are moved out-doors to the lakeside and you can contemplate the city from afar over a relaxing drink. In winter, service moves inside to a cosy cellar. There's good-value food in the *Siden af Front Page* restaurant next door.

Café Gokken & Kokken

Map 6, D5. Nørrebrogade 114. Bus #5 or #16.

Mon–Thurs 10am–midnight, Fri & Sat 10am–2am, Sun 10am–11pm.

Close to Assistens Kirkegården, with a varied (if not exactly stylish) clientele, this thoroughly unpretentious bar offers solid entertainment at weekends, when the volume on the small sound system is turned up and everyone sings along, and cosy lazing around during the week. Reasonably priced food available too.

Mexibar

Map 6, D7. Elmegade 27. Bus #3.

Mon–Thurs 5pm–2am, Fri & Sat, Sun 6pm–1am.

On the corner of Skt Hans Torv and Elmegade, this small and easily missed basement venue looks from the outside rather like an abandoned travel agency, with a dusty Mexican sombrero and a string of colourful Christmas lights in the window. Step inside, though, to find one of the best-value cocktail bars in town, with superb drinks and a lively mix of tourists and locals.

Pussy Galore's Flying Circus

Map 6, E7. Skt Hans Torv 30. Bus #3.

Mon–Fri 8am–2am, Sat & Sun 9am–2am.

Named after the nubile hero-ine of the James Bond movie *Goldfinger*, you'll be stirred if not shaken by unusual cock-tails like Cuban *mojritos* (rum, lemon and lime, mint and soda water), an extensive list of schnapps, tasty wok dishes and outdoor seating on one of Nørrebro's hippest squares – definitely a place to be seen.

Café Rust

Map 6, D7. Guldbergsgade 8. Bus #3, #5, #16.

Mon 6pm–midnight, Tues–Sat 6pm–5am.

Crowded, multi-level dive

named after Mathias Rust, who cheated advanced radar systems and sleeping Russian bureaucrats when landing his small Cessna plane on Moscow's Red Square in 1987. His adventure resulted in the pan-Scadinavian peace initiative, the Next Stop Sovjet, which was based in this building. *Rust* subsequently began to host live bands, and is still one of the city's most popular music venues (see p.191). Features include a new dance floor, with stage and bar, a popular and laid-back minimalistic cocktail bar and, in the basement, one of Copenhagen's hippest DJ-ing venues.

Sebastopol

Map 6, E7. Skt Hans Torv 2. Bus #3.

Mon–Wed & Sun 9am–1am, Thurs–Sat 9am–2am.

Classy Parisian-style café crowded at weekends with well-groomed professionals warming up for a night out. As the evening moves on, the outdoor drinking area on Skt Hans Torv gradually expands to include the cobblestones.

The more budget-minded join the crowd with beer from the cornershop across the road.

ØSTERBRO

Circus

Map 6, J8. Rosenvængets Alle 7. Bus #1 or #6.

Mon–Wed & Sun 11am–1am, Thurs–Sat 11am–2am.

Formerly a butcher's – look out for the impressive frieze illustrating the life of a cow from green field to butcher's knife – *Circus* has recently been converted into an unusual combination of deli shop, hair dressing salon and bar-restaurant, all under one roof. Food here, predominantly Danish cuisine, is a tad pricey, but the bar is comfy.

Kruts Karport

Map 6, G9. Øster Farimagsgade 12. Bus #14 or #40.

Mon–Sat 11am–2am, Sun 12am–1am.

Small Parisian-style neighbourhood café-bar which prides itself on having Denmark's largest whisky selection (mainly Scotch single malts) and on being the only bar in Copenhagen selling absinthe. Arranges whisky tastings and cigar evenings, with accompanying talks, during the winter.

Park Café

Map 6, K7. Østerbrogade 71.
Bus #4 or #16.
Mon & Sun 11am–midnight, Tues & Wed 11am–2am, Thurs 11am–5am, Fri & Sat 11am–6am.

One of Denmark's largest cafés, with a classical interior of high stucco ceilings, polished rotating doors, crystal chandeliers and marble pillars. Quiet in the day, it transforms by evening into a vibrant pick-up joint, while a drinks list as long as your arm, live music a couple of nights a week, and a disco from Thursday to Saturday all add to the party atmosphere – expect queues at weekends. There's a great view of Østerbro from the rooftop terrace.

Rytme Hans

Map 6, J8. Østerbrogade 35.
Bus #1 or #14.
Mon–Wed 2pm–2am, Thurs 2pm–3am, Fri 2pm–4am, Sat 11am–4am, Sun 11am–2am.

Small and cosy neighbourhood café-bar with cheap drinks, named after a music groupie who, in the 1970s, spent years following the popular Danish band Gnags around to all their gigs on a small moped.

Café Theodors

Map 6, K7. Østerbrogade 106.
Bus #6 or #14.
Mon–Wed 11am–midnight, Thurs 11am–2am, Fri & Sat 11am–4am, Sun noon–7pm.

Combined venue with a top-class, pricey French restaurant at the back and a cool, Art Deco-ish café-bar at the front. Quiet and sedate during the day, the clientele becomes younger and a lot louder at evenings and weekends, as it fills up with disillusioned swingers opting out of the hectic meat market across the road at *Park*.

Live music and clubs

Copenhagen is Scandinavia's party town, and has a nightlife to suit the widest – and wildest – tastes, at least at weekends, although things can be fairly subdued during the week. The city's liberal drinking laws, the most relaxed in Scandinavia, pull in punters from far and wide – it's particularly popular with Swedes, who descend on the city en masse in search of a good time. A wide range of **bars** (see p.172) and **clubs** cater to fun-lovers of all ages, with every sort of music from bebop to bhangra; entrance is usually around 40–50kr.

There's also a healthy raft of **live music** venues. Traditionally, the **jazz** scene has always been the city's liveliest – a legacy of the number of respected American jazz musicians such as Dexter Gordon and Ben Webster who lived here during the 1960s and 1970s – and the annual jazz festival is world renowned, whilst there are a number of other festivals worth investigating (see box on p.189). There's also a healthy local **rock** music scene, while many big-name international acts include Copenhagen on their tours (while many more turn up for the huge Roskilde

Festival – see p.129). A number of the smaller venues double as cafés during the day and bars in the evening, before becoming live music venues or nightclub after midnight.

Many of the larger venues sell **tickets** through **Billetnet** (credit card booking line ☎ 70 15 65 65), at Vesterbrogade 3 beside Tivoli's main entrance and in all post offices (10kr booking fee). You can also **book online** at many of the venues listed below – we've given Web sites where they exist.

LIVE MUSIC

We've divided our live music listings into the following areas: Indre By (below), Tivoli and around (p.190), Christianshavn (p.190), Vesterbro (p.191), Nørrebro and Østerbro (p.191), Amager (p.192).

INDRE BY

Copenhagen Jazzhouse/Natclub

Map 3, F5. Niels Hemmingsensgade 10.
☎ 33 15 26 00
ⓦ www.jazzhouse.dk
Bus #5, #29 or Nørreport S-Tog.
Mon–Wed & Sun 6pm–midnight, Thurs–Sat 6pm–5am.
Copenhagen's premier jazz venue, this large, smart, two-level club is frequented by jazz lovers of all ages. Club nights feature a mix of live blue note, R 'n' B and soul, after which a DJ takes over and the venue turns into a nightclub.

JazzHuset Vognporten

Map 3, F6. Rådhusstræde 13.
☎ 33 15 63 53
Bus #5 or #29.
Mon–Sat 11am–1am.
Located in the same building as Huset and Use It. Monday to Thursday are for bebop and mainstream, whilst Friday and Saturday feature old-fashioned

LIVE MUSIC: INDRE BY

JAZZ FESTIVALS

Copenhagen's premier jazz event, the **Copenhagen Jazz Festival** (early to mid-July; ⓦ *www.djf.dk*), stages free concerts on the city's main squares, plus evening concerts at venues throughout the city. Music ranges from traditional Dixieland to modern experimental jazz, performed by local musicians and big international names. In September, the **Swinging Copenhagen Jazz Festival** puts the emphasis on traditional Dixieland: more than a hundred indoor and open-air jazz concerts are held over four days throughout the city at around forty venues. Most of the open-air events are free; big indoor events at places like the Copenhagen Jazzhouse cost up to 150kr. The week-long **Autumn Jazz** (early November), held in a dozen of the city's top music venues, offers everything from mainstream bebop to traditional swing. Full programmes for all these festivals are available at tourist offices in the city.

jazz to dance to. It's a small and laidback venue, though it manages to squeeze in a surprisingly large dance floor.

La Fontaine
Map 3, F6. Kompagnistræde 11.
ⓣ 23 44 97 77
Bus #5 or #29.
Daily 10pm–5am.
Frequented largely by up-and-coming Danish hopefuls, this is the place to come if you're into small smoky rooms and surprise appearances by the

big boys of jazz when they're visiting the city. Later in the evening the stage is thrown open to aspiring performers in the audience.

Mojo
Map 3, F7. Løngangsstræde 21c.
ⓣ 33 11 64 53
ⓦ *www.mojo.dk*
Bus #5 or #29.
Daily 8pm–5am.
Live music nightly in this small blues venue with plenty of down-at-heel

ambience, popular with aficionados of all ages. Less established local acts get things going before the big names come on stage.

TIVOLI AND AROUND

Cirkus
Map 3, C7. Jernbanegade 8.
ⓣ 33 16 37 00
ⓦ *www.cirkusbygningen.dk*
Bus #8, #13, #14 or #46.
Historic early twentieth-century venue (see p.80) hosting established rock acts in an intimate atmosphere, with excellent acoustics and steeply tiered seating which gets you right up close to the performers.

Pumpehuset
Map 3, C7. Studiestræde 52.
ⓣ 33 93 19 09
ⓦ *www.pumpehuset.dk*
Bus #5, #14, #16 or Vesterport S-Tog.
The city's spacious former pumphouse offers a broad sweep of middle-of-the-road rock, hip-hop and funk from Denmark and abroad about eight times a month.

Tivoli
Map 3, D8–E8. Central Station.
ⓣ 33 15 10 01
ⓦ *www.tivoli.dk*
Surprisingly good, sometimes even groundbreaking, live outdoor rock-pop every Friday night during summer – with a good crowd and decent weather it can be great fun. Entry is free with general Tivoli admittance.

CHRISTIANSHAVN

Base Camp
Map 3, N2. Halvtolv bygningen 148, Holmen.
ⓣ 70 23 23 18
ⓦ *www.basecamp.dk*
Bus #8.
Mon–Thurs 6pm–1am, Fri 6pm–5am, Sat 11am–5am, Sun 11am–1pm.
Housed in the former Holmen naval base, this cavernous complex hosts mainstream pop and rock concerts once or twice a month on its main stage, plus live jazz on the patio during Sunday brunch (see p.164).

Loppen
Map 3, M5. Christiania.

ⓣ 32 57 84 22

ⓦ www.loppen.dk

Bus #8.

Wed & Thurs 9pm–3am, Fri &
Sat 10pm–5am.

On Wednesday nights this
cool converted warehouse on
the edge of Christiania hosts
both established and experimental Danish rock, jazz and
performance artists, and quite
a few visiting British and
American ones too. Thursdays
to Sundays are disco nights,
popular with Christiania
residents.

Sofies Kælder

Map 3, L7. Sofiegade1,
Christianshavn.

ⓣ 32 54 29 45

Bus #2, #3, #8, #9, #19, #28,
#31, #37, #350S.

Daily 2pm–2am.

An old favourite among fol-
lowers of Danish rock, this
popular and laidback bar transforms at weekends into a live-
music venue: Fridays feature
local rock acts, while Saturdays
are devoted to folk, and
Sundays to jazz jam sessions.
There's a small dance floor
too.

VESTERBRO

Vega

Map 5, I6. Enghavevej 40,
Vesterbro.

ⓣ 33 25 80 12

ⓦ www.vega.dk

Bus #3, #16 or Enghave S-Tog.

In a former union hall, this
newish music venue retains its
1950s and 1960s decor –
zigzag tiles and red plastic sofas
– while showcasing plenty of
modern alternative rock. Keep
your eye out for local and
visiting luminaries: Björk
apparently loves the place, as
does Lene from Aqua.

NØRREBRO AND
ØSTERBRO

Café Rust

Map 6, D7. Guldbergsgade 8,
Nørrebro.

ⓣ 35 24 52 00

ⓦ www.rust.dk

Bus #3, #5, #16.

Mon & Tues 7.30pm–2am,
Wed–Sat 11pm–5am.

One of the best-known venues
in town, this multifaceted
place right on busy Skt Hans

Torv hosts up-and-coming live music acts on its main stage. Downstairs is the very hip *Bassment* nightclub (see p.195) specializing in hip-hop and cool, funky grooves. It's also a popular bar (see p.184).

Pavillonen

Map 6, J5. Fælled Park, Østerbro.

ⓣ 35 26 01 11

ⓦ *www.pavillonen.dk*

Bus #1.

Mid-May to mid-Sept Mon–Wed & Sun 11am–11pm, Thurs–Sat 11am–5pm.

Summer-only open-air venue in Fælled Park. Sunday to Tuesday it's an ordinary café, but from Wednesday to Saturday there's a barbecue followed by a diverse selection of Danish rock bands at 8pm and a DJ playing funk and acid from 10pm.

Ungdomshuset

Map 6, D5. Jagtvej 69,

Nørrebro. Bus #5, #16 or #18. This famous venue (see p.101) has long been a meeting place for the city's wilder youth subcultures, and having survived the threat of demolition it's now enjoying a resurgence of fortunes, even hosting part of the eminently respectable Copenhagen Jazz Festival. Come here if you want non-commercial underground music – check the posters plastered all over the building's front for details.

AMAGER

Femøren

Map 1, D6. Amager Strandpark.

Bus #12 or #13.

Huge, inexpensive open-air rock concerts by top local bands and international acts from June to August on a big, temporary stage a stone's throw from Amager beach.

Check with the tourist office and see p.106 for details of free outdoor summer concerts and festivals at Fælled Park.

CLUBS

We've divided our club listings into the following areas:
Indre By (below), Tivoli and around (p.194), Vesterbro and
Frederiksberg (p.195), Nørrebro and Østerbro (p.195).

INDRE BY

Krasnapolsky
Map 3, E6. Vestergade 10.
ⓣ 33 32 88 00
ⓦ www.krasnapolsky.dk
Bus #5.
Mon–Wed 10am–2am,
Thurs–Sat 10am–5am, Sun
2pm–midnight.
This ultra-cool bar is also home
to a weekend disco (Thurs, Fri
& Sat) where the terminally
fashionable come to dance
away the night to mainly ambi-
ent house and techno sounds.

Nasa-Slide-Fever
Map 3, H3. Boltens Gård.
ⓣ 33 93 74 15
Bus #31, #42 or #43.
Thurs 11pm–3am, Fri & Sat mid-
night–5am.
You don't have to be rich and
famous to come here, but it

helps, and you'll certainly need
to dress up to have any chance
of getting in. Of the three
clubs, *Nasa*, on the top floor –
the haunt of Danish and visiting international movie and
music stars – is by far the most
exclusive. Downstairs, *Slide*
and *Fever* are marginally more
relaxed and easier to get into,
though you'll still need to slip
on a posh party frock.

Sabor Latino
Map 3, D7. Vester Voldgade 85.
ⓣ 33 11 97 66
ⓦ www.saborlatino.dk
Bus #5, #14, #16, #150S.
Thurs 9pm–3am, Fri & Sat
9am–5am.
Salsa bar, long popular among
the city's small South
American community and
now increasingly hip as
Copenhagen discovers Latin
fever. Free Salsa classes every

Friday and Saturday between 10pm and 11pm.

Stereo Bar

Map 3, C4. Linnésgade 16.
ⓣ 33 13 61 13
Bus #5, #14, #16 or Nørreport S-Tog.
Wed–Sat 8pm–3am.
Right on up-and-coming Israel Plads, this is *the* Nørrebro place for 1970s retro music – illuminated by lava lamps – plus Latino, jazz and world-music nights.

Subsonic

Map 3, E5. Skindergade 45.
ⓣ 33 13 26 25
ⓦ *www.subsonic.dk*
Bus #5.
Fri & Sat 11pm–5am.
DJs pump out a 1980s groove in this very funky place with a big dance floor, a beer cellar and copy of an old SAS airport lounge, including original airplane seats.

Woodstock

Map 3, E6. Vestergade 12.
ⓣ 33 11 20 71
ⓦ *www.woodstock.dk*
Bus #5.
Thurs 9pm–5am, Fri & Sat 7pm–5am.
Basically a large dance floor and not much else, *Woodstock* pulls in a large, fun-loving older crowd willing to bop to anything with a beat, though the music is predominantly retro, from Abba all the way back to Elvis.

TIVOLI AND AROUND

Mantra

Map 3, D8. Bernstorffsgade 3.
ⓣ 33 11 11 13
ⓦ *www.mantra.dk*
Central Station.
Thurs–Sat 11pm–7am.
Right beside Tivoli Gardens in a former jazz club, this is one of the best and most central disco and house music nightspots in town; Thursday is reggae night; Friday and Saturday are for soul and R 'n' B. The decor features leather sofas and a gorgeous panoramic mural of the city. Thursdays is Reggae Dub Club.

Q-House of Dance

Map 3, C7. Axeltorv 5.
ⓣ 33 11 19 15
Bus #1, #12, #13, #14, #46 or Vesterport S-Tog.

Thurs 11pm–5am, Fri & Sat
11pm–6am.

Unmissable, multicoloured
dance club, easily reachable
(and visible) from Central
Station. A bit staid, with an
older clientele, but fine if
you're looking to tango until
dawn.

Rosie McGee's

Map 3, D8. Vesterbrogade 2a.
Ⓣ 33 32 19 23
Bus #6, #28, Central Station or
Vesterpot S-Tog.
Mon–Wed 11am–2am, Thurs
11am–4am, Fri & Sat 11am–5am,
Sun 11am–midnight.
A stone's throw from
Rådhuspladsen, *Rosie McGee's*
pub-style venue attracts many
Anglophone visitors. There's a
restaurant and bar downstairs,
but it's the upstairs disco that
gives life to the place, pump-
ing out mainstream pop until
dawn to a diverse crowd.

VESTERBRO AND FREDERIKSBERG

- - - - - - - - - - - - - - - - - - - -

Ideal Bar & Night Club

Map 5, I6. Enghavevej 40,
Vesterbro.

Ⓣ 33 25 80 12
Ⓦ *www.vega.dk*
Bus #3, #16 or Enghave S-Tog.
Fri & Sat 11pm–5am.
Latin and swing music club in
Vesterbro; part of the
immensely popular *Vega* (see
p.191). DJs play funky beats
and soulful sounds in this large
bar with lot of dancing space.
Gets very busy after 1am.

Kellerdirk

Map 5, E5. Frederiksberg Allé
102, Frederiksberg.
Ⓣ 33 25 22 53
Ⓦ *www.kellerdirk.dk*
Bus #18 or #28.
Mon–Thurs & Sun noon–mid-
night, Fri & Sat noon–5am.
A restaurant and theatre café
during the week, at 11pm on
Fridays and Saturdays *Kellerdirk*
throws open its spacious back-
room disco, sometimes featuring live jam sessions, but mostly
with danceable disco, house,
mainstream, Latin and Afro.

NØRREBRO AND ØSTERBRO

- - - - - - - - - - - - - - - - - - - -

Bassment and Club Lust

Map 6, D7. Guldbergsgade 8,

Nørrebro.

ⓣ 35 24 52 00

ⓦ *www.rust.dk*

Bus #3, #5 or #16.

Wed–Sat 11pm–5am.

Part of the *Rust* complex (see p.191) near Skt Hans Torv, *Bassment* is a small and cosy downstairs club which focuses on serious dancing. Thursday is house night, Friday progressive acid, and Saturday jazz funk, Afro and Latin, house and breakbeat. On Wednesdays the venue becomes *Club Lust*, geared towards a slightly older clientele, with music ranging from hip-hop to drum 'n' bass.

Park Diskotek

Map 6, K7. Østerbrogade 79, Østerbro.

ⓣ 35 42 62 48

ⓦ *www.parkcafe.dk*

Bus #6, #14 or #650S.

Thurs 10pm–5am, Fri & Sat 10am–6pm.

Popular club with disco and house music, plus bar and café, catering to a fun, diverse crowd, who jam the place, especially the open deck during summer.

Stengade 30

Map 6, C7. Stengade 18, Nørrebro.

ⓣ 35 36 09 38

ⓦ *www.subcity.dk/stengade30/*

Bus #3, #15, #16 or #350S.

Wed & Sun 2pm–2am, Thurs–Sat 2pm–5am.

Popular among a younger local crowd, rough-and-ready *Stengade 30* stages alternative live garage and hardcore acts followed by all-night dance parties, mainly to techno.

Performing arts and film

I n cultural terms, Copenhagen entered the new millennium at a crossroads. On the one hand there are those who want to see the city continue as a stronghold of conservative Danish traditions; on the other, those who would like it to reinvent itself as a cosmopolitan regional hub, drawing on its burgeoning immigrant community and its new links via the Øresund Bridge with Malmö in Sweden, which has increased the city's catchment area by half a million. At the moment, however, Copenhagen still delivers a relatively conservative array of culture, and it's the traditional "high" arts – **opera**, **classical music** and mainstream **theatre** – which get most of the government's enormous subsidies, with more experimental ventures struggling to survive even on the fringe. An exception in recent years has been the lively film industry, and to some to degree alternative theatre, both of which have managed to escape the city's often parochial mindset.

Tickets to many live performances can be bought through **Billetnet** (credit card booking line ☎ 70 15 65 65), at Vesterbrogade 3 beside Tivoli's main entrance and in

A HOME FOR THE ARTS?

One symbol of Copenhagen's current cultural uncertainties are the arguments surrounding the city's various performing arts venues. The possible closure or redevelopment of Tivoli's concert hall, a major venue for orchestral music, and the size limitations of Det Kongelige Teater, have led to plans to build a massive, purpose-built auditorium for opera, music and ballet in the new suburb of Ørestad (see p.115) – although many have wondered how sensible it would be to have the city's main concert hall in such an out-of-the-way suburb. To add to the general uncertainty, octogenarian Maersk McKinney Møller, Denmark's richest man, has recently announced plans to build a huge new opera house-cum-concert hall at the northern end of Holmen, a project which, if it goes ahead, will radically alter the cultural landscape of Copenhagen.

all post offices (10kr booking fee). **ARTE** sell tickets – including same-day tickets at half price – for theatre performances and concerts through its outlet at the Tivoli ticket office on Vesterbrogade (April–Sept daily 10am–10pm; Oct–March Mon–Fri 10am–7pm, Sat 10am–5pm). For **listings** information, pick up a copy of the English-language *Copenhagen Post* (15kr) from the Wonderful Copenhagen tourist office near Tivoli.

CLASSICAL MUSIC AND OPERA

Copenhagen boasts a wide range of **classical music** and is home to a number of top-class ensembles – including the Zealand Symphony Orchestra, the Academic Orchestra and Choir, and the Danish Radio Symphony Orchestra and Choir – and two **opera** companies, based at Det Kongelige Teater and Den Anden Opera. Thanks to subsidies, **tickets** are fairly cheap: there are many free concerts in the city, though seats for big opera productions can run as high as 1200kr – tickets for most performances are available through Billetnet.

There are also regular classical music concerts in many of Copenhagen's grandest **churches**, including Vor Frue Kirke, Vor Frelsers Kirke, Marmorkirken, Skt Petri Kirke and the church in Kastellet – a free quarterly programme listing all these concerts is available from the churches themselves or from the Wonderful Copenhagen tourist office; most are either free or very modestly priced. Look out, too, for concerts in the city's **museums** (including Ny Carlsberg Glyptotek, Louisiana, Arken, the Statens Museum for Kunst and the National Museum) and in the Queen's Hall of the Black Diamond.

An excellent resource on classical music in Copenhagen is the Danish Music Information Centre, at Gråbrødretorv 16 (Ⓣ 33 11 20 66, Ⓦ *www.mic.dk*), which has information on all aspects of Danish music.

Den Anden Opera
Map 3, G4. Kronprinsensgade 7, Indre By
Ⓣ 33 93 60 93
Bus #31, #42 or #43.
An offbeat alternative to Det Kongelige Teater (see opposite), Den Anden Opera ("The Other Opera") stages small-scale new chamber operas by contemporary Danish composers.

Det Kongelige Teater
Map 3, I4. Kongens Nytorv, Indre By
Ⓣ 33 69 69 69
Ⓦ *www.kgl-teater.dk*
Bus #1, #6, #10 or #31.
Copenhagen's grandest theatre and opera house, with prices to match, stages a fairly conservative range of mainstream operas and classical concerts. Prices rise according to the scale of the production

(100–1200kr), and tickets for popular works sell out very fast. Tickets bought from the box office after 5pm on the day of performance are reduced by 50 percent, and you can book online seven days in advance. Tickets not available through Billetnet.

Radiohuset Koncertsal
Map 5, K1. Rosenørns Allé 22, Frederiksberg
ⓣ 35 20 30 40
Bus #2, #3, #8, #11, #13, #68, #69 or #250S.
A classic of twentieth-century Danish architecture – all wood panelling and sweeping curves – Radiohuset is also something of a white elephant, having been built ten metres shorter than originally planned due to lack of funds, a shortcut which drastically affected the hall's acoustics. Now hosts regular performances by the Danish Radio Symphony Orchestra.

Rundetårn
Map 3, E4. Købmagergade, Indre By
ⓣ 33 73 03 73
Bus #5 or Nørreport Station.
Regular chamber-music recitals (50–80kr), generally at weekends, with a free concert in the observatory every full moon.

Tivolis Koncertsal
Map 3, E9. Tietgensgade 20, Indre By
ⓣ 33 15 10 01
ⓦ *www.tivoli.dk*
Bus #1, #2, #6, #8, #28, #29, #550S, #650S, Vesterport S-Tog or Central Station.
Inside Tivoli, the garden's concert hall stages a variety of classical performances, often featuring the major national orchestras. Tickets are available through Billetnet, except for concerts put on by Det Kongelige Teater (see p.199), which must be bought direct from them.

FILM

The Danes' love affair with celluloid stretches back to the 1920s, when the country's thriving film studios looked for a time as though they would become Europe's answer to Hollywood. Now, at the start of the new millennium, the Danish film industry is booming again, with the country's filmmakers achieving international critical acclaim, culminating in May 2000, when Lars von Trier won the Palme d'Or at Cannes with his film *Dancer in the Dark*.

> The weekly *Film Kalenderen* programme (in Danish only) includes details of almost all of Copenhagen's cinematic offerings and is available free in most cinemas.

Despite all this, however, most cinemas in Copenhagen offer the standard repertoire of mainstream Hollywood flicks, though you may find more offbeat offerings at the city's arthouse cinemas, particularly the Posthuset Teater and Filmhuset. Nearly all films in Copenhagen are screened in their original language, with Danish subtitles. Most cinemas offer reductions earlier in the day, with prices being staggered up to the most expensive evening and weekend screenings – from about 30–40kr to 60–80kr. At weekends, it's definitely worth booking ahead. Cinemas are not part of the Billetnet system.

From early to mid-March the city takes part in the **Night Film Festival**, during which cinemas across the country screen large numbers of mostly foreign films (with English subtitles) which wouldn't otherwise be seen in Denmark, along with a few previews, and retrospectives showcasing the work of particular actors.

FILM

Cinemateket at Filmhuset

Map 3, F3. Gothersgade 55, Indre By

ⓣ 33 74 34 12

ⓦ *www.dfi.dk*

Bus #31, #42, #43, #350S or Nørreport S-Tog

Closed Mon.

Three-screen, state-of-the-art cinema showing the best of Danish and international art-house film – the more eagerly anticipated films sell out quickly, so bookings are advisable. The Benjamin theatre shows children's films and free documentaries, and the complex also houses a reasonable café, a decent film bookshop and fantastic cinematic archives (see p.66).

Dagmar

Map 3, D7. Jernbanegade 2, Indre By

ⓣ 33 14 32 22

ⓦ *www.dagmar.dk*

Bus #8, #12, #14, #16, #150S or Vesterport S-Tog.

Mainstream arthouse cinema in the heart of Copenhagen containing five theatres and a bust of Carl Theodore Dreyer, the Danish director of the Oscar-winning *The Last Passion of Joan of Arc*, who was the cinema's manager for a short period.

Gloria

Map 3, E7. Rådhuspladsen 59, Indre By

ⓣ 33 12 82 32

ⓦ *www.gloria.aok.dk*

Bus #5, #8, #12, #14, #16, #29, #150S or S-Tog Vesterport.

Recently refurbished cinema excellently located right in the centre of the city, with an eclectic programme of specially imported films and arthouse favourites. Also sells a range of arthouse films through its own video distribution arm, some of which can be hard to find elsewhere. A cine buff's delight.

Imperial

Map 3, C8. Ved Vesterport, Vesterbro

ⓣ 70 13 12 11

Vesterport S-Tog.

Copenhagen's largest cinema, and the usual site for gala openings and premieres. The enormous single screen – the biggest in Scandinavia – shows mainly middle-of-the-road Hollywood blockbusters, with reclining seats and a stunning sound system.

FILM

DOGME 95

Established in 1995 by Lars von Trier, the golden boy of Danish film, **Dogme 95** is perhaps the most distinctive European film movement of recent years. Founded in reaction to the usual Hollywood reliance on special effects and massive budgets, Dogme 95 is basically a set of rules designed to enhance cinematic realism – only hand-held cameras and natural lighting are allowed, and no special costumes, special effects or extraneous soundtracks are permitted. Three of the best known Dogme films are Danish: *Idiots*, by von Trier himself, *Festen* by Thomas Vinterberg and *Mifune's Last Chance* by Søren Kragh Jacobsen. Some commentators have derided Dogme 95 as cheap gimmick, but although at first it was largely ignored outside the European arthouse scene, it's now attracting international interest – at the last count, no less than fourteen accredited Dogme films had been created, including ones from as far afield as Korea and Argentina.

Palads
Map 3, C8. Axeltorv 9, Indre By
Ⓣ 70 13 12 11
Vesterport S-Tog.
One of the world's first and largest multiplexes, this Copenhagen landmark, with its famously gaudy exterior, shows Hollywood-blockbuster fare on all seventeen of its screens.

Park Bio
Map 6, K7. Østerbrogade 79, Østerbro
Ⓣ 35 38 33 62

Bus #6, #14, #650S.
One of the oldest in town, this atmospheric single-screen cinema tends to show the more commercial arthouse films towards the end of their runs. Also has a decent café-bar.

Posthuset Teater
Map 3, F6. Rådhusstræde 1, Indre By
Ⓣ 33 11 66 11
Bus #5, #29, Nørreport S-Tog or Vesterport S-Tog.
A must for cine-buffs – look

FILM

out for British director Peter Greenaway's signature on the ceiling – Posthuset is a labour of love, kept running on a very limited budget by its film-fanatic owner. Typically screens long runs – it holds the Danish record of three years – of specially imported films, though lack of funds forces it to close periodically. Also has a cosy café.

Vester Vov Vov

Map 5, K6. Absalonsgade 5, Vesterbro

ⓣ 33 24 42 00

ⓦ *www.vester.vov-vov.dk*

Bus #6, #16, #28 or Central Station.

Three-screen arthouse cinema, with a decent bar and café for pre-screen nibbles. Also has a large and fairly comprehensive collection of film posters, some of them for sale.

THEATRE AND DANCE

Whilst the state subsidizes every ticket at the showpiece Det Kongelige Teater to the tune of 2000kr, the majority of the city's **theatres** have to compete for limited government funds – more alternative performance groups often struggle to compete with traditional, state-funded ensembles or theatres. A few youthful and dynamic theatres and companies have recently appeared, though as they only stage Danish-language productions, they're unlikely to be of interest to most visitors. London Toast Theatre is a British company that performs English-language light comedies and musicals in the mainstream city theatres. Copenhagen has a small but thriving **dance** scene – although there's only one venue, Dansescenen, specifically devoted to this, other theatres occasionally stage dance performances.

Ticket prices can be steep even for fringe performances: expect to pay at least 150kr, though seats may be cheaper if bought late on the day of performance. A free monthly programme, *Teater Kalendern*, is available at the theatres themselves and at the Wonderful Copenhagen and

Use It tourist offices. Tickets to nearly all performances can be bought via Billetnet (see p.197).

Dansescenen

Map 6, L6. Øster Fælled Torv 34, Østerbro

☎ 35 43 58 58

Bus #6, #14, #18, #650S.

The only place in Copenhagen with regular performances of modern dance, showcasing top Scandinavian ensembles on its two stages.

Folketeatret

Map 3, D5. Nørregade 39, Indre By

☎ 33 93 96 93

Bus #5, #14, #16 or Nørreport S-Tog.

One of the oldest theatres in town, with three auditoriums. The main stage (Store Scene) tends to show family-oriented stuff; the smaller Hippodromen shows more experimental work; while the tiny youth stage (Ung Scene) maintains a low entry price (60kr) for its avowedly fringe performances.

Det Kongelige Teater

Map 3, I4. Kongens Nytorv, Indre By

☎ 33 69 69 69

ⓦ www.kgl-teater.dk

Bus #1, #6, #10 or #31.

Copenhagen's flagship state theatre, with two stages and a permanent troupe who perform a variety of mainstream contemporary and older plays. Tickets bought from the box office after 5pm on the day of performance are reduced by fifty percent, and you can also book online up to seven days in advance. Tickets not available through Billetnet.

Østre Gasværk

Map 2, F3. Nyborggade 17, Østerbro

☎ 39 27 71 77

ⓦ www.oestre-gasvaerk.dk

Bus #6, #14, #650S or Svanemøllen S-Tog.

Set in an old gasworks, this is one of the hippest theatres in town, with new plays aimed largely at a younger audience – don't expect weighty classics. Also hosts modern dance shows from time to time.

THEATRE AND DANCE

Gay Copenhagen

Being the capital of a country where homosexuality has long been legal, and where gay and lesbian couples are allowed to marry, has led to Copenhagen becoming one of the world's premier gay cities. Heads don't generally turn if a gay or lesbian couple are seen kissing or holding hands, and many Copenhageners pride themselves on their liberal attitudes, although occasional cases of gay-bashing do take place. An example of the city's emancipated attitude is the way its main cruising spot, H.C. Ørstedsparken, has been equipped with "birdboxes" containing condoms and lubricating gel, while police patrols here are designed not to chase out cottaging men, but to protect them from homophobic violence.

Look out in all major gay hangouts for the English-language
Guide to Gay and Lesbian Denmark, published annually.
The monthly, Danish-language *PAN Bladet* has dozens
of useful listings – fairly easy to decipher even if you
don't speak Danish.

Paradoxically, Copenhagen's liberal traditions mean that there are fewer specifically gay and lesbian venues than in less tolerant cities. For general **information**, the national organization for gays and lesbians, the Landforeningen for

Bøsser og Lesbiske (LBL) at Teglgårdsstræde 13 (map 3, C6; Tues & Sun 1pm–3am, Thurs 1pm–4am, Fri 1pm–5am, Sat 1pm–6am; ⓣ 33 13 19 48, ⓦ *www.lbl.dk*) provides a very well-run advice service and is an excellent place to pick up news of any gay- or lesbian-oriented events in the city. Alternatively, the telephone service PAN INFO (Mon, Thurs & Sun 8pm–11pm; ⓣ 33 36 00 86) offers information on any aspect of the gay and lesbian scene in Denmark. For **rooms** (from 300kr) in gay or gay-friendly private accommodation call Enjoy on ⓣ 32 96 02 06 or email *jope.rainbow@sol.dk*. Copenhagen's annual **gay pride march** takes place at the beginning of August, though it's only been going for a few years and numbers are still quite low. For further details visit *www.mermaidpride.dk*.

For an explanation of the accommodation price codes used here, see p.135.

ACCOMMODATION

Carsten's Guest House

Map 3, H8. Christians Bygge 28, 5th floor (ring the bell marked "Carsten Appel") ⓣ 33 14 91 07 or 40 50 91 07 ⓦ www.copenhagen-gay-life.dk/atcarstens Bus #1, #2, #3, #11–13 or #40. Guesthouse with a very friendly and international atmosphere, though the rooms are a bit small and the walls thin. There's a great roof garden, a

comfortable and attractive lounge, plus a kitchen for guests' use; breakfast costs 40kr. Dorm beds 125kr, doubles ❹.

Copenhagen Rainbow

Map 3, E6. Frederiksberggade 25, Indre By ⓣ 33 14 10 25 ⓕ 33 14 10 25 ⓦ www.copenhagen-rainbow.dk Bus #5, #8, #12–#14, #16, #150S or Vesterport S-Tog. Brand new, gay-only guesthouse in an excellent position just off Strøget near

Rådhuspladsen. There's a mixture of rooms with and without en suite, though all have TV and tea- and coffee-making facilities, and the room rate includes a buffet breakfast. There's also free Internet access in reception. ❹.

Hotel Windsor
Map 3, C3. Frederiksborggade 30, Indre By
⊤ 33 11 08 30
Bus #5, #14, #16, #31, #42, #43, #350S or Nørreport S-Tog. Well-placed, long-established and unpretentious gay hotel with well-kept, though slightly run-down, rooms; shower and toilets are shared. Continental breakfast is included in the room rate. ❹.

RESTAURANTS, BARS AND CLUBS

Centralhjørnet
Map 3, E6. Kattesundet 18, Indre By. Bus #5, #8, #12–14, #16, #150S or Vesterport S-Tog.
Daily noon–1am.
Unpretentious and very cheap bar with a lively atmosphere and a famous jukebox

featuring a vast selection of kitsch pop.

Masken
Map 3, D6. Studiestræde 33, Indre By. Bus #5, #8, #12–14, #16, #150S or Vesterport S-Tog.
Mon–Fri 4pm–2am, Sat & Sun 3pm–2am.
Nearly every segment of the city's gay and lesbian population makes it to this raucous bar at some point during the week. There's a "girls' night" on Thursdays from 8pm, whilst Fridays are for young gays and lesbians.

Mens Bar
Map 3, D6. Teglgårdsstræde 3, Indre By. Bus #5, #8, #12–14, #16, #150S or Nørreport S-Tog.
Daily 3pm–2am.
The city's most macho bar, popular with leather men and those who enjoy a walk on the butch side – you won't find any women or straights here.

PAN
Map 3, F6. Knabrostræde 3, Indre By. Bus #5 or #29.
Mon–Wed & Sun 8pm–5am, Fri & Sat 8pm–6am.
Vibrant, loud, raunchy and

cruisy, *PAN* is Copenhagen's only permanent gay nightclub, though it attracts a straight crowd too. Friday and Saturday it offers a variety of groovy beats for disco divas; on other days it's a popular karaoke bar.

Sebastian
Map 3, F5. Hyskenstræde 10, Indre By. Bus #5 or #29.
Daily noon–2am.
A traditional first port of call on a night out, the very popular *Sebastian* serves good traditional Danish food as well as every kind of soft and alcoholic drink imaginable. Can get cruisy late in the evening.

Queen Victoria
Map 3, F6. Snaregade 4, Indre By
℡ 33 91 01 91. Bus #5 or #29.
Daily 5pm–midnight.
Owned by well-known drag queen Queen Victoria, this extremely popular and gay-friendly central Copenhagen restaurant has good service, and a traditional Danish and international menu served in a tolerant atmosphere that attracts Danish celebrities and politicians.

GAY COPENHAGEN: RESTAURANTS, BARS AND CLUBS

Shopping

Shopping is undoubtedly one of the highlights of a visit to Copenhagen, with a raft of eclectic and original shops, including dozens of small businesses which offer a refreshing alternative to the usual selection of bland chain stores. Quality is very high – as are, for that matter, prices. Exclusive handmade and luxury goods abound, often bearing witness to Denmark's fine traditions of innovative design, something which can be seen in products as diverse as clothing, glassware, stereo equipment and handmade bicycles.

Most of the city's top shops are in Indre By, traversed by Strøget, the world's longest (and oldest) pedestrianized shopping street – with no real traffic to dodge or excessive distances to cover, shopping here can be a real pleasure. Kronprinsensgade, off Købmagergade, has some of the city's best **designer clothes** shops, while for the best selection of **antique shops**, take a stroll down Kompagniestræde. Larsbjørnstræde and Skt Peder Stræde have the broadest selection of cheap **secondhand** and **ethnic clothes** shops, and the area around **Nansensgade** has become increasingly popular for its small designer clothes shops, quality restaurants and quirky businesses such as body-piercing salons.

Away from Indre By, the small street of Værnedamsvej in Vesterbro, lined with an array of delicatessens, bakeries and colourful fruit and veg shops, is the place to hunt out gourmet **food**. When the weather is good, the city's outdoor Saturday **flea markets** are well worth a visit, while the city's **galleries** and **museum shops** offer a multitude of shopping options for the artistically inclined.

Opening hours for most shops are roughly Monday to Friday 9.30am or 10am to 5.30pm or 7pm, Saturday 9am to 4pm. If you're shopping for wine or beer, note that shops aren't allowed to sell alcohol after 8pm.

We've divided our listings into the following categories: clothes and jewellery (below), crafts and design (p.214), department stores (p.215), food and drink (p.215), galleries (p.217), markets (p.218), museum shops (p.219), speciality shops (p.220).

CLOTHES AND JEWELLERY

Bruuns Bazaar

Map 3, F4. Kronprinsensgade 8, Indre By. Bus #31, #42 or #43. Mon–Thurs 10am–6pm, Fri 10am–7pm, Sat 10am–4pm.

Following a successful debut at the Paris Fashion Show in 1999, Bruuns is rapidly establishing itself as one of the city's most fashionable designer clothes shops, catering for both men and women, though it's as expensive and exclusive as you'd expect.

Casmose

Map 3, A5. Kjeld Langes Gade 1, Indre By. Bus #5 or #16. Tues–Fri 10am–5.30pm, Sat 10am–2pm.

In a basement shop just off Nansensgade, Casmose sells its own exclusive – and expensive – range of practical but stylish clothes for all ages.

Figaros Bryllup

Map 3, G3. Store Regnegade 2, Indre By. Bus #1, #6, #9 or #19. Tues–Thurs 11am–5.30pm, Fri

11am–6pm, Sat 11am–2pm.
Light, unpolished handmade jewellery using a variety of different metals including 22-carat gold, pink gold and platinum.

Heartmade
Map 3, G4. Pilestræde 45, Indre By. Bus #31, #42 or #43.
Tues & Wed 11am–4pm, Thurs & Fri 11am–5.30pm, Sat 11am–1pm.
Featuring sleek and simple clothes by Julie Fagerholdt, every item here is a uniquely designed one-off, with every-day garments alongside evening gowns and wedding dresses, often adorned with elegant embroidery and glass pearls.

Louise Grønlykke
Map 4, L9. Store Standstræde 19, Frederikstad. Bus #1, #6, #19 or #29.
Mon–Fri 11.30am–5.30pm, Sat 10am–2pm.
Beautiful handmade jewellery, mostly of gold, inspired by Japanese and North African ornamental styles. Everything is created by Louise Grønlykke herself, a fully trained goldsmith who has exhibited internationally.

Munthe plus Simonsen
Map 3, F4. Kronprinsensgade 11–12, Indre By. Bus #31, #42 or #43.
Mon–Thurs 10am–6pm, Fri & Sat 10am–7pm.
Hot fashion to burn a hole in your pocket – the catalogue was photographed by super-model Helena Christensen and features Iben Hjejle, one of the stars of the film *High Fidelity*. The clothes are by Danish designers Munthe and Simonsen, who are quickly establishing an international reputation with garments that blend Far Eastern influences with Scandinavian simplicity.

Museums Kopi Smykker
Map 3, G3. Grønnegade 6, Indre By. Bus #31, #42 or #43.
Mon–Thurs 10am–6pm, Fri & Sat 10am–7pm.
If you've been admiring the amazing Viking jewellery on display at the National Museum, this excellent, if pricey, shop produces out-standing handmade copies of these and other jewellery finds

CLOTHES AND JEWELLERY

BOOKSHOPS

There are dozens of good **bookshops** in Copenhagen, mainly in Indre By, most of which stock at least a few English-language paperbacks. Many of the city's bookstores are in the area around Fiolstræde (opposite Nørreport Station) and Købmagergade in Indre By. The Book Trader, Skindergade 23, has a varied selection of old and new books in English; Kupeen DIS Rejser, Skindergade 28, has guidebooks and maps for budget travellers. Chief places for new books are GAD, on Strøget at Vimmelskaftet 32 and inside Central Station; Arnold Busck, Købmagergade 49 (with a discount branch at Østergade 16); and Boghallen i Politikens Hus, Rådhuspladsen 37.

from the Bronze Age onwards. There's another branch on Strøget at Frederiksberggade 2.

ParaDigm
Map 3, F4. Klarebodrene 10, Indre By. Bus #31, #42 or #43. Tues–Fri 11am–6pm, Sat 10am–2pm.

Sustainable design is the popular new concept developed by the three women behind ParaDigm. They only produce clothes made from recyclable materials – anything from organic linen to old plastic bottles – which are transformed into a surprisingly light and elegant range of women's fashions, featuring eco-friendly everyday wear and party gear.

Pisces
Map 3, B4. Nansensgade 53, Indre By. Bus #5 or #16. Mon–Thurs 11am–7pm, Fri 11am–8pm, Sat 11am–4pm.

Small boutique run by three women who produce their own clothes and jewellery. The light and comfortable clothes use unusual fabrics like plastic and hemp; the simple jewellery is mostly silver, but also features copper, gold and a variety of semi-precious and precious stones. They also make clothes to order.

CLOTHES AND JEWELLERY

213

CRAFTS AND DESIGN

Butik til Borddækning

Map 3, F3. Møntergade 5, Indre By. Bus #31, #42 or #43. Tues–Fri noon–6pm, Sat 11am–2pm.

Dedicated to the important Danish tradition of table setting – it's believed that elegantly served food actually tastes better – Butik til Borddækning serves up a unique selection of table-top items, most of them made by the shop owner herself from a combination of tin, glass, wood and porcelain.

Illums Bolighus

Map 3, G5. Amagertorv 10, Indre By. Bus #5 or #29. Mon–Thurs 10am–6pm, Fri 10am–7pm, Sat 10am–5pm.

Two elegant floors overflowing with an eye-catching assortment of Danish design, from fabulous kitchenware to slimline PH lamps and the famously simple Kaare Klint furniture, though none of it's cheap.

Keramik- & Glasværkstedet

Map 4, I7. Kronprinsessegade 38, Frederikstad. Bus #10. Tues–Fri noon–6pm, Sat noon–3pm.

One of Kronprinsensgade's many delightful small shops, offering a beautiful selection of simple, functional ceramics and glassware for the dining table. Everything's made in the workshop out the back: you may be lucky enough to be invited in to see the four owners – three potters and a glass blower – in action.

Kvindesmedien

Map 3, N4. Christiania, Christianshavn. Bus #8. Mon–Fri 9am–5pm, Sat 11am–3pm.

One of Christiania's many cottage industries: here you can watch the owners creating a variety of handmade and moderately priced steel and iron objects such as mirrors, candlesticks, tables and sculptures to their own unique designs. They also make pieces to order.

CRAFTS AND DESIGN

DEPARTMENT STORES

Illums
Map 3, G4. Østergade 52, Indre By. Bus #1 or #6.
Mon–Thurs 10am–6pm, Fri 10am–7pm, Sat 10am–5pm.
The city's most exclusive department store, with elegant displays of top-of-the-range consumer desirables – everything from men's underwear to quirky bottle openers – at equally top-of-the-range prices. There's also a delightful café on the top floor.

Magasin du Nord
Map 3, H4. Kongens Nytorv 13, Indre By. Bus #1, #6, #9, #10 or #29.
Mon–Thurs 10am–6pm, Fri 10am–7pm, Sat 10am–5am.
Dating back to 1871, the redoubtable Magasin du Nord on fashionable Kongens Nytorv is the oldest department store in the city, running Illums (see above) a close second in both exclusivity and price.

FOOD AND DRINK

A.C. Perch's Thehandel
Map 3, F4. Kronprinsensgade 5, Indre By. Bus #31, #42 or #43.
Mon–Thurs 9am–5.30pm, Fri 9am–7pm, Sat 9.30am–2.30pm.
One of Europe's oldest tea shops, founded in 1835, Perch's retains much of its delightful original wooden interior, around which waft the wonderful aromas of specially imported teas from around the globe.

Boyesen
Map 5, J5. Værnedamsvej 10, Frederiksberg. Bus #1, #14 or #28.
Mon–Fri & Sun noon–11pm, Sat 11am–11pm.
Delicatessen and restaurant known for its eccentric range of chocolates flavoured using ingredients as outlandish as thyme, vervain, nutmeg and curry powder – they're tastier than you'd think.

Circus

Map 6, J8. Rosenvængets Allé 7a, Østerbro. Bus #6.

Mon–Fri 10am–8pm, Sat & Sun 10am–6pm.

One of the most original shops in town, Circus triples up as a great restaurant (see p.170), decent hairdressers and wonderful delicatessen stocking a great array of Danish and foreign sausages, cheeses and wines.

Frederiksberg Chocolade

Map 5, I5. Frederiksberg Allé 64, Frederiksberg. Bus #28.

Mon–Fri 11am–6pm, Sat 10am–2pm.

Mouthwatering homemade chocolates and truffles created without artificial colourings or preservatives.

J. Chr. Andersens Efterfølger

Map 3, E4. Købmagergade 32, Indre By. Bus #5.

Mon–Thurs 10am–5.30pm, Fri 10am–6.30pm, Sat 10am–2pm.

Follow the pungent odours emanating from Andersens' shop to discover Copenhagen's finest selection of cheeses, alongside some delicious homemade salads and an array of exotic fresh fruit.

Kana Vin

Map 3, B5. Nansensgade 24, Indre By. Bus #5 or #16.

Mon–Thurs 3.30–7pm, Fri noon–7pm, Sat 10.30am–3pm.

A labour of love for its friendly owners, this shop offers a fantastic selection of Italian wines, with most of that country's regions and grapes represented. If you're lucky you may coincide with an impromptu free wine tasting.

Props Wine Shop

Map 5, J5. Vesterbrogade 114, Vesterbro. Bus #6.

Thurs 3–6pm, Fri 4–8pm, Sat 11am–2pm.

Possibly Copenhagen's smallest wine shop, but it crams in an incredibly wide selection of excellent vintages and often has cheap special offers too. Also has hand-rolled cigars – if you're feeling flash you can even have your name inscribed on each tube.

Shark House Deli

Map 6, C8. Blågårdsgade 3, Nørrebro. Bus #5 or #16.

Mon–Fri 11am–8pm, Sat 11am–4pm.

Great Italian, French and Danish homemade fare such as pesto, sausages, jam and bread. There's also a small selection of Italian- and French-inspired takeaway meals, usually including a vegetarian option.

Sømods Bolscher
Map 3, D5. Nørregade 36, Indre By. Bus #5 or Nørreport Station.

Mon–Thurs 9.15am–5.30pm, Fri 9.15am–6pm, Sat 10am–2.30pm.

Using century-old recipes – no chemical additives – this shop makes a range of flavoursome traditional boiled sweets; you can also watch the elaborate sweet-making process during which millimetre-thin strands of multicoloured mixture are coiled together to make the rainbow-coloured candy.

GALLERIES

Den Frie Udstilling
Map 4, H4. Oslo Plads 1, Østerbro. Bus #1, #6, #9 or Østerport S-Tog.
Daily mid-Aug to May 10am–5pm.

Opened in 1898, this is one of Copenhagen's oldest galleries (see p.72) and usually displays a smattering of contemporary Danish art, most of it for sale.

Galleri Nicolai Wallner
Map 2, F11. Building 15, Njalsgade 21, Amager. Bus #12, #13, #34 or #40.

Tues–Fri noon–5pm, Sat & Sun noon–3pm.

In an old red warehouse on Islands Brygge on Amager, this gallery gives promising younger Danish and international artists an opportunity to display and sell their work in a congenial atmosphere.

Starving Artistz
Map 6, D7. Elmegade17, Nørrebro. Bus #5 or #16.
Mon–Fri 2pm–6.30pm, Sat noon–5pm.

Set up on the principle that all artists should be able to sell their work, and everybody should be able to afford to buy it, this eclectic and original gallery just off Skt Hans

Torv offers a variable bunch of work, with pieces by established artists alongside those by students and amateurs.

MARKETS

Det Blå Pakhus
Map 2, I12. Holmbladsgade 113, Amager. Bus #5 or #37. Sat & Sun 10am–5pm.

A year-round weekend fixture, Copenhagen's largest indoor flea market boasts four-and-a-half-thousand square metres of uninhibited clutter, featuring objects of every conceivable size, shape, form and value.

Christiania Christmas market
Map 3, N5. Christiania, Christianshavn. Bus #8. Second Mon in Dec until Dec 20: Mon–Fri 2–8pm, Sat & Sun noon–8pm.

Held at Christiania's Grå Hal, this is where Copenhagen's more alternative shoppers fill up their Christmas stockings. You can find some great stuff here, including many items created in the Free City's workshops – cast-iron candle-

sticks, colourful batik clothes and much more.

Frederiksberg Rådhus
Map 5. D3. Gammel Kongevej, Frederiksberg. Bus #1 or #14. Sat mid-April to mid-Oct 8am–2pm.

Popular trading place for locals of all ages – and thanks to this prosperous neighbourhood's wealthier residents, you might turn up a few better-than-usual wares, anything from antique jewellery to train sets.

Israels Plads
Map 3, C4. Israels Plads, Indre By. Bus #5 or #16. Sat May–Sept 8am–2pm.

On the children's playground behind the fruit and veg market just off Frederiksborggade, this Saturday flea market is rumoured to be the place where Copenhagen's high-street shops get rid of stuff they can't sell, and is a good spot to hunt out unused clothes and jewellery.

Nørrebro market

Map 6, C6–D5. Along the wall of Assistens Kirkegården,

Nørrebro. Bus #5 or #16.

Sat May–Sept 8am–2pm.

This is the city flea market that most resembles a traditional car-boot sale – search patiently and you may unearth some real bargains.

MUSEUM SHOPS

Arken

Map 1, C6. Ishøj S-Tog, and then bus #128 or a 25-minute walk.

Tues–Sun 10am–5pm.

Excellent selection of art books, with a large section on special offer – some real bargains can be had – along with a variety of designer items ranging from umbrellas to ashtrays, some handmade specially for the museum.

Botanisk Have

Map 4, D9–F7. Bus #5, #7, #14, #16, #24, #40, #43, #84, #384 or Nørreport S-Tog.

Summer daily 8.30am–6pm; winter daily 8.30am–4pm.

Situated in a small building near the botanic gardens' main gate on Øster Farimagsgade, with orchids and other exotic

cuttings alongside assorted cacti and a vast array of seeds.

Danish Design Centre

Map 3, F8. H.C. Andersens Boulevard, Indre By. Bus #1, #2, #5, #8, #10, #16, #28, #29 or Central Station.

Mon–Fri 10am–5pm, Sat & Sun 11am–4pm.

The best part of the otherwise disappointing Design Centre and a good place to acquire some chic but affordable Danish designs of everyday objects including bags, T-shirts and pens. There's also a good selection of books and postcards.

Danish Museum of Decorative Art

Map 4, L5. Bus #1, #6, #9, #19, #29 or Østerport S-Tog.

Daily 1pm–4pm.

Good selection of excellent books on Danish and international design, as well as scale models of design classics and various other desirable ornaments.

Ny Carlsberg Glyptotek

Map 3, F8. Bus #1, #2, #5, #8, #10, #16, #28, #29 or Central Station.

Tues–Sun 10am–4pm.

Bag a memento of the magical Ny Carlsberg Glyptotek here from its shop's collection of postcards, posters and reproductions of the museum's finest busts and sculptures. There are also in-depth catalogues of the Glyptotek's massive col-lection, plus a plethora of art books.

Louisiana

Map 1, D3. Gamle Strandvej 13, Humlebæk. Local train to Humlebæk every 20min from Central Station, then a seven-minute signposted walk.

Daily 10am–5pm, Wed until 10pm.

One of the best art bookshops in the Copenhagen area, and also stocks high-quality repro-ductions of classic works – Warhol's Marilyn literally flies off the shelves. Like the muse-um, it's always packed, with eager shoppers snapping up Louisiana bags and T-shirts, but don't come looking for bargains, as it's rather pricey.

SPECIALITY SHOPS

Bang & Olufsen

Map 3, H4. Østergade 3–5, Indre By. Bus #1, #6, #9, #10 or #29.

Mon–Thurs 9.30am–5pm, Fri 9.30am–7pm, Sat 10am–2pm.

On Strøget, just around the corner from Kongens Nytorv, this is a shrine to Denmark's famous makers of chic hi-fi.

Christiania Cykler

Map 3, N5. Christiania, Christianshavn. Bus #8.

Mon–Fri 10am–5pm.

Next door to the *Månefiskeren* music café and bar, the Christiania bicycle workshop is the home of the well-known (at least to bicycle enthusiasts)

Pedersen bike, an age-old design created to make cycling on cobbled streets more comfortable, which is produced and sold here.

Games
Map 3, E5. Jorcks Passage, Indre By. Bus #5.
Mon–Thurs 10am–6pm, Fri 10am–7pm, Sat 10am–3pm.
All kinds of traditional board games and toys, ranging from functional pocket chess sets to suave Italian leather backgammon boards.

Sögreni of Copenhagen
Map 3, D6. Skt Peders Stræde 30, Indre By. Bus #14 or #16.

Mon–Thurs 10am–6pm, Fri 10am–7pm, Sat 10am–4pm.
Beautiful handmade bicycles are produced here; they can also make bikes to your own specifications.

Zübeil Body Piercing
Map 3, B5. Nansengade 42, Indre By. Bus #5 or #16.
Mon–Fri noon–7pm, Sat noon–4pm.
If in a moment of terrible clarity you decide that a navel- or tongue-piercing is what is needed to make your visit to Copenhagen complete, then this is the place to get clean, professional holes made in you.

Sport and outdoor activities

I n terms of health and fitness the Danes are a contradic-
tory lot: the country has one of Europe's highest rates of
smoking- and drinking-related deaths, yet also, thanks
to massive government funding, boasts some of the best
public sports facilities in the world. Far and away the country's most popular sport is **football**, an enthusiasm which
has been nourished by the excellent performances of the
national team during the past two decades. Recreational
sports like **golf**, **tennis** and **swimming** are also well
catered for, while Copenhagen's proximity to the sea means
there are plenty of opportunities for **water-based activities** like windsurfing, kayaking, diving and fishing. All the
venues listed here are within easy reach of the city centre.

FOOTBALL

Thanks to the Danish national team's success over the past
decade – they were European champions in 1992 and
World Cup quarter-finalists in 1998 – and the number of
players who have forged successful careers at Europe's

largest clubs – Peter Schmeichel at Manchester United, Brian and Michael Laudrup at AC Milan and Barcelona – **football** has become the country's most popular sport. Having said that, the domestic game in Denmark is fairly low-key compared to the big European leagues: there were no professional clubs in the country until as recently as 1985, and though there's plenty of football played in the Copenhagen area, you shouldn't expect big crowds or high-quality games unless you're going to a match involving the national side or the local derby between the city's two biggest teams, Brøndby and FC København (usually known as FCK). Matches are played on Saturdays, Sundays and Mondays and the season lasts roughly from late July to June, with a winter break from December to February. **Tickets** for Brøndby, FCK and national team games are available through Billetnet (see p.197) or at the respective stadiums. Danish football fans are noted for their relaxed behaviour, and the laid-back atmosphere is enhanced by the availability of beer inside the stadium, as well as surprisingly good hotdogs.

Founded in 1991, **FCK** is the country's richest club – they recently acquired ex-Inter Milan coach Roy Hodgson as manager and aspire to break into big-time European football, though they've struggled in recent years even to hold their own in the Danish premier division. Games are well attended, with an average gate of about 14,000, though they can't create much atmosphere in the vast 40,000-capacity Parken stadium (map 6, J6; tickets from 100kr; bus #1, #6 or #14). If you want a more intimate atmosphere, try next door at Østerbro Stadium (map 6, K6), where **B93** – a team in Denmark's semi-professional second-division – play; tickets (80kr) are available on the gate.

FCK's main rivals are **Brøndby**, from the working-class suburbs to the south of the city. Founded in 1964, they

FOOTBALL

ROLIGANS

During the 1986 World Cup in Mexico – the first the Danes had ever qualified for – the Danish football team's exemplary performances on the field were matched by the country's football fans off it. These supporters of the national team became known as the **Roligans** – a play on the words *rolig* ("relaxed") and "hooligan" – and their good humour, colourful hats and face paintings compared strikingly to the boorish behaviour of many rival fans. The Roligans' finest hour came during Denmark's victory at the 1992 European Championship, leading to the biggest street party ever seen in the country, and they still turn up in large numbers to all Denmark's home games in Parken stadium, though you might find their antics a bit annoying if you've come to watch the football, rather than to Mexican wave. Check out their website at ⓦ*www.roligan.dk*, where you can purchase Viking hats decked out in the red and white of the national team.

became the country's first professional football club when they turned pro in 1985. Brøndby are presently Denmark's most successful club in recent years, winning the league eight times in the fifteen years since they turned pro, and having several successful campaigns in European football, including reaching the semi-finals of the Uefa Cup. Brøndby's smaller stadium has atmosphere, but crowds have dwindled, though numbers still rival FCK – a team they consider overpaid prima donnas. Tickets cost from 80kr; take the S-Tog to Glostrup and then bus #131.

GOLF

The city boasts a wonderful eighteen-hole course at the **Copenhagen Golf Club** (☎ 39 63 04 83; daily 8am until

30min before sunset; green fees 280kr Mon–Fri, 350kr at weekends, club hire 200kr per day; S-Tog or local train to Klampenborg station, then bus #388) is set in the middle of a deer sanctuary, beautiful woodlands and meadows. It's the oldest club in Scandinavia, and has a friendly atmosphere, along with a restaurant and bar.

During the colder winter months try the **Copenhagen Indoor Golf Centre** at Refshalevej 177b, Christianshavn (ⓣ 32 54 43 32; mid-Sept to mid-Oct Mon–Fri 4–9pm, Sat & Sun noon–5pm; mid-Oct to April Mon & Fri 11am–9pm, Tues–Thurs 11am–10pm, Sat & Sun 9am–7pm; 63–126kr, club hire 30kr; bus #8), where there's a driving range, putting green and a state-of-the-art golf simulator.

SWIMMING

Copenhagen has plentiful and well-maintained public **swimming pools**; some also have saunas, and others form part of sports centres offering a range of different activities; most rent swimming costumes for a small fee. Easily the best, right in the heart of the city and set in a state-of-the-art complex, is the wonderful **DGI-byen Swim Centre** (Vandkulturhuset), at Tietensgade 65 (map 5, N6; Mon & Wed 7am–7pm, Tues & Thurs 10am–5pm, Fri 7am–5pm, Sat & Sun 9am–5pm; 40kr; S-Tog to Central Station; ⓦ *www.dgi-byen.dk*), including five pools (one with a climbing wall above it, another shooting up massaging bubbles). If you really want pampering visit the *kurbadet* (spa), where 60kr buys you access to a sauna, steam rooms, plunge pools, complimentary fresh fruit and mineral water, and robes and towels; a variety of treatments such as massages are also available.

Other pools in the city include Fælledbadet in Fælledparken, just off Nørre Alle (Mon & Thurs 7am–6pm, Tues 7am–8pm, Wed 10am–6pm, Fri 7am–3pm, Sat & Sun

COPENHAGEN MARATHON

On the third Sunday of May many of the prettiest areas of Copenhagen are cordoned off to make way for the **Copenhagen Marathon**, during which around six thousand participants of all ages and abilities, from professional athletes to fun runners, take over the streets, cheered by more than twice that number of spectators. If you're fit enough and want to give it a try, contact Sparta (Ⓦ *www.sparta.dk*; entry fee 325kr).

9am–3pm; 24kr; bus #1, #3, #6 or #14), Vesterbro Swimming Baths at Angelgade 4 (Mon 10am–9pm, Tues & Thurs 7am–5pm, Wed 7am–7pm, Fri 7am–4pm, Sat & Sun 9am–2pm; 25kr; bus #3, #10, #16, #650S or Enghave S-Tog) and the pleasant outdoor pool at Bellahøj (mid-May to mid-Aug daily 10am–5pm; 20kr; bus #5, #8, #11, #67, #68, #250S or #350S).

TENNIS

Copenhagen's one notable **tennis** tournament, the indoor ATP **Copenhagen Open** (last week of Feb), has attracted top players like Greg Rusedski and Pat Cash, who have come to KB-Hallen on Peter Bangsvej in Frederiksberg to have a stab at the US$350,000 first prize. The week-long tournament is now one of Denmark's biggest sporting events, and the country comes to a virtual standstill when Danish players such as Frederik Fetterlein and Kenneth Carlsen try to make it just a little bit further than they did last year. KB-Hallen's beautiful interior provides the perfect surroundings. **Tickets** start at 120kr early in the tournament, rising to 250kr for the finals, and are available at any post office through Billetnet or at the ticket office at KB-Hallen (☎ 38 71 14 18).

If you want to play tennis yourself, there are indoor and outdoor courts available at the B93 tennis club at Svanemølleanlæggct 10, Østcrbro (Mon Fri 7am 11pm, Sat & Sun 8am–6pm; ☎39 27 18 90; 130–150kr per court per hour; bus #1, #6, #14 or Svanemøllen S-Tog). Book in advance, as it gets busy, and you'll need to bring rackets and balls, as there are none for hire.

WATERSPORTS AND FISHING

With its strong links with the sea, Copenhagen should be an excellent place to indulge in **watersports**, though unfortunately the waters around the city have more than their fair share of crazed speedboaters and kamikaze jet skiers, a fact which, coupled to a complete absence of policing, makes the whole harbour area feel like an accident waiting to happen. If you're in a small craft such as a kayak or dinghy it's best to go with a guide.

Copenhagen Adventure Tours (Gammel Strand, Indre By, look for the sign, ☎40 50 40 06, ⓦ *www.kajakole.dk*) run excellent and affordable guided **kayak** tours around the harbour area on safe and easy-to-use individual kayaks. The guides' local knowledge is excellent, and they offer both group and individual tours to set or negotiated time scales – expect to pay 120kr an hour.

The Surf and Snowboard School (June–Oct; ☎32 84 04 53, ⓦ *www.surfsnowboard.dk*) at Amager Beach rents out everything you need for **windsurfing**, a very popular activity in Denmark; prices start at 80kr per hour for equipment hire, and beginners' lessons are also available.

For **diving**, head 25km south along the coast to Karlslunde and the exceptionally well equipped Nautic Diving (Mosede Strandvej 51 ☎43 90 02 22, ⓦ *www.nautic-diving.dk*), who run dozens of courses from PADI to divemaster, rent out equipment to qualified divers and organize wreck diving trips. Prices start at 350kr for equipment rental, a wreck diving trip costs an extra 250kr. If you really want to get out to sea, Baltic, at Lautrupkaj, Østerbro (℡ 33 22 00 25; bus #29 or Nordhavn S-Tog) organize day-long **fishing trips** (150–170kr, tackle 50kr) out into the Øresund – remember to bring warm, waterproof clothing as the weather can be fierce even during summer.

Kids' Copenhagen

openhagen is a child-friendly city, and a recent baby boom has meant that places without facilities for children are few and far between – even the more exclusive cafés and restaurants now have high-chairs and children's menus. The low level of traffic makes the city easy and relaxing to explore with **kids**, while if your children are into cycling, there are cycle lanes throughout the city, and it's generally very safe (see p.14 for a list of bike hire places). Boat trips around the harbour and canal (see p.15) are also a surefire hit.

Most of Copenhagen's **museums** cater for children in some way, so travelling with kids doesn't mean you have to miss out on the city's cultural side. Some, like the National Museum (see p.230), have made a special effort to involve children and make sure they have a memorable experience. A number of galleries, such as Louisiana (p.121) and the Royal Museum of Fine Arts (p.63), also have good children's sections where you can unload your children while you go off and do your own exploring.

Fælled Park (see p.105) is especially popular with kids, and its wide, open areas are ideal for relaxing and letting the children loose. **Kongens Have** (see p.61) is also very child friendly, staging free puppet shows every summer (June–Aug daily at 2pm & 3pm) on the Kronprinsessegade side of the park; on the other side, by the Hercules Pavilion, there's a novel children's play area complete with dragons for clambering on. During winter, **ice skating** is a favourite pastime for the city's children – there are free outdoor rinks at Kongens Nytorv (see p.46) and Frederiksberg Rundel (see p.94) (skates can be hired at both).

ATTRACTIONS

Copenhagen Zoo
Map 5, A5–B6. Bus #28, #39 or #550S.

March Mon–Fri 9am–4pm, Sat & Sun 9am–5pm; April, May & Sept Mon–Fri 9am–5pm, Sat & Sun 9am–6pm; June–Aug daily 9am–6pm; Oct daily 9am–5pm; Nov–Feb daily 9am–4pm; adults 70kr, children 35kr.

In addition to its fine selection of exotic animals (see p.98), the Copenhagen Zoo has an excellent children's "stroking zoo" section where kids can touch young rabbits and deer. Pony rides are also available, and there's a playground if your kids get fed up with animals.

DGI-byen
Map 5, N6–N7. Bus #10, #550S or Central Station.
ⓦ *www.dgi-byen.dk*

Mon–Thurs 6.30am–9pm, Fri 6.30am–7pm, Sat & Sun 9am–5pm; adults 40kr, under-14s 25kr.

The city's flashest swimming complex, with pleasantly warm water, geysers, bubble columns, wave machines and diving platforms spread around three unusually shaped pools.

MUSEUMS

Children's Museum at the National Museum
Map 3, F7–G7. Bus #5 or #28.
ⓦ *www.natmus.dk*

Tues–Sun 10am–5pm; 40kr, free Wed and for under-16s.

Aimed specifically at children between 6 and 12, with a

variety of attractions including a full-size model of a Tuareg camp in the Sahara; copies of a Viking ship (kids can dress up in Viking costumes too) and a small medieval castle; and an "aroma" section with exotic spices where kids can learn where the different smells come from.

Experimentarium

Map 2, F1. Bus #6, #21, #650S or S-Tog to Hellerup or Svanemøllen then a 10min walk.
ⓦ www.experimentarium.dk
Mon & Wed–Fri 9am–5pm, Tues 9am–9pm, Sat & Sun 11am–5pm; adults 79kr, children 3–14 years 57kr, under-3s free.
This fascinating, hands-on science centre lets children explore the laws of nature by performing their own experiments. There are over 300 experiments in total, using easy to follow guidelines – helpful instructors are on hand if you get stuck – and covering topics such as magnetism, aerodynamics, anatomy,

astronomy and environmental science. Regular scientific demonstrations are given throughout the day, and there's a special kids' pavilion for 3- to 6-year olds, with mechanical bubble-making machines.

Post and Tele Museum

Map 3, F4. Bus #5 or Nørreport S-Tog
ⓦ www.ptt-museum.dk
Tues & Thurs–Sun 10am–5pm, Wed 10am–8pm; adults 30kr, under-12s free, free on Wed.
The children's section of this informative museum has old postal uniforms for kids to dress up in and telegraph equipment and bits of other antiquated telecommunications equipment for them to play with, including a morse-code transmitter. For older children, the museum's "B@lkony" section is dedicated to computers and the Internet, with lots of fun programmes to fiddle around with. There's also a children's playroom in the rooftop café.

AMUSEMENT PARKS

Bakken

Map 1, D4. Klampenborg S-Tog. ⓦ *www.bakken.dk*

April–Aug daily noon–midnight; free.

The world's oldest amusement park, Bakken's attractions include Denmark's longest and highest big-dipper, assorted merry-go-rounds and many other fun and breathtaking rides (8–15kr each) including a ghost train and a waltzer. There's also a free children's play park (look for "*børnelege-plads*") with seesaws and swings. All rides are half price on Wednesdays from mid-June to early August. It's also located on the edge of Dyrehaven park – a great picnic spot.

Tivoli

Map 3, D8–E8. Bus #1, #2, #6, #8, #28, #29, #550S, #650S, Vesterport S-Tog or Central Station. ⓦ *www.tivoli.dk*

Mid-April to Sept & first three weeks of Dec Mon–Thurs & Sun 11am–midnight, Fri & Sat 11am–1am; 39kr, mid-June to mid-Aug 49kr.

An absolute must for families with children, this famous amusement park offers everything a child could ever want: 26 fun rides (10–20kr each), sweets of all descriptions, spectacular fireworks at midnight, and plenty of opportunities to win colourful and completely useless plastic gadgets.

SIGHTS AND SHOPS

Changing of the guard at Amalienborg

Map 4, L6–M7. Bus #1, #6, #9, #10 or #29.

Daily at noon; free.

The changing of the guard at Amalienborg (see p.69) is

always a big children's pull, as one set of splendidly costumed guards marches off and another arrives, sometimes to the accompaniment of a band. At other times, kids can have fun trying to outstare the mannequin-like guards as they stand to attention outside the palace.

Sømods Bolscher

Map 3, D4. Nørregade 36. Bus #5 or Nørreport Station. Mon–Thurs 9.15am–5.30pm, Fri 9.15am–6pm, Sat 10am–2.30pm. Confectionery-loving kids will enjoy a visit to this famous sweet shop, where you can watch the skilful process of traditional sweet-making before sampling some of scrumptious, rainbow-coloured end-products.

Directory

AIRLINES Aer Lingus, Jernbanegade 4 (ⓣ33 12 60 55); Air France, 2nd floor, Ved Vesterport (ⓣ33 13 76 76); Alitalia, Vesterbrogade 6d (ⓣ33 36 93 69); Austrian Airlines, Vester Farimagsgade 6 (ⓣ33 32 16 37); British Airways, Rådhuspladsen 16 (ⓣ80 20 80 22); Finnair, Nyropsgade 47 (ⓣ33 36 45 45); Icelandair, Vester Farimagsgade 1 (ⓣ33 12 33 88); Lithuanian Airlines, Copenhagen Airport (ⓣ32 52 81 50); LOT, Vester Farimagsgade 21 (ⓣ33 14 58 11); Lufthansa & SAS, Hammerichsgade 1–5 (ⓣ70 10 20 00); Swissair, Vester Farimagsgade 6 (ⓣ33 32 16 37).

AIRPORT INFORMATION ⓣ32 31 32 31; information on arrivals and departures is also shown on teletext p.490 on DR1.

ATMS Nearly all ATMs in Copenhagen take Visa, Mastercard and Maestro-marked bankcards.

BANKS AND EXCHANGE Exchange bureaux offer better rates for changing money than banks. Central bureaux include American Express, 3rd floor, 7a Nørregade (Mon–Fri 9am–5pm, Sat 9am–2pm); Forex, Vesterbrogade 28 (Mon–Fri 10am–6pm) and Central Station (daily 8am–9pm); The Change Group, Nyhavn 35 (daily 10am–6pm) and Frederiksberggade 5 (Mon–Thurs 9am–8pm, Fri & Sat 9am–9pm, Sun 10am–6pm). In an emergency there are a number of 24hr currency-exchange machines, though rates are poor. Machines can be found at:

Arbejdernes Landsbank, Vesterbrogade 5; Den Danske Bank, Central Station; Jyske Bank, Vesterbrogade 9; Unibank, Axelborg Torv 35 and Rådhuspladsen.

CAR PARKING A pay-and-display system operates on the city's streets, with rates varying depending on which colour-coded zone you are in. Stretching out from the city centre, the zones are red (20kr per hour), yellow (12kr), green (9kr), blue (5kr) and white (free). Each pay-and-display meter has a map on it detailing the extent of each zone. "STOPFORBUD" means no stopping, whilst "PAKERING FORBUDT" means no parking unless a time limit is displayed. It's usually easy to find street parking space, but note that your car will be towed away if you overstay or park where you shouldn't. Downtown car parks are thin on the ground: there's a handy one at the Statoil petrol station on Israel Plads, (12kr for 1hr, 65kr per day), and another attached to the Q8 station near Vesterport Station at Nyropsgade 42 (7–10kr per hour, 55kr per day).

CAR RENTAL Avis, Kampmannsgade 1 (☏ 33 15 22 99); Europcar, Gyldenløvesgade 17 (☏ 33 11 62 00); Hertz, Ved Vesterport (☏ 33 17 90 20).

CREDIT CARDS Strangely for a Western European capital, the chance to flex your plastic is limited. Supermarkets, many bars, cafés, smaller shops and some restaurants don't accept either Visa or Mastercard – many only take the local Dankort card.

DENTIST Tandlægevagten, Oslo Plads 14 (☏ 35 38 02 51). Open for emergencies (Mon–Fri 8–9.30pm, Sat & Sun 10am–noon). Be prepared to pay at least 150kr on the spot.

DISABLED VISITORS Provision for disabled visitors throughout Denmark is excellent, and public transport and most museums and many hotels are wheelchair accessible. The Danish Tourist Board, Vesterbrogade 6d (☏ 33 11 14 15) publish a free and full list of accessible places throughout Copenhagen.

ELECTRICITY The Danish electricity supply runs at 220–240V, 50Hz AC; sockets generally require a two-pin plug. Visitors from the UK will need an adaptor; visitors from outside the EU may need a transformer.

EMAIL AND INTERNET ACCESS There are a few good Internet cafés around the centre of Copenhagen (most include free coffee in their rates): Cyber Space Net Café, Jagtvej 55, Nørrebro (open 24hr; 10–15kr per hour; ☎ 35 83 11 45); Drop Zone, Frederiksborggade 41, Frederiksborg (Mon–Fri noon–midnight, Sat & Sun noon–8am; 20kr per hour; ☎ 33 93 68 88); GameStation Øst, Strandboulevarden 151, Østerbro (daily noon–midnight, Fri & Sat until 8am; 35kr per hour; ☎ 35 43 97 96); GameStation Vest, Vesterbrogade 115, Vesterbro (daily noon–midnight, Fri & Sat until 8am; 35kr per hour; ☎ 33 25 97 96); NetPoint Royal, inside the SAS Royal Hotel, Hammerichsgade 3, Indre By (Mon–Fri 9am–10pm; 20kr per hour; ☎ 70 22 10 08). There's a free Internet service at the Use It office on Rådhusstræde (see p.7) and at Hovedbiblioteket, Krystalgade 15–17 (Mon–Fri 10am–7pm, Sat 10am–2pm) – you'll need to book in advance for both.

EMBASSIES Australia, Strandboulevarden 122 (☎ 39 29 20 77); Canada, Kristen Bernikows Gade 1 (☎ 33 48 32 00); Finland, Skt Annæ Plads 24 (☎ 33 13 42 14); Germany, Stockholmsgade 57 (☎ 35 45 99 00); Ireland, Østbanegade 21 (☎ 35 42 32 33); New Zealand, c/o the UK embassy (see below); Norway, Amaliegade 39 (☎ 33 14 01 24); Sweden, Skt Annæ Plads 15a (☎ 33 36 03 70); UK, Kastelsvej 40 (☎ 35 44 52 00); USA, Dag Hammerskjölds Allé 24 (☎ 35 55 31 44).

EMERGENCIES ☎ 112 for police, fire or ambulance. There are police stations at Halmtorvet 20 (☎ 33 25 14 48) and Store Kongensgade 100 (☎ 33 93 14 48), as well as Central Station.

HEALTH ☎ 112 for medical emergencies. The local

emergency department is at Rigshospitalet, Blegdamsvej 9 (☎ 35 45 35 45), with free treatment for EU and Scandinavian nationals, though citizens of other countries are unlikely to have to pay. If you need a doctor, call ☎ 33 93 63 00 (Mon–Fri 8am–4pm) and you'll be given the name of one in your area; outside these hours, call ☎ 38 88 60 41, unless you're in Christianshavn, in which case call ☎ 32 84 00 41. Doctors' fees range from 120kr to 350kr, to be paid in cash. If you're a UK national and you have an E111 form, you can claim back doctors' fees and charges for medicine from the local health department. You'll need to produce the relevant receipts and your E111 – they're available from any UK post office, where you should get your copy stamped and validated before travel.

LATE-OPENING SHOPS The supermarket at Central Station is open daily from 8am until midnight.

LAUNDRY Central places to do washing include: Alaska Vask & Rens, Borgergade 2 ; Møntvask, Istedgade 29; Quickvask, Istedgade 45; and Vasketeria, Dronningensgade 42. An average load costs about 40kr.

LEFT LUGGAGE The DSB Garderobe office downstairs in Central Station stores luggage for 20kr per item per day and has lockers for 25–35kr per day. There are also lockers (same price) in the InterRail Centre in Central Station and at Use It, Rådhusstræde 13.

LIBRARIES Hovedbiblioteket, Krystalgade 15–17, (Mon–Fri 10am–7pm, Sat 10am–2pm), is the main city library and stocks some English-language books, magazines and newspapers. Huset, Rådhusstræde 13, also has a very well-stocked reading room, with international magazines and newspapers.

LOST PROPERTY The police department's lost property office is at Slotherrensvej 113, Vanløse (☎ 38 74 88 22). For items lost on a bus, contact the bus information line (☎ 36 13 14

HEALTH–LOST PROPERTY

15); lost on a train, the DSB office at Central Station (☎ 33 16 21 10); lost on a plane, contact Kastrup Airport (☎ 32 31 32 31).

NEWSPAPERS AND NEWS IN ENGLISH Overseas newspapers are sold at the Magasin du Nord department store (see p.215), the stall on the eastern side of Rådhuspladsen, and some newsagents along Strøget. Also check any of the newsagents in Central Station, which stock a large range of foreign newspapers and magazines. News in English is broadcast on Radio Denmark 1062MHz medium wave (Mon–Fri at 8.40am, 11am, 5.10pm & 10pm). The BBC World Service can be picked up on short wave 6195KHz, 9410KHz and 12,095KHz; you may also be able to pick up BBC Radio 4 on long wave 198Mhz.

PHARMACIES Steno Apotek, Vesterbrogade 6C (☎ 33 14 82 66) and Sønderbro Apotek, Amagerbrogade 158 (☎ 32 58 01 40) are open 24 hours.
POST OFFICES The main office is at Tietgensgade 35–39,

right behind Central Station (Mon–Fri 11am–6pm, Sat 10am–1pm) and there's another office inside Central Station (Mon–Fri 8am–10pm, Sat 9am–4pm, Sun 10am–4pm). Poste restante not addressed to a named post office is sent automatically to the main office. Postal rates for items up to 20g are 4.50kr to EU countries, 5.50kr elsewhere; items up to 100g cost 13kr to EU countries, 18kr elsewhere. To send a telegram, phone ☎ 122 (information ☎ 168).

PUBLIC HOLIDAYS New Year's Day; Maundy Thursday; Good Friday; Easter Sunday; Easter Monday; Common Prayer Day (fourth Friday after Easter); Ascension Day (fifth Thursday after Easter); Whit Sunday and Whit Monday (seven weeks after Easter); Constitution Day (June 5); Christmas (December 24–26). Most shops and businesses are closed on these days, and transport services are reduced.

TAX A luxury tax, MOMS, of 25 percent is added to many goods. Non-EU citizens can claim a refund at the airport provided you fill out the correct form at the point of purchase.

TELEPHONES There are plentiful well-maintained public telephone boxes throughout the city. Coin-operated phones require two 1kr coins to make a connection; phonecards can be bought from post offices in 20kr, 50kr and 100kr denominations. If you take your UK mobile phone you can choose one of four local Danish networks. Telia are currently the cheapest (roughly 22p/min to the UK and 15p/min to call within Copenhagen – similar to charges from phone boxes). Before you travel you will need to contact your UK network provider to have any international blocks removed. Most importantly,

remember that for any call you receive whilst on a foreign network you will be charged at about £1 a minute.

TIME Denmark is one hour ahead of GMT, six hours ahead of US Eastern Standard Time, and nine ahead of US Pacific Standard Time.

TRAVEL AGENTS KILROY Travels, Skindergade 28 (ⓣ 33 11 00 44), have good general information on travelling around Denmark, the rest of Scandinavia and Europe. DFDS Seaways, Skt Annæ Plads 30 (ⓣ 33 42 33 42) provide information on various car ferry services from Denmark, whilst the DSB Rejsebureau at the Central Station (ⓣ 33 14 11 26) has information on train services.

CONTEXTS

A brief history of Copenhagen

Beginnings

Archeological evidence suggests that humans may have arrived in Denmark as early as 50,000 BC, though the first permanent settlements were probably not established until much later, around 12,000 BC, when the ice sheets which had previously covered the country began to recede, and nomadic hunters arrived in pursuit of the herds of reindeer that grazed the tundra. As the climate gradually warmed and the reindeer headed north, a Stone Age village culture developed, until by around 4000 BC agricultural settlements covered the country.

Bronze was introduced from southern Europe around 1800 BC – the richness of some pieces, such as the bronze sun chariot now on display in the National Museum, suggests that even at this early date there was contact between Denmark and the Mediterranean cultures of Crete and Mycenae. From this period also come the famous Danish *lurs*, curved metal horns which were blown to call villagers to meetings – a statue of two *lurs* blowers stands outside Copenhagen's Rådhus.

The Vikings

The Danes trace their origins back to the northern Germanic tribes who arrived in Denmark from southern Sweden in around 500 AD, part of a group of peoples who became collectively known as the **Vikings**. The Vikings were seamen, warriors and peasants, and they quickly became notorious for their opportunistic raids on surrounding countries – at their peak they travelled as far as North America and the Caspian Sea.

The **first Danish state**, established by the Viking Gotfred, King of Jutland, emerged some time around 800 AD, based in – and encompassing most of – the Jutland peninsula. A century later, the Norwegian chieftain Hardegon conquered the peninsula and began to expand eastwards over the rest of Denmark, establishing the foundations of the modern Danish nation, the oldest in Europe – the present Danish monarchy can be traced back to his son, Gorm the Old. Shortly afterwards, **Christianity** became the national religion. Benedictine monks had started arriving in Denmark in 826, but it wasn't until 961 that Gorm the Old's son, Harald Bluetooth, made Christianity Denmark's state religion – even if his reasons for doing so (to make peace with the Franks to the south) were not entirely spiritual.

During the late tenth century Danish power expanded: in 1016, Knud (Canute) the Great became King of England, and by 1033 the Danes controlled most of southern Sweden, the whole of England and Normandy, and dominated trade in the Baltic. From this period dates the first historical record of the small fishing village of **Havn** (literally "Haven" or "Harbour"), which would later develop into the city of Copenhagen – mentioned for the first time in 1043, when the Norwegian King Magnus sought refuge in it after losing a sea battle in the Øresund.

The Middle Ages

A century of internal political struggle weakened Viking power in Denmark, and it wasn't until the accession of Valdemar the Great in 1157 that the country was once again united and free of factional fighting. One of Valdemar's key supporters, his foster-brother **Bishop Absalon**, was given the village of Havn, strategically located on the **Øresund** – the narrow sea channel that divides Denmark from Sweden, and the main entrance to the Baltic – which was soon to become one of the main trading routes of medieval Europe.

Within a decade, Absalon had built a castle on the small island (today's Slotsholmen) opposite Havn, from where he countered the Wendish pirates, based in eastern Germany, who had previously raided the coast with impunity. Havn developed rapidly following the castle's construction. In 1209, Vor Frue Kirke – later to become the city's cathedral – was consecrated by Bishop Absalon's successor (Absalon had died in 1201), and in 1238 the city's first monastery was established on Gråbrødretorv. Despite increasing competition with – and attacks by – the Hanseatic League, by 1254 it had acquired its modern name, **København** ("Merchants Port"), a fortified market town with full municipal rights.

Thirty years later, following a German invasion of Jutland, the Danish nobles seized the opportunity to curb the powers of the monarch, forcing Erik V in 1282 to sign a charter under which he agreed to rule together with the nobles of the **Council of the Danish Realm**, an institution which was to survive as a major influence in Danish government until 1660. Almost a century of civil war followed, as the nobles fought against the king and one another, during which Copenhagen was passed back and forth between the warring factions. In 1369, the city fell to Hanseatic forces, and stonemasons from the city of Lübeck proceeded to dismantle Bishop Absalon's castle brick by brick, with the intention of ending Danish control of the Øresund once and for all.

The Kalmar Union

Despite the temporary loss of its castle, however, Copenhagen's fortunes continued to prosper. In 1397, **Margrete I**, one of Denmark's shrewdest rulers, formed the Kalmar Union, creating an alliance between Denmark, Norway and Sweden aimed at countering the Hanseatic League's influence on regional trade – the union was largely administered from, and dominated by, Copenhagen. A new fort to replace Absalon's dismantled castle was completed in 1417, and made the seat of Danish rule and residence of the royal family by Magarethe's grandson, Erik of Pomerania. Erik also ensured Copenhagen's further growth by imposing the **Sound Toll** tax on all vessels passing through the Øresund, an endless source of revenue which would underpin Copenhagen's fortunes for the next four centuries. Revenues from the toll allowed an increasingly self-confident Copenhagen to seize growing amounts of trade from the declining ports of the Hanseatic League and to establish itself as the Baltic's principal harbour.

In 1443, Copenhagen was made the **capital of Denmark** by Erik's son, Christoffer III of Bavaria, decisively shifting the national balance of power away from the former capital and ecclesiastical centre of Roskilde. Thirty years later, the first **university** in Scandinavia was founded in Copenhagen by Christian I, helping to establish the city as the nation's cultural as well as administrative hub. At the same time, **Kronborg Slot**, just north of Copenhagen at Helsingør was built to control the Øresund and enforce payment of the Sound Toll, further entrenching Copenhagen's pre-eminent position in the region.

The Reformation to the Thirty Years' War

The wealthy and corrupt Catholic church was already unpopular in Denmark, and in 1534, in the wake of increasing religious discontent, the country burst into **civil war**. Peasant uprisings spread across the country, and the Hanseatic city of Lübeck sent mercenaries to Copenhagen, where they sided with the city's anti-clerical merchants. A year-long siege of the city followed: Copenhagen's defensive ramparts held up, but many of its citizens starved to death or died during the epidemics that ravaged the city. Copenhagen finally surrendered in the summer of 1536, signalling the end of the civil war. After the dust had settled, the nobles found themselves back in control, but obliged to accept religious reform. In 1536, Lutheranism became the official state religion.

Following the travails of the Reformation, Copenhagen experienced a period of relative peace and prosperity. The city was now home to the Danish navy – during the fifteenth and sixteenth centuries the largest in northern Europe – and revenue from the Sound Toll provided a continuous source of income for Danish coffers. It was in this atmosphere of wealth and stability that **Christian IV**, known as the "Great Builder", became king. Ruling from 1588 (when he was 10) until 1648, he became the Danish monarch who made the most lasting contribution to Copenhagen's skyline, ordering the creation of buildings including the Rundetårn, Børsen and Rosenborg Slot, along with the district of Nyboder and the fortress of

Kastellet. In addition, he almost doubled the city's size by moving the defensive fortifications outwards to include Frederikstad and Nyboder to the north and the newly reclaimed island of Christianshavn to the east.

Unfortunately, Christian IV's architectural vision was not matched by his political skill. As Denmark's arch-rival Sweden became increasingly powerful, Danish military prowess steadily declined. In 1625, Christian IV took Denmark into the disastrous **Thirty Years' War** – by 1657, at the conclusion of hostilities, the west coast of the Øresund (the province of Skåne) was lost to Sweden, splitting the Sound down the middle.

Absolute monarchy

The conflict with Sweden and the loss of Skåne left Denmark heavily in debt and, to make matters worse, the nobles of the Council of the Danish Reign were reluctant to impose the taxes needed to rescue the state's finances. In response, in 1660 Christian's successor **Frederik III** compelled the nobles to sign a charter reinstating the king as absolute monarch, removing all powers from the Council. An efficient central bureaucracy was established and Copenhagen made a free city, with commoners being accorded the same privileges as nobles. Frederik III started rebuilding the military and, following three minor wars with Sweden, a peaceful coexistence was finally achieved.

Meanwhile, in 1711, bubonic plague wiped out a third of Copenhagen's population, whilst two devastating **fires** in 1728 and 1795 forced the reconstruction of most of the city, during which the basis of the present-day street plan was established. Despite these disasters, however, the reign of Frederik V (from 1746) saw a great cultural awakening as the new royal district of **Frederikstad**, with the grand royal palace of Amalienborg and the Marmorkirke church, was erected (though the latter wasn't finished until 1894).

The Napoleonic Wars

Despite its improving domestic position, Denmark found itself once again embroiled in the mire of international power struggles with the outbreak of the **Napoleonic Wars** (1796–1815). Denmark at first reluctantly sided with the League of Armed Neutrality – Russia, Sweden and Prussia – in an attempt to stay out of the conflict between expansionist Britain and revolutionary France. Considering the treaty potentially hostile, the British sent a fleet under admirals Nelson and Parker to Copenhagen in 1801, damaging the powerful Danish navy and forcing them to withdraw from the agreement. In 1807 the British returned, worried that Napoleon's advancing armies would take over the newly rebuilt Danish fleet if they didn't, and demanded Danish surrender. When Christian VII refused, the British blockaded the city, subjecting it to a murderous three-day bombardment before towing away what was left of the Danish fleet. Denmark understandably rejected the subsequent British offer of an alliance, siding instead with France. With the eventual defeat of the French, however, the luckless Danes were left bankrupt and without allies, and Norway had to be handed over to Sweden as payment for war debts.

Despite this terrible beginning to the century, by the 1830s Copenhagen had recovered, becoming the centre of the Danish **Golden Age**. For two decades the nation's arts flourished as never before (or since): Hans Christian Andersen charmed the world with his colourful fairy tales, while Søren Kirkegaard scandalized it with his philosophical works. At the same time, the nation's visual arts reached new heights under the auspices of sculptor Bertel Thorvaldsen, and C.W. Eckersberg, who led the emergence of the first specifically Danish school of painting. From this period date many of the city's most notable Neoclassical buildings, such as Christiansborg Slotskirke, the Domhus (Law Courts) and Vor Frue Kirke.

Social changes were in the air too. In the early nineteenth century, the theologian **N.F.S. Grundtvig** developed a new form of Christianity which aimed to draw its strength and inspiration from the people – a precursor of liberal traditions to come – while the example of the French revolution of 1848 forced Frederik VII to relinquish absolute rule and hand over power to the National Liberal Party. The first Danish constitution was drawn up and signed, transforming the country at a stroke from one of the most autocratic to one of the most liberal in Europe.

In 1856, Copenhagen's fortifications were demolished, finally allowing the cramped city to expand beyond its medieval limits and sowing the seed for the new industrial era. Railways, factories and shipyards began to change the face of the city, and Copenhagen gradually developed into a thriving manufacturing centre, while the new working-class districts of Nørrebro and Vesterbro were flung up, with Copenhagen's workers packed into slum tenements which would subsequently become hotbeds of left-wing politics. The second half of the nineteenth century also saw the establishment of the **Carlsberg Brewery** on the then desolate Valby Bakke, along with the rapid growth of the Royal Danish Porcelain factory and the founding of the city's two main department stores – the Magasin du Nord and Illums – two of the growing number of recreational possibilities available for the city's aspiring bourgeoisie, which also included the newly constructed Royal Theatre on Kongens Nytorv and the recently established city zoo.

To World War II

Parliamentary reforms at the turn of the century and the enfranchisement of women and servants in 1915 further extended Denmark's liberal traditions, while industrial unrest in the years following World War I (during which Denmark managed to stay neutral) brought further power to unions and left-wing political groups – it was during these early postwar years that the foundations of Denmark's comprehensive social welfare system were established.

When **World War II** broke out Denmark again tried to remain neutral, this time unsuccessfully. On April 9, 1940, the country was invaded by German troops, who marched up Nordre Frihavnsgade to the royal palaces at Amalienborg and took power the same day. The Danish parliament was left to operate purely as an administrative body and the economy was geared towards the German market. At first, the Danes could do little but comply, but growing resistance made life difficult for the Nazi forces. Passive non-cooperation gradually turned to armed struggle, and by the war's end, thousands of citizens had fought for the Danish resistance, many of them losing their lives in the process. In Copenhagen, the effect of the war was felt mainly in food and fuel rationing, and, apart from the occasional air-raid, the city largely escaped the devastation visited on other European cities – its finest moment came when a British air-raid on the Nazi headquarters on Rådhuspladsen allowed most of the captured members of the Danish Resistance to escape.

The post-war years

Following the war, Denmark succeeded in creating one of the world's most successful **welfare states**, with a comprehensive programme of cradle-to-grave benefits. Quality of life in Denmark soon ranked among the highest in the world.

The final decades of the millennium saw further enormous changes in the social and physical make-up of Copenhagen. In 1971 the old military base on the eastern side of Christianshavn was taken over by squatters, who created the "Free City" of **Christiania**. Initial, unsuccessful attempts by the police to clear the squatters out were followed by a twelve-year trial period, after which the city was legally recognized, even to the point where "Pusherstreet" is now marked on official maps of the city.

The 1980s and 1990s saw further huge changes to the city's physical fabric, as attempts were made to clean up the derelict areas of **Nørrebro** and **Vesterbro**. In Nørrebro the result was disastrous, as blocks of ramshackle but characterful buildings were torn down and replaced by concrete housing estates, until mass protests forced the city to desist. The remaining buildings in Nørrebro and most of Vesterbro were restored rather than torn down – with the result that housing in these areas increased enormously in value, in many cases forcing the original inhabitants out, with waves of Copenhagen yuppies taking the places of the districts' formerly working-class inhabitants.

None of these changes, however, rivalled the latest and most spectacular addition to the Copenhagen landscape, the **Øresund Bridge**, a road-and-rail link opened in 2000 and connecting Copenhagen with Sweden. As well as significantly enhancing Copenhagen's connections with the rest of Scandinavia, the bridge has brought the nearby Swedish city of Malmö within thirty minutes of central Copenhagen, adding at a stroke half a million people to the city's catchment area and establishing it as a major regional hub.

Recent changes in the city's physical make-up have been mirrored in arguments about its culture and character. The arrival since the 1960s of substantial numbers of immigrants

– the so-called **new Danes**, as they have become known –
continues to raise questions about the future identity of
Copenhagen. Immigrants, mainly from Yugoslavia and
Turkey, brought in during the boom years of the 1960s to fill
the city's menial jobs became suddenly less welcome in the
1970s, as unemployment rates began to rise and the ugly face
of racism raised its head. The resulting tensions continue
to simmer to this day, as in recent arguments over a supermarket chain's decision to ban its Muslim women staff from
wearing headscarves at work, or in the riots that erupted
in Nørrebro in 1999 to protest against the extradition of a
second-generation Turkish immigrant. Whether the city's
ethnic communities – often faced with overweening pressure
to conform to the Danish way of life – will succeed in bringing true cultural diversity to the city remains to be seen.

The major barometer of national feeling in Denmark,
however, has been the way in which people have seen the
country's role in Europe. Despite being a founding member
of the **European Union** in 1972, the Danish people have
in recent years constantly rocked the European boat, first in
a 1992 referendum, when the Danes rejected the Maastricht
Treaty. A second referendum in 1993, backed by massive
state propaganda, established the necessary majority, but so
inflamed popular opinion in parts of Copenhagen that it led
to a riot in Nørrebro during which eleven people were shot
and injured. At a third referendum, in late 2000, the Danes
again shocked fellow EU member states by chosing to opt
out of monetary union, as right-wing politicians stirred up
nationalist emotions, claiming that giving up the Danish
krone was equivalent to relinquishing national sovereignty
(the fact that the krone was already linked to the deutsch-
mark was conveniently overlooked). How this might affect
Copenhagen's position – newly enhanced by the Øresund
Bridge – at the crossroads of Europe and Scandinavia, is the
first major question of the new millennium.

THE POST-WAR YEARS

Books

There are relatively few English-language books on Copenhagen – the list below represents a fairly comprehensive selection of what's available. Where titles are published by different publishers in the UK and US, we've given both, separated by an oblique slash; where only one publisher is given, this covers both the UK and US, unless specifically stated. Out-of-print titles are marked "o/p".

Hans Christian Andersen, *Hans Andersen's Fairy Tales* (Oxford UP). Still the most internationally prominent figure of Danish literature, Andersen's fairytales are so widely translated and read that the full clout of their allegorical content is often overlooked: interestingly, his first collection of tales (published in 1835) was condemned for its "violence and questionable morals". *A Visit to Germany, Italy and Malta, 1840–1841* (Peter Owen, UK) is the most enduring of his travel works, while his autobiography, *The Fairy Tale of My Life* (o/p), is a fine alternative to the numerous sycophantic portraits which have appeared since.

Karen Blixen (Isak Dinesen), *Out of Africa*; *Letters from Africa*; *Seven Gothic Tales* (Penguin). *Out of Africa*, the account of Blixen's attempts to run a coffee farm in Kenya after divorce from her husband, is a lyrical and moving tale. But it's in *Seven Gothic Tales* that

Blixen's fiction is at its zenith: a flawlessly executed, weird, emotive work, full of twists in plot and strange, ambiguous characterization.

Elias Bredsdorff, *Hans Christian Andersen* (Souvenir Press, UK). One of the better biographies out of a huge raft of works on the life and times of the great fairy tale writer.

Robert Bretall, *A Kierkegaard Anthology* (Princeton University Press). An excellent cross-section of Kirkegaard's work, reflecting all the major themes of his proto-existential philosophy.

Inga Dahlsgård, *Women in Denmark, Yesterday and Today* (o/p). A refreshing presentation of Danish history from the point of view of its women.

Tove Ditlevsen, *Early Spring* (Seal Press). An autobiographical novel of growing up in the working-class Vesterbro district of Copenhagen during the 1930s. As an evocation of childhood and early adulthood, it's totally captivating.

James Graham-Campbell, *The Viking World* (Facts on File/Checkmark Books). A wonderfully colourful book full of photographs of excavated Viking sites and artefacts. Also gives a broadly-written account of the history of the seafaring warriors.

Peter Høeg, *Miss Smilla's Feeling for Snow* (published in the US as *Miss Smilla's Sense of Snow;* Harvill/Delta). A worldwide bestseller, this compelling thriller deals with Danish colonialism in Greenland and the issue of cultural identity.

Johannes V. Jensen, *The Fall of the King* (o/p). The 1944 Nobel prize winner Johannes V. Jensen's masterpiece vividly depicts an overlooked period of Danish history covering the tumultuous reign of Christian II (1513–1523) and his many years in captivity at Sønderborg Slot, superbly described through the eyes of his servant and friend, Mikkel Thøgersen.

W. Glyn Jones, *Denmark: A Modern History* (o/p). A valuable account of the twentieth-century (up until 1984) history of Denmark. Strong on politics, useful on social history and the arts, but disappointingly brief on grassroots movements.

Søren Kierkegaard, *Either/Or* (Penguin). Kierkegaard's most approachable work, packed with wry and wise musings on love, life and death in nineteenth-century Danish society; includes the (in)famous "Seducer's Diary".

Dea Trier Mørch, *Winter's Child* (Nebraska University Press, US). A wonderfully lucid sketch of modern Denmark as seen through the eyes of several women in the maternity ward of a Copenhagen hospital. See also *Evening Star*, which deals with the effect of old age and death on a Danish family.

Roger Poole and Henrik Stangerup (eds), *A Kierkegaard Reader* (Fourth Estate, UK). By far the best and most accessible introduction to this notoriously difficult nineteenth-century Danish philosopher and writer, with a sparkling introductory essay.

Judith Thurman, *Isak Dinesen: The Life of Karen Blixen*

(Penguin, UK). The most penetrating biography of Blixen, elucidating details of the Kenyan farm period not found in the two "Africa" books.

Rose Tremain, *Music and Silence* (Vintage). Captivating historical novel that follows the lives of Christian IV, his consort, his English lutenist and their lovers. Life in the many castles around Copenhagen is brilliantly described, and the novel provides a delightful insight into Danish aspirations and superstitions during the period.

Jackie Wullschlager, *Hans Christian Andersen: The Life of a Storyteller* (Penguin/Allen Lane). The most recent biographical study of Hans Christian Andersen, this finely documented and insightful biography examines the misery of Andersen's childhood, his subsequent rapid success and his troubled sexuality, arguing that it was the shock and power of these experiences that fuelled many of his mournful fairytales.

Glossary

Båd Boat

Bakke Hill

Bro Bridge

By Town

-et/-en suffixes denoting "the"

Fælled Common

Folketing Danish Parliament

Gade Street

Gammel Old

Gård Yard

Have Garden

Havn Harbour

Hus House

Kanal Canal

Kirke Church

Kongens King's, royal

Lille Little, small

Museet Museum

Nørre Northern

Ny New

Ø Island

Øster Eastern

Plads Square

Port Gate

Rådhus Town Hall

Sankt (Skt) Saint

Slot Castle

Sø Lake, sea

Sønder Southern

Stor Big

Stræde Street

Strand Beach or shore

Tårn Tower

Tog Train

Torv Square

Vej Road

Vester Western

Index

Stay in touch with us!

ROUGHNEWS is Rough Guides'
free newsletter.
In three issues a year we give you
news, travel issues, music reviews,
readers' letters and the latest
dispatches from authors on the road.

I would like to receive ROUGHNEWS: please put me on your free mailing list.

NAME . . . .

ADDRESS . . . .

Please clip or photocopy and send to: Rough Guides, 62-70 Shorts Gardens,
London WC2H 9AH, England

or Rough Guides, 375 Hudson Street, New York, NY 10014, USA.

ROUGH GUIDES: Travel

ROUGH GUIDES: Mini Guides, Travel Specials and Phrasebooks

Seattle
Sydney
Tokyo
Toronto

German
Greek
Hindi & Urdu
Hungarian
Indonesian
Italian
Japanese
Mandarin
  Chinese
Mexican
  Spanish
Polish
Portuguese
Russian
Spanish
Swahili
Thai
Turkish
Vietnamese

MINI GUIDES
Antigua
Bangkok
Barbados
Big Island of Hawaii
Boston
Brussels
Budapest
Dublin
Edinburgh
Florence
Honolulu
Lisbon
London Restaurants
Madrid
Maui
Melbourne
New Orleans
St Lucia

TRAVEL SPECIALS
First-Time Asia
First-Time Europe
More Women Travel

PHRASEBOOKS
Czech
Dutch
Egyptian Arabic
European
French

AVAILABLE AT ALL GOOD BOOKSHOPS

ROUGH GUIDES:
Reference and Music CDs

REFERENCE
Classical Music
Classical:
  100 Essential CDs
Drum'n'bass
House Music

World Music:
  100 Essential CDs
English Football
European Football
Internet
Millennium

**ROUGH GUIDE
  MUSIC CDs**
Music of the Andes
Australian
  Aboriginal
Brazilian Music
Cajun & Zydeco
Classic Jazz
Music of Colombia
Cuban Music
Eastern Europe
Music of Egypt
English Roots
  Music
Flamenco
India & Pakistan
Irish Music
Music of Japan
Kenya & Tanzania
Native American
North African
Music of Portugal

Jazz
Music USA
Opera
Opera:
  100 Essential CDs
Reggae
Rock
Rock:
  100 Essential CDs
Techno
World Music

Reggae
Salsa
Scottish Music
South African
  Music
Music of Spain
Tango
Tex-Mex
West African Music
World Music
World Music Vol 2
Music of Zimbabwe

100
Essential
CDs

Eight titles,
one name

ROUGH GUIDES

Will you have enough stories to tell your grandchildren?

©2000 Yahoo! Inc.

Yahoo! Travel

DO YOU YAHOO!?

🚲 Daily departures all summer.

🚲 Young enthusiastic guides who know the city.

🚲 Special night tours for Copenhagen night life.

🚲 Special group tours according to your wishes.

CITY SAFARI

GUIDED BIKE TOURS
IN THE CITY JUNGLE

City Safari
citysafari@citysafari.dk
www.citysafari.dk
+ 45 33 23 94 90

Rough Guides
on the Web

www.travel.roughguides.com

We keep getting bigger and better! The Rough Guide to Travel Online
now covers more than 14,000 searchable locations. You're just a click
away from access to the most in-depth travel content, weekly
destination features, online reservation services, and an outspoken
community of fellow travelers. Whether you're looking for ideas for
your next holiday or you know exactly where you're going, join us online.

You can also find us on Yahoo!® Travel (http://travel.yahoo.com) and
Microsoft Expedia® UK (http://www.expediauk.com).

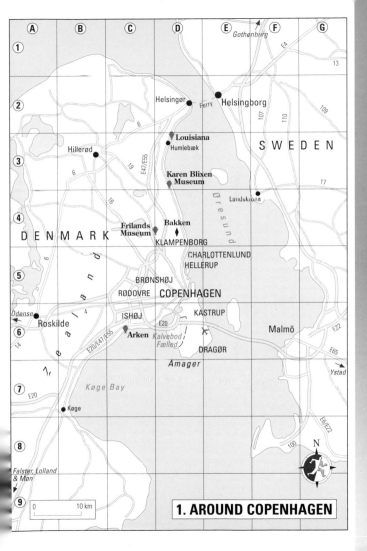

1. AROUND COPENHAGEN

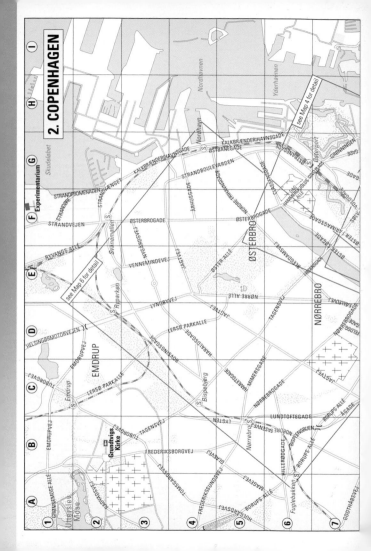

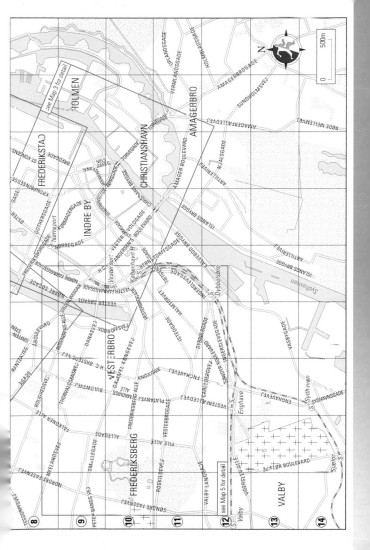

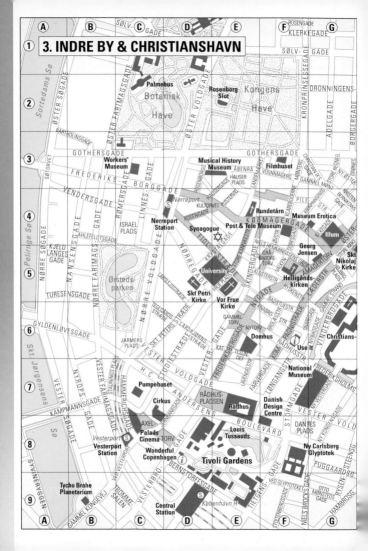

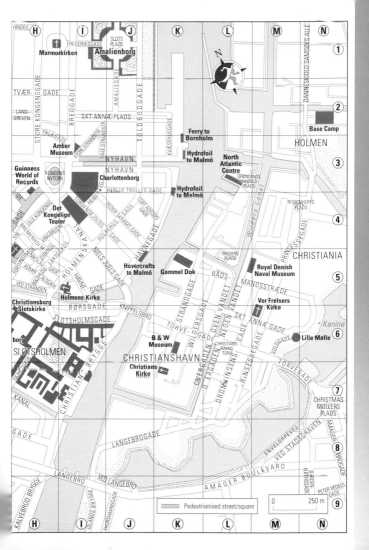

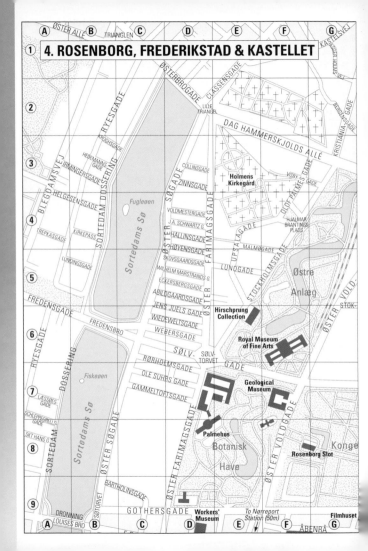

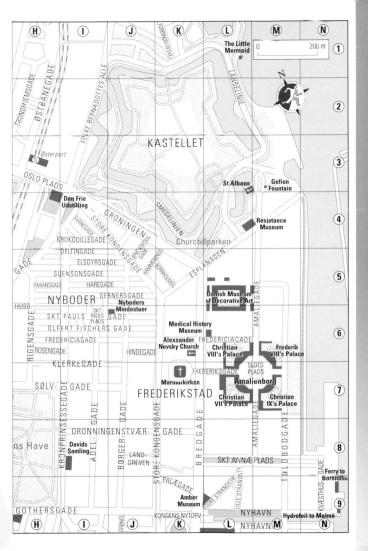

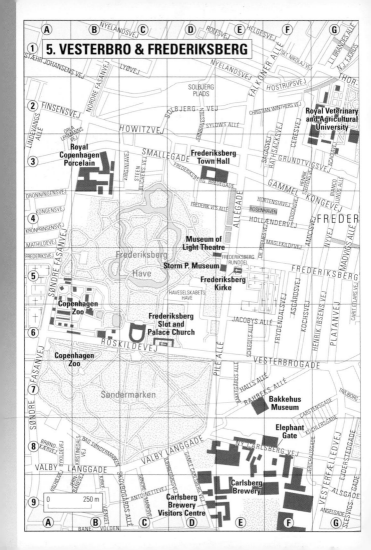

5. VESTERBRO & FREDERIKSBERG

Royal Veterinary and Agricultural University

Royal Copenhagen Porcelain

Frederiksberg Town Hall

Museum of Light Theatre

Storm P. Museum

Frederiksberg Kirke

Frederiksberg Have

Copenhagen Zoo

Frederiksberg Slot and Palace Church

Copenhagen Zoo

Søndermarken

Bakkehus Museum

Elephant Gate

Carlsberg Brewery

Carlsberg Brewery Visitors Centre

0   250 m

FREDER

FREDERIKSBERG

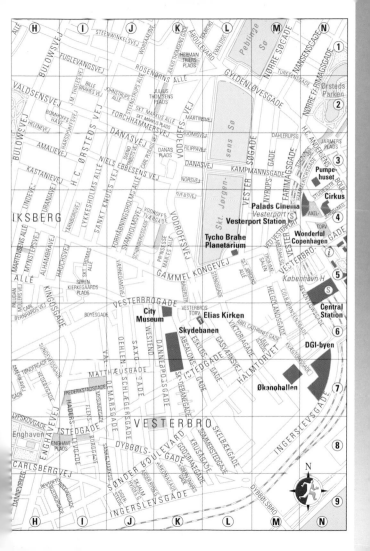

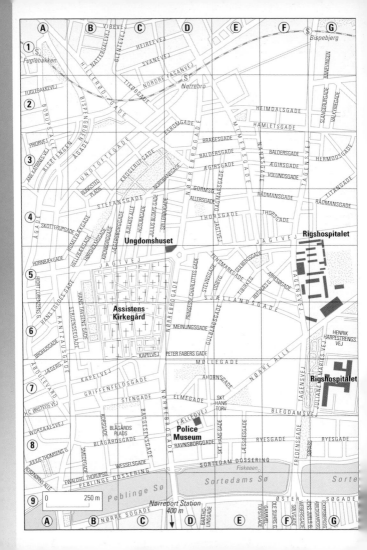

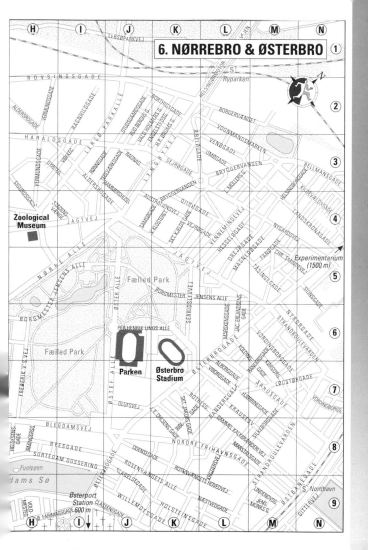

7. S-TOG AND REGIONAL TRAIN NETWORK

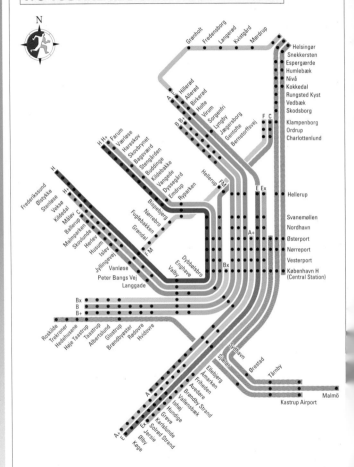